Private Virtues, Public Vices

Private Virtues, Public Vices

Philanthropy and Democratic Equality

EMMA SAUNDERS-HASTINGS

THE UNIVERSITY OF CHICAGO PRESS   CHICAGO AND LONDON

The University of Chicago Press, Chicago 60637
The University of Chicago Press, Ltd., London
© 2022 by The University of Chicago
Published 2022
Printed in the United States of America

31 30 29 28 27 26 25 24 23 22   1 2 3 4 5

ISBN-13: 978-0-226-81614-2 (cloth)
ISBN-13: 978-0-226-81615-9 (paper)
ISBN-13: 978-0-226-81613-5 (e-book)
DOI: https://doi.org/10.7208/chicago/9780226816135.001.0001

Library of Congress Cataloging-in-Publication Data

Names: Saunders-Hastings, Emma, author.
Title: Private virtues, public vices : philanthropy and democratic equity /
    Emma Saunders-Hastings.
Description: Chicago : University of Chicago Press, 2022. | Includes index.
Identifiers: LCCN 2021034597 | ISBN 9780226816142 (cloth) |
    ISBN 9780226816159 (paperback) | ISBN 9780226816135 (ebook)
Subjects: LCSH: Charity organization—Political aspects. | Humanitarianism—
    Political aspects. | Democracy—Social aspects.
Classification: LCC HV70 .S48 2022 | DDC 361.7—dc23
LC record available at https://lccn.loc.gov/2021034597

Contents

Introduction

Nearly two thousand years ago, the Stoic philosopher Lucius Annaeus Seneca lamented that "among the numerous faults of those who pass their lives recklessly and without due reflexion . . . I should say that there is hardly any one so hurtful to society as this, that we neither know how to bestow or how to receive a benefit."[1]

Seneca's questions, and the normative and practical challenges they present, remain with us today. A person who wishes to bestow a benefit on particular persons or on society must decide what and how much to give and with what expectation of reward; how to choose among possible recipients; and what terms (if any) to attach to the gift. Potential recipients must decide how to greet the proffered benefit; what conditions to accept; what attitudes to take toward the giver; and what expressions of gratitude (or attempts at repayment) to make. And political communities must decide how (if at all) to regulate the exchanges of benefits among members.

Seneca, like many champions and critics of what we now call charity or philanthropy, focuses on the virtues of givers, of recipients, and of individuals seeking to live a good life. These virtues and questions of individual ethics will play a role in my account of philanthropy as well. Any contemplation of philanthropy must give due consideration to its wide-ranging value for givers, recipients, and communities, as well as due respect to the serious moral purposes that acts of philanthropy often express and promote.

But my larger purpose is to ask how the individual virtues expressed in acts of philanthropy interact with the virtues of democratic institutions and egalitarian social relations—hence the different questions implied by my designating philanthropy as a problem of "private virtues and public vices." Is some charity less private (and less virtuous) than it seems? Can it create objectionable hierarchies and subordinating relationships? Can genuine private virtues like generosity and compassion threaten justice and democratic equality? Does this give citizens reason to regulate exchanges of benefits that are permissible and even praiseworthy at the level of individual ethics? Or is the attempt to regulate private virtues itself a public vice?

The title of this book is also, of course, a transposition of Bernard Mandeville's famous maxim that private vices yield public benefits.[2] In alluding to this capitalist article of faith, I do not mean to endorse an ethic of egoism or selfish indifference in the place of philanthropic benevolence. Nor do I wish to deny that philanthropy and its associated virtues can yield important public benefits. But just as private greed may sometimes generate public wealth, personal generosity can contribute to objectionable inequalities of power and status. I invoke Mandeville as shorthand for the insight that the relationship between individual ethics and the quality of public outcomes is complicated and often counterintuitive.[3]

Philanthropy Today

The definition of philanthropy that I will use in this book is simple, inclusive, and nonmoralized: by philanthropy, I mean voluntary contributions of private resources for broadly public purposes and for which the giver does not receive payment.[4] "Private resources" can include goods and services as well as money. "Public purposes" exclude most gifts to friends and family members, but otherwise I adopt a wide view of what counts as a philanthropic purpose.[5] On my definition, philanthropy need not arise from or express a particular motive (e.g., altruism, love of humanity, or concern for the public good).[6] This stipulation allows us to classify acts as philanthropic (or not) based on more accessible and less controversial factors than a donor's motives. Finally, except where otherwise noted, I use the terms *philanthropy*, *charity*, and *voluntary giving* interchangeably. While these sometimes have different connotations (outside of religious traditions, *charity* often has more negative or pejorative rhetorical baggage), I do not distinguish between them by definition.

Philanthropy today is largely directed toward nonprofit organizations— that is, organizations that are prohibited by law or barred by internal governance rules from distributing profits to their members (the so-called nondistribution constraint).[7] But I will be using the term more broadly to also cover donations to (or time volunteered toward) governmental and intergovernmental institutions, to public agencies, and to individuals. Though

I will focus on philanthropy by individuals, associations, and private foundations, much of what I say applies to corporate philanthropy as well.

Philanthropic giving amounts to some $450 billion a year in the United States alone.[8] Billions more are given worldwide or held in trust and in philanthropic foundations. This giving fuels a tremendous variety of organizations and an enormous range of activities. It may be helpful to provide some examples of the kinds of philanthropy that will concern us in the chapters that follow.

In January 2014, federal mediators involved in Detroit's bankruptcy proceedings announced that nine local and national foundations had committed $330 million in grants to shore up the city's pension program; by relieving some of Detroit's debt obligations, the philanthropic commitment helped avoid the necessity of selling off parts of the art collection of the city-owned Detroit Institute of the Arts.[9] This was a rare case of private foundations moving to fund public-sector pensions, and the deal came with conditions attached: the money would be earmarked for city workers' pensions, control of the museum would pass to a nonprofit, the state of Michigan would be required to contribute to the pension fund, and property taxes that local counties had enacted to help fund the museum were to remain in effect.[10] Partly because of these conditions, and partly because of the novelty of private foundations so explicitly taking over public programs, praise for the philanthropic commitments was mixed with discomfort. William Schambra, a *Chronicle of Philanthropy* columnist and director of the Bradley Center for Philanthropy and Civic Renewal at the Hudson Institute, expressed his own ambivalence: "On the one hand, you have to applaud the foundations for being willing to step into something of a vacuum in public leadership. . . . On the other hand, have we really arrived at this point where foundations can dictate terms and conditions to state and city government?"[11] This mixed reaction captures important features of the debate about both the Detroit case and contemporary large-scale philanthropy more generally. Recognition of good intentions and even good effects mingles with misgivings about donors' exercise of power. The worry here is that philanthropy could function as a Trojan horse for elite influence in an unusually exact sense: that acceptance of some gifts could involve ceding control of a city to the givers.

Philanthropic action in the Detroit case was exceptional, but in other areas it has become routine. In particular, philanthropy has played a visible and influential role in shaping not only higher education but, increasingly, primary and secondary education as well. Grants in the area of U.S.

education account for the Bill and Melinda Gates Foundation's major domestic spending; other large-scale philanthropists seeking to improve educational outcomes and reform the U.S. school system include the Walton Family Foundation and the Eli and Edythe Broad Foundation. The education sector has also attracted highly publicized one-off donations: Mark Zuckerberg's $100 million donation to the Newark, New Jersey, school system, for example, drew attention both for the departure it represented from Zuckerberg's previously low philanthropic profile and for the involvement of political actors and political ramifications.[12] In sectors like education and health, philanthropy is an underexamined aspect of movements toward private influence and privatization—movements that proceed against a backdrop of skepticism about the efficacy of democratically enacted solutions to social problems.

Perhaps the most-publicized cases of large-scale philanthropy are international in their targets and their ambitions. No single gift did as much to reignite public attention to elite philanthropy as Warren Buffett's record-breaking donation to the Bill and Melinda Gates Foundation in 2006. While the Gates Foundation funds a range of domestic and international programs, it is probably best known for its grants in the area of global health (and especially on communicable diseases). In addition to the range of organizations focused on combating the worst effects of global poverty, other philanthropists have focused more explicitly on international political goals: George Soros's Open Society Foundations (formerly Open Society Institute), for example, came to prominence after Soros made donations in an attempt to help build democracy in Eastern Europe after the fall of the Soviet Union. In exceptional cases, philanthropists have even moved to fund government responsibilities in the international arena: having already pledged $1 billion of his fortune over ten years to fund UN international programs, Ted Turner agreed in December 2000 to pay an additional $35 million to make up a shortfall in the United States' UN dues.[13] At the international level, as at the domestic one, disillusionment with public action and democracy may play a role in expanding philanthropic ambitions.

And, of course, philanthropy is practiced by ordinary citizens as well as by the stratospherically wealthy. In the United States, the largest share of philanthropic dollars goes to religious organizations and is composed of a high volume of relatively small-dollar-amount contributions. Millions of people, with a range of motivations, contribute to philanthropic causes at the local, national, and international levels. The enormous volume of charitable contributions collected in the wake of disasters like the Indian Ocean earthquake and tsunami of 2004, Hurricane Katrina in 2005, and the Haiti earthquake of 2010; the charitable donations made by people inspired by Peter Singer and the "effective altruism" movement to try to do "the most good" possible; the millions collected by bail funds in the spring and summer of 2020, following the murder of George Floyd by a Minneapolis police officer and nationwide protests against racism in the American police and legal systems—all underscore the point that today, for ordinary citizens as well as for elites, moral and political commitments often find expression in philanthropic action.

Philanthropy thus raises a host of questions familiar to political theorists—questions about social and economic inequality, democratic control, elite influence, the boundaries between public and private, and the connection between personal moral duties and demands of justice. However, political theorists are only now beginning to turn their attention to philanthropy,[14] and they continue to overlook what can be distinctively democratically troubling about it. Enormous philanthropic resources stand ready to confer benefits on the public, and this fact naturally focuses debate on how those resources might be used (or wasted) in the promotion of good public outcomes. But philanthropy is more than a potential contributor to good outcomes; it is also an important source of power that can be exercised in undemocratic and paternalistic ways. Philanthropy gives donors influence and authority, in public life and over particular beneficiaries. It shapes public options and the choices available to individuals. And it is often governed in ways that magnify the control of wealthy donors over beneficiaries and relative to the broader public. Philanthropy can promote or reinforce objectionably hierarchical social and political relationships, even when donors pursue morally appropriate ends. These problems are not addressed by theories that focus on evaluating donor altruism or on specifying the outcomes that donors (and especially rich donors) should be trying to bring about. Rather, the hierarchical dimensions of philanthropic relationships must be recognized for what they are and addressed directly if philanthropy is to be made compatible with a democratic society of equals. Democratic equality demands of philanthropy and philanthropic regulation not (or not only) better outcomes but changes in the ways that power is distributed and exercised within philanthropic relationships.

With that goal in mind, this book shows how philanthropy might avoid both the usurpation of control over public outcomes and subordinating relationships between philanthropists and the people they seek to benefit. Philanthropy's compatibility with democratic equality depends on how philanthropy is practiced, governed, and regarded within political communities: what entitlements and regulatory leeway are accorded to philanthropists, nonprofit organizations, and public charities; how philanthropists exercise their power; how beneficiaries navigate their position; and what attitudes members of society take toward philanthropy. Philanthropy can supply important benefits to individuals and communities. A democratic philanthropy should aim to provide those benefits without subverting relationships of social and political equality. As we will see, this is no simple task.

Theoretical Context and Some Contrasts

Political theory can inform our understanding of philanthropy. And engagement with philanthropy can illuminate broader issues in political theory concerning the meaning of democratic equality, its requirements both within and beyond formal political institutions, and the grounds of objections to (even) benevolent social and political hierarchies. But although philanthropy speaks to central issues in political theory, thinking politically about philanthropy requires breaking some habits. This book develops a theory of philanthropy that is political, not just ethical; that applies across multiple levels of idealization; and that is oriented to relational equality. Understanding how this approach contrasts with its alternatives also helps to explain why contemporary political theorists have generally not treated philanthropy as an important problem for democracy or for equality.

Ethical and Political Theories

As the examples surveyed above may have already suggested, philanthropy can elicit conflicting moral and political intuitions. In particular, it can elicit conflict *between* moral and political intuitions. Surveying the signatories to Bill and Melinda Gates and Warren Buffett's "Giving Pledge" for billionaire donors, many people will be tempted both to praise the generosity of the individuals involved and to feel uneasy about a system in which the life outcomes of millions of people come to *depend* on that generosity. Our moral evaluations of particular philanthropists and their activities can diverge—sometimes dramatically—from our assessments of the justice of the distributions of wealth and power that lie in the background.

What this suggests is a need to supplement our ethical theories of phi-lanthropy—which address themselves to well-motivated individuals and generally focus on where, how much, and in what spirit a person ought to give—with political and, especially, democratic theories of philanthropy that ask how philanthropy ought to be governed by public institutions and what kinds of philanthropy are compatible with democratic norms.

Political theories often focus on formal institutional questions. Demo-cratic or not, any political theory of philanthropy can include principles for how states and public officials ought to treat philanthropy: where to per-mit, restrict, or incentivize giving (e.g., by offering tax deductions for char-itable contributions) and how the philanthropic sector should be defined and governed by legal and political institutions.[15] A democratic theory must consider these questions with reference to principles of political equality, and its answers need not track judgments about the personal morality of donors. Regulating private giving in ways consistent with political equality might involve limiting some ethically good kinds of philanthropy and permit-ting or even subsidizing some morally dubious kinds. This disconnect between moral value and just political regulation is familiar in other areas of demo-cratic theory and practice. In political campaigns, it may be morally praise-worthy for a donor to contribute to the candidate most likely to improve public outcomes or outcomes for the worst-off people. Yet there might none-theless be good political reason to limit campaign contributions (without attempting to discriminate between just and unjust donors or candidates). Similarly, it may be morally indecent, or at least suboptimal, to spend mil-lions of dollars on a yacht in a world where people starve—but there might nonetheless be good political reasons to permit extravagant consumption. We cannot straightforwardly infer the appropriate political regulation of philanthropy from its moral value: political theory does not amount to ap-plied moral philosophy.

Political theories do more than articulate normative principles for for-mal political institutions. More broadly, they address the organization of common life and the distribution of power and authority within it. Po-litical theories engage questions about the public norms and social rela-tionships appropriate for members of a political community (in their in-teractions with each other and with nonmembers). Democratic theories, centrally concerned with affirming citizens' status as political equals, must be attentive to the ways that status can be promoted or subverted outside formal political institutions as well as within them. The relationship of these concerns to (other) ethical ones is often complex: even people acting to promote morally good ends might, in the process, violate expectations about how members of a democratic society should relate to each other and how they should share authority over important features of their common life.

Levels and Sites of Idealization

The distinction between ethical and political theorizing must be understood with reference to a second family of distinctions—that is, between ideal and nonideal, and between ideal and realist, political theories.[16] More than ethical theories, political theories of philanthropy face questions about what idealizing assumptions (if any) to adopt. While facts about social institutions, background inequalities, and other agents' behavior will affect how moral principles apply to particular circumstances, ethical principles themselves ("Give from purely altruistic rather than selfish motives" or "Give until the marginal welfare cost of giving to you exceeds its benefit to others") generally travel with relative ease across levels of idealization. This is less true of political theorizing. Highly demanding moral principles can be adopted by individuals even in far-from-ideal circumstances; on the other hand, theorizing the norms and institutions that should regulate philanthropy may seem to force choices between normative ambition and real-world applicability.

Political philosophy has, in general, prioritized normative ambition. One possible explanation for the relative dearth of political theorizing about philanthropy is that philanthropy has been understood as a problem of nonideal theory and so has been treated as less interesting or urgent. Anglo-American political philosophy since John Rawls has given priority to ideal theory, investigating "the nature and aims of a perfectly just society."[17] Ideal theory focuses on specifying principles of justice (for Rawlsians, principles of justice applying to the "basic structure" of society and the ways that major social institutions distribute rights, opportunities, benefits, and burdens), assuming full compliance with those principles and relatively favorable social conditions.[18] In this tradition, nonideal theory, dealing with noncompliance or unfavorable social conditions must be set out with reference to political ideals. Even if unlikely to be realized (in the near term or ever), principles of justice developed under idealizing assumptions provide standards for evaluating existing social institutions and help set targets for reform.[19]

But specifying the roles that philanthropy might play in a fully just society does not provide very useful guidance for the practice and regulation of philanthropy in existing societies. Compared with existing democracies, a just society might have significantly less economic and political inequality—and this, we might think, would greatly reduce both the scope for and the urgency of philanthropy. Indeed, philanthropy in such a society might be unrecognizable. We could rely on just social institutions to secure a fair distribution of resources and opportunities; we could be confident that donors exercised no improper influence over political institutions and officials; we would know that philanthropists spent only money that was justly theirs. But once these background assumptions are violated, the ability of an ideal theory to guide philanthropic giving and regulation declines precipitously. This problem is not unique to philanthropy, but because philanthropy is so often thought of as either the product of serious distributive injustice or as a necessary response to unjust or inadequate social institutions, it opens questions about the application of ideal to nonideal theorizing in an especially vivid way.

Some authors have argued that we should instead take nonideal circumstances and actually existing injustices rather than a conception of fully-realized social justice as the point of departure for political theorizing.[20] And "realist" arguments have charged "moralists" (including Rawlsians) with neglecting the inevitability of deep moral disagreement and the paramount importance of securing a political order that can contain and manage such disagreement.[21] On these views, the problem is not just that ideal theory lacks direct application to nonideal theory but rather that "views that assume away the problems that political institutions are supposed to solve are not in fact political at all."[22]

The political theory of philanthropy that I develop in this book applies across multiple levels of idealization. It is meant to guide (and, sometimes, to change) our responses to philanthropy in societies that are less than fully just or democratic, and where the magnitude of that shortfall is a matter of disagreement. In the assumptions that I adopt, I therefore try to cast a wide net. I appeal to democratic and egalitarian principles, but in doing so I do not mean to presuppose the truth of any specific democratic or egalitarian theory. I assume that in a democratic society, the practice and regulation of philanthropy should be consistent both with the protection of extensive individual liberties and with some conception of political equality (although, in the societies I have in mind, commitments to liberty and equality may be imperfectly realized in practice). I assume both the existence of private property and also some redistributive taxation and social welfare programs: that is, I do not provide general arguments defending private property on the one hand or redistributive taxation and social programs on the other, since imagining either a property-less or a minimal state would foreclose many of the questions about philanthropy and its regulation that I want to consider. (However, the assumptions that I adopt are compatible with a very wide range of views about *what* should be privately owned and *how much* redistributive taxation should occur.)

The other background assumptions I adopt are similarly related to the practical questions I want to investigate. At most points in the book, I assume that I am presenting arguments for a society in which (despite some redistributive taxation and the existence of a welfare state) there are significant economic inequalities between members of society and that those inequalities threaten to introduce at least some inequalities in people's influence over political institutions and other aspects of common life.[23] Importantly, I also assume that in this society there is disagreement about whether social institutions and the levels of economic and political inequality they permit are just. I mostly avoid relying in my arguments on either the presupposition that a society's wealthiest members hold that wealth justly or that they do so unjustly: while it can be useful to consider what changes in our arguments if we adopt either of those presuppositions, we can derive important guidance for the democratization of philanthropy from less controversial premises that do not rely on a publicly shared conception of distributive justice.

With all that said, I assume that in this society—indeed, perhaps in any society—some people wish to contribute resources for broadly public purposes.[24] In short, I assume societies facing problems much like our own.

A central methodological objective of the book is to balance realism about actually existing philanthropy with realism about actually existing states. It would be naive to assume that philanthropy can do no wrong. But it would be equally foolish to idealize government and to reserve our suspicion for philanthropists who are at least (we might think) trying to increase welfare or approximate justice—and certainly trying harder than many governments and public officials. Disenchantment with democracy, and loss of faith in democratic political action, is something that, for many people, enhances philanthropy's appeal. And we must bear in mind that, in the real world, the power to regulate philanthropy will lie in the hands of states that are not fully just or democratic and that do not adequately represent even all their own citizens (much less other affected interests). This does not mean that no improvements in the regulation of philanthropy are possible or that we must limit ourselves to taking laws as they are and billionaires as they might be. The method adopted here combines appeals to conceptions of democratic equality and of egalitarian relationships with a realistic assessment of the motives, effects, and prospects for philanthropy; it is from this perspective that I advance some strategic (if preliminary) proposals for more democratic governance.

Distributive and Relational Conceptions of Equality

A third contrast, related to the foregoing ones, will be important in the chapters to follow: the contrast between distributive and relational conceptions of equality. A central argument of this book is that a relational conception provides the more appropriate lens through which to evaluate philanthropy and the ways it may promote or subvert equality.

Distributive conceptions of equality focus on the just distribution of some set of goods, resources, and opportunities (with long-standing debate about what exactly is the *equalisandum* or "currency" of a just distributive pattern: welfare, opportunities for welfare, resources, "primary goods," capabilities, etc.).[25] G. A. Cohen expresses a strongly distributive conception of equality when he announces that he will "take for granted that there is something which justice requires people to have equal amounts of."[26] Relational conceptions of equality do not take this for granted in the same way: as Elizabeth Anderson puts it, they object not primarily to the unfair or unequal distribution of any particular good (or set of goods) but to "forms of social relationship by which some people dominate, exploit, marginalize, demean, and inflict violence on others."[27] In positive terms, relational egalitarians "seek a social order in which persons stand in relations of equality. They seek to live together in a democratic community, as opposed to a hierarchical one."[28] While distributive and relational egalitarian ideals are often compatible,[29] it would be misleading to reduce the relational egalitarian concern for respecting and securing people's status as equals to distributive terms (e.g., to attempting to secure for people equal *amounts* of status or standing). Equality is fundamentally a social rather than a distributive ideal.[30] It requires that members of society relate to each other as social and political equals rather than as superiors and inferiors.

Proponents of distributive conceptions of equality generally prioritize ideal theory for reasons that should be clear: the justice of social institutions and the overall pattern of distribution cannot be secured by individual actions, only assessed with reference to the question of whether the basic structure as a whole satisfies principles of justice. So the focus is on getting that structure, and those principles, right. And for this reason, though distributive conceptions may be friendlier to philanthropy in practice (so long as money is flowing from the better-off toward the worse-off), they will be less interested in it as part of a political ideal or as an object of political critique. For a distributive egalitarian, the obvious thought will be that I am specifying the object of concern incorrectly—there would be no worry about philanthropy if there were no unjust background inequality. The unease about the billionaire donors, the thought goes, is an objection not to philanthropy but to billionaires.

On a relational conception there are other concerns, including philanthropy's effects on democratic institutions, on the ways that people interact in public and private life, and on the prospects for "a community in which people stand in relations of equality to each other."[31] Of course, relational egalitarians care about the ways that social institutions distribute resources, opportunities, and power, and (like distributive egalitarians) they generally seek to reduce economic inequality (often motivated by what Martin O'Neill calls the "deep social fact" that significant material inequalities reliably compromise people's ability to live together as equals).[32] But even absent the achievement of distributive justice, we may be able to close some avenues of unequal influence in our democracies and to erode the ways that some citizens exercise private power over others. In all probability, the democratic challenges presented by private philanthropy would be mitigated under conditions of distributive equality. But that is not a reason for inattention to those challenges in existing, significantly unequal societies—societies where philanthropists *can* exercise vitally important influence over people's lives and common institutions. The amount of power that a wealthy American can exercise philanthropically is partly the product of economic inequality, but it is also the product of permissive regulation and of laws and attitudes that are overwhelmingly deferential to donors' preferences. So what would be false in an already just society may be true in actually existing ones: that we can make important progress toward equality by seeking to reduce inequalities that occur within, or in ways shaped by, philanthropic relationships.

This project requires attention to a plurality of relational vices. Neorepublicans have developed a kind of relational ethic centered on the concept of domination, or vulnerability to arbitrary interference from other agents.[33] Such a perspective captures some important objections to philanthropic power—for example, it can explain how reliance on private philanthropy for important social services could establish relations of domination and subordination between providers of those services and the people most dependent on them.[34] But domination is not the only kind of objectionable social and political relation, and a more capacious relational egalitarianism is more useful for theorizing philanthropy.[35]

The core of relational egalitarian ideals consists in the claim that it is important for members of a society to stand in relations of social and political equality.[36] The importance of egalitarian relations may be easiest to understand in negative terms—that is, with reference to the range of ways that hierarchical social relations can be disrespectful and harmful to people.[37] These include, but are not limited to, the effects of some hierarchical relationships on people's access to resources and opportunities; on the quality of collective decisions; and on people's sense of self-worth and what Rawls calls "the social bases of self-respect."[38] Relational egalitarians appeal to the badness of being dominated (and the forms of servility or "bowing and scraping" that this may encourage) but also to the badness of being exploited, paternalized, insulted, marginalized, stigmatized, and deprived of power or status. Some argue that inappropriately hierarchical relations are bad for *both* superiors and inferiors (e.g., because relating on terms of inequality corrupts the character or inhibits the happiness and flourishing of all parties involved).[39] Relating as equals, on this view, would be better for everyone. I think that such claims are plausible, but I avoid relying on them in the arguments that follow. I assume that our reasons to reject objectionably hierarchical relationships can be adequately grounded in concern for the subordinated parties and in appeals to the badness of being subordinated.

I do not claim that egalitarian relations are necessarily characterized by other goods such as friendship, warm feelings, community, and solidarity. Egalitarian relations require a minimum threshold of goodwill and reciprocity in order to recognize and uphold people's status as equals, but I want to leave open the possibility that in some contexts there could be trade-offs between the equality and the warmth of social relations. Further, what matters, on my account, is that the social and political relationships in which people find themselves and that are salient in people's lives be arranged on terms of equality—not that people enter into new (egalitarian) relationships where there were no relationships before. I claim that egalitarian relations are generally preferable to hierarchical ones, but I do not make the stronger claim that an egalitarian relationship is (always, or generally) preferable to no relationship at all or to reducing the salience of some social relationships. Democratic individualism can be as much a relational egalitarian ideal as views emphasizing communal solidarity.

Relating as social and political equals does not require that people understand themselves to be equal in all respects. It is compatible with thinking that some people are superior to others in their talents or moral characters. It is also compatible with some people exercising powers that others do not (e.g., when the relevant powers serve legitimate purposes and are appropriately circumscribed and where access to them is not decided in morally objectionable ways). Relational egalitarian views must therefore help us to distinguish between objectionable and unobjectionable inequalities in status and esteem and between legitimate and illegitimate inequalities in influence and authority. This book's analysis of philanthropy aims to do this by developing and testing relational conceptions outside some of the familiar political contexts. As I will argue, philanthropy may subvert valuable relations of equality in two ways.

One is more overtly political than the other. As equals, members of a society should share authority over their common life and matters of common concern. (This includes sharing authority over what *counts* as a matter of common concern.) It is for this reason that relational egalitarian ideals give central place to conceptions of democratic equality, to the point where the terms *relational equality* and *democratic equality* are often used synonymously.[40] Philanthropy raises democratic concerns when it permits the usurpation of control over matters of common concern, especially by the very rich. Chapter 3 develops this argument about what democratic equality requires and how elite philanthropy can subvert it. It distinguishes the central *democratic* objection to elite authority from objections to the ways that authority is exercised and from questions about whether and how to subsidize it.

I also argue that the moral and political significance of philanthropy is not confined to its influence over what are usually thought of as (or ought formally to be) collective, political decisions. The second dimension of relational equality that I stress (in particular in chapter 4) is a commitment to antipaternalism—a commitment binding not only on governments but also on other social actors. Recognizing people's equal status and relating as social equals requires sharing authority over common life. It also requires treating people's judgments about how best to live their *own* lives as equally deserving of respect. While social equality permits (indeed, requires) some limits on individual autonomy, it is hostile to the differentiated or hierarchical deployment of paternalist restrictions and incentives.

Chapter 4 explains in more detail how philanthropy can run afoul of these commitments.

I do not claim that these relational harms are exhaustive of the problems with philanthropy: rather, they are dimensions that have been overlooked or underemphasized in existing critiques. Nor is it my principal objective to use these strands of relational critique of philanthropy to reverse engineer a comprehensive relational egalitarian ideal. (In fact, I take it to be an advantage that relational egalitarian arguments, unlike distributive egalitarian ones, are often modular. People with different ideal theories—or none—can find the same relational vices objectionable, even if they disagree about the underlying reasons for and relative weight of the objections; accordingly, some readers may be much more troubled by some strands of my relational critique of philanthropy than others.) But, as I will argue, the relational lessons that we can draw from philanthropy have wider application: through a close consideration of particular relational vices as they operate in philanthropic contexts, we can gain a better understanding of how they operate in democratic life more broadly.

Chapter Outline

In chapter 1, I describe the unusual deference that philanthropy enjoys both in public discourse and from public institutions, with particular reference to the United States. I ask whether we can explain this deference with reference to the reasons that we have for valuing philanthropy and argue that we cannot: while there are important reasons why liberal democrats might value philanthropy in some form, these reasons tell us little about the appropriate shape of public regulation and the appropriate character of public attitudes toward philanthropy. Moreover, some of the reasons surveyed are more persuasive than others, and none provide a master defense of everything that currently goes under the name "philanthropy": we need to disaggregate the philanthropic sector and our reasons for valuing it or according it deference.

In chapter 2, I elaborate a distinction between distributive and relational perspectives on voluntary giving. I argue that distributive perspectives dominate the existing normative discussion of philanthropy, focusing attention on considerations such as the kinds of goods that philanthropy (as opposed to the state) ought to provide and the demandingness of individuals' obligations to give. I also argue that this is a narrow and historically anomalous way of evaluating voluntary giving. I reconstruct historical perspectives that evaluate philanthropy by its impact on social and political relationships as well as its distributive consequences. The project of the rest of the book is to develop a relational egalitarian perspective on contemporary philanthropy.

Chapters 3 and 4 explain in more detail how philanthropy can threaten the equality of political and social relationships. Chapter 3 focuses on the democratic challenges raised by elite philanthropy and its distinctive element of donor control. I argue that philanthropy represents a plutocratic institution in contemporary democracies—an area where we rely, for public benefits, on the judgment and authority of the rich. I use examples of philanthropic gifts with "strings attached" to show how philanthropy can be an avenue through which elites exercise undue influence in the polity at large. I also argue that expansive donor control need not be taken as an inevitable feature of philanthropy. To say that we want to permit or encourage philanthropy in some issue areas does not yet answer the question of how control over philanthropic gifts is to be distributed between the donor, recipients, and the public. In contrast with existing approaches to elite philanthropy, which often focus on identifying sectors where philanthropic influence should be blocked or on redistributing tax subsidies for philanthropy, I give particular attention to the goal of redistributing control over gifts.

Chapter 4 develops a second strand of the relational egalitarian argument against philanthropy. I argue that philanthropy can be objectionable where it is paternalistic. This will strike some readers as deeply wrong: on some influential views, since philanthropy adds to rather than restricts the options open to people, it cannot be paternalistic. I argue that this objection rests on a truncated understanding of what paternalism involves and show how a consideration of philanthropy can help us to better understand what paternalism is and why we should resist it. Paternalism involves not only judgments about an agent's *absolute* incompetence, which represent an affront to autonomy; it also involves judgments about an agent's incompetence *relative* to the paternalist and so represents an affront to equality. Such insults to equality can arise even when one merely "adds an option" to a paternalized person or group's choice set.

Chapter 5 turns from elite philanthropy to mass and associational philanthropy and asks whether the latter kinds of philanthropy automatically avoid the problems of undemocratic influence and private paternalism. I argue that the relevant problems are not overcome simply by opening philanthropy to more citizens (e.g., through a high volume of small-dollar-amount donations) or outweighed by the civic benefits produced by voluntary associations. I attempt to get clearer on the conditions under which associational philanthropy (and philanthropy of other kinds) is consistent with social and political equality. In the process, I call attention to the errors of some existing conceptions of democracy that focus on mass participation rather than the egalitarian or inegalitarian character of social and political relationships.

Chapter 6 considers international philanthropy and the significance of shared and unshared political membership for the problems identified in earlier chapters.

Throughout the book, I offer suggestions about how we might improve philanthropic regulation and adjust our attitudes toward philanthropy. I also show how philanthropy can illuminate broader issues in political theory, and the conclusion draws together some of the central lessons for democratic theory in particular. Philanthropy presents a set of normative and practical questions that are interesting and important in their own right, but it also helps us to think more generally about what democracy and equality require. It directs our attention to an old, but still vital, set of problems for political theory and practice: how to understand the interplay of private wealth and power, how to criticize hierarchies coded as benevolent, and what entitlements accrue to a person attempting to benefit others.

CHAPTER ONE

Donations and Deference

Before Parisian firefighters had fully extinguished the blaze that ravaged Notre-Dame in April 2019, lavish pledges rolled in from philanthropists eager to support the cathedral's reconstruction: €100 million from Bernard Arnault, France's richest person; double that amount—each—from François-Henri Pinault and from the Bettencourt Meyers family; and further commitments in the millions and tens of millions of euros from individual and corporate donors in France and abroad.[1] The pledges were greeted with a mixed reception: conventional expressions of gratitude in some quarters but swift criticism from others. Why, some skeptics asked, were private funds so readily available to repair a building but not to address rising inequality in French society? Nick Tedesco, a philanthropic advisor at J. P. Morgan Private Bank, gave plaintive voice to donor reaction: "Instead of praising the act of philanthropy itself, people are saying it's not the highest and best use of that capital. When did we get to a place where we feel comfortable criticizing other people's altruism?"[2]

A study of philanthropy should not be uncharitable. It must give due consideration to the many reasons for endorsing philanthropy as an individual virtue and public benefit. At the same time, thinking politically about philanthropy requires questioning the deference habitually extended to philanthropy and philanthropists.

I use the term *deference* broadly to refer both to informal norms (e.g., that donors should be treated with respect, esteem, and gratitude rather than subjected to scrutiny and criticism) and to legal and economic advantages that institutions confer on philanthropic donations. While it will be important to disaggregate these different dimensions of deference as the argument proceeds, they are jointly important to the puzzle I explore in this chapter: how and why we single out a category of spending called "philanthropy" for differential treatment (formal and informal) from other uses of private money.

I begin the chapter by canvassing the kinds of public attitudes and institutional treatment of philanthropy that I count as deferential. Next, I survey some important contemporary sources of deference: the reasons that people committed to broadly liberal democratic values have for thinking that philanthropy is (at least in general) a virtuous or beneficial practice, worthy of respect and encouragement. I argue that these reasons do not justify (and sometimes stand in tension with) existing forms of social and institutional deference.

Over the course of the chapter, I also note some of the ways that deference to philanthropy has varied over time and across political contexts.[3] Deference to philanthropy is a political phenomenon—the product of both institutional choices and social norms. By analyzing and disaggregating existing forms of deference, we can begin to see how different norms and institutions would better and more consistently reflect democratic commitments.[4]

The Shape of Deference

Deference to philanthropy has not been universal and departures from it have sometimes been dramatic. Following Livy, Machiavelli tells the story of Spurius Maelius, a wealthy Roman who used his own money to purchase grain to distribute to the plebs in a time of famine. The Roman Senate's response to this act of charity was singularly ungrateful: because Spurius "had such a crowd of people in his favor . . . the Senate, thinking of the inconvenience that could arise from that liberality of his, so as to crush it before it could pick up more strength, created a dictator over him and had him killed."[5] Machiavelli approves of the Senate's course of action and mildly comments that "many times works that appear merciful, which cannot reasonably be condemned, become cruel and are very dangerous for a republic if they are not corrected in good time."[6] He draws a distinction between two ways or "modes" of acquiring reputation:

> The public modes are when one individual by counseling well, by working better in the common benefit, acquires reputation. . . . The private ways are doing benefit to this and to that other private individual. . . . A well-ordered republic ought, therefore, to open the ways, as was said, to whoever seeks support

through public ways and close them to whoever seeks it through private ways, as one sees Rome did.[7]

The language of public and private is Machiavelli's gloss on the source material, but Livy, too, is concerned that Spurius had used his wealth to acquire a following that gave him "an air of dignity and importance far beyond what was due to a man who held no official position."[8] Whether or not Spurius's motivation was colored by political opportunism, summary execution is an overly intrusive way of regulating philanthropy. But Livy's and Machiavelli's total lack of interest in the charitable character of Spurius's spending is also striking. To them, his actions represent an exercise of concentrated private power, no less threatening for its charitable form.

American politicians have been friendlier than the Roman Senate was to philanthropists, but degrees of political deference to philanthropy nevertheless ebb and flow. Political actors in earlier eras were often vocal in their suspicions of philanthropic activity. John D. Rockefeller failed to obtain a federal charter for his foundation (which was later incorporated in New York) due to intense political opposition to the "bill to incorporate Mr. Rockefeller."[9] And critics of philanthropy have not been motivated only by fears of corruption and undue personal influence, of the kind that Livy and Machiavelli express. Worries about philanthropy appear even in debates over government accepting open-ended bequests from the dead. The 1829 will of James Smithson—an Englishman who had never visited the United States and the illegitimate son of the Duke of Northumberland—bequeathed his fortune "to the United States of America, to found at Washington, under the name of the Smithsonian Institution, an establishment for the increase and diffusion of knowledge among men."[10] At the time, U.S. senators questioned the propriety of accepting the gift in striking terms: John C. Calhoun believed that "it was beneath the dignity of the United States to receive presents of this kind from *anyone*," and William C. Preston likewise argued that "it was not consistent with the dignity of the country to accept even the grant of a man of noble birth."[11]

To many readers, some of this resistance to philanthropy will sound strange and unmotivated; the natural response will be to side with Spurius, Smithson, and (by extension) the people they were trying to benefit and against political elites asserting their exclusive authority or national dignity. But some of the concerns are more familiar. While deference to and celebration of philanthropy are common today, suspicion and criticism of philanthropy are again on the rise. A broadside against "the elite charade of changing the world" recently hit best-seller lists, and there is renewed debate in the popular media about philanthropy's role in preserving the status quo and legitimating inequality.[12] Worries about the political influence of the rich have also led to increased scrutiny of their charitable contributions: critics of the Koch network (a conservative donor consortium founded by billionaire brothers Charles Koch and the late David Koch) and of the Clinton Foundation decry potentially corrupt forms of private influence in the public sphere. Suspicion of philanthropy is not always well grounded and can devolve into conspiracism: Bill Gates, an active donor to public health research, has become a focal point of public fears that a vaccine for COVID-19 will be used to implant microchips in recipients; George Soros has been a long-standing target of anti-Semitic and anti-immigration conspiracy theories.[13] I will not hazard an empirical explanation of when and why deference to philanthropy waxes or wanes, but deference to philanthropy is at this moment not only a political question but an increasingly open one. This makes it especially important to untangle the forms that deference can take, to evaluate their warrant, and to think carefully about the institutions and attitudes that ought to replace them.

Social Deference

Philanthropists generally lack formal authority over other people and in public life. (There are exceptions, where large-scale philanthropists also hold political office—for example, the former Mayor of New York City, Michael Bloomberg.) But while philanthropists cannot command obedience, they benefit from deference by reason of both the economic incentives they are able to extend and the forms of social respect that philanthropy enjoys. I begin by focusing on the latter (without, of course, denying that norms and attitudes of respect may be motivated or reinforced by economic incentives).[14]

One might object that I am misidentifying the source and scope of deference here: perhaps whatever social deference philanthropists enjoy is due simply to their wealth, not to what they choose to do with it. But at least some social deference is underdetermined by net worth. Elite philanthropy attracts appreciation and calms criticism in ways that extravagant consumption spending does not and, in doing so, contributes to the social legitimation of large fortunes.

In public discourse, it is still conventional to praise—and bad manners to criticize—philanthropists. Philanthropists and philanthropic consultants sometimes police this norm.[15] But most of us do not need reminding that we lack standing to criticize what philanthropists choose to do with their money; we anticipate the rejoinder—"What have *you* contributed lately?" Even in avowedly critical treatments of philanthropy, one frequently encounters disclaimers about not wanting to seem churlish or to deter generosity. (I insert such disclaimers myself.)

If violating norms against criticizing philanthropy often makes critics themselves uncomfortable, it also induces discomfort and sometimes even outrage in observers. Peter Singer and proponents of the effective altruism movement often support their arguments for increasing the volume and efficiency of welfare-improving charity by comparing relatively efficient and inefficient ways of donating. Consider the case of charities that train guide dogs for people with disabilities: it can take two years and between $45,000 and $60,000 to train a single dog, almost half of the dogs trained do not qualify for placement as guide dogs, and a single client might need five or more dogs over the course of her life.[16] These programs therefore fare poorly by the lights of the effective altruism movement: Singer often notes that the money required to train a single guide dog could cure blindness for hundreds of people in lower-income countries.[17] These kinds of observations by effective altruists frequently draw hostile reactions.[18] My question here is not whether Singer's or effective altruists' standards are the correct ones to apply in evaluating charitable donations; it is, rather, why engaging in comparative evaluations of philanthropic donations in the first place strikes many people as ill mannered or out of line.[19] This is also a case where deference is difficult to explain simply as a matter of class position. Singer and effective altruists are critical of welfare-inefficient donating by small donors, not just by elite ones, and their arguments seem at least as capable of giving offense when they are aimed at ordinary people as when they target the wealthy.

Philanthropists enjoy some forms of social deference from the public at large; others may arise within a more restricted circle of beneficiaries or recipient organizations. Indeed, a donor might forgo public deference by giving anonymously but nevertheless be treated with deference by a recipient organization: fundraisers might flatter and court the donor, and staff might be reluctant to challenge her views about how best to pursue the organization's mission. And, importantly, deference need not be elicited by the explicit or even tacit demands of donors. Given nonprofits' incentives to appeal to donors—to respond to their priorities and even to anticipate their wishes in hopes of attracting donations—some forms of deference may be difficult to overcome even for donors who sincerely wish to do so.

For now, I want simply to notice these examples of social deference. Some forms of social deference to philanthropy may reflect and reinforce objectionably hierarchical relations that we should work to overcome. Others might be harmless in themselves and compatible with democratic equality. That question will depend partly on the forms of institutional deference that accompany social norms around giving.

Institutional Deference

Like the social norms canvassed above, institutional deference to philanthropy varies both within and between political communities. In this section, I focus on the forms that institutional deference takes in contemporary liberal democracies (and that are especially pronounced in the United States). These include privileged tax treatment for philanthropic enterprises (e.g., tax-exempt status for nonprofit organizations and tax deductions for charitable contributions); weak oversight of organizations that enjoy those benefits; institutional creations like the private foundation that facilitate giving; and legal protection of the intent of charitable donors (that exceeds the protections enjoyed by other uses of private money).

Institutions in the United States (and, to a lesser degree, in other liberal democracies) combine the designation of philanthropy as a privileged category (benefiting from special legal or tax treatment) with a nonjudgmental attitude toward the question of what *counts* as philanthropy. Philanthropic organizations are often celebrated for their diversity. Some are fantastically wealthy and others modest; some are endowed by a single individual or family, while others are assembled from an accumulation of small donations; some are expansive in focus, while others concentrate their efforts on a single issue or in a small community. There are organizations dedicated to every conceivable issue; they vary widely in their missions, their effectiveness (and even in the degree to which "effectiveness" is a goal that they would recognize), and their internal structure, membership rules, and inclusiveness. But in the United States, the diversity of the philanthropic sector does not correspond to a similar variety in the legal and financial treatment of philanthropy and nonprofit organizations: it is the "nondistribution constraint" and other formal features rather than the substantive purposes or effects of different organizations that determine their eligibility for nonprofit status.[20]

Section 501(c) of the U.S. Internal Revenue Code sets out over two dozen types of nonprofit organizations that are exempt from federal income taxation. 501(c)(3) public charities, in addition to the income tax exemption, are eligible to receive tax-deductible contributions; this amounts to a subsidy for charitable donations and costs the U.S. Treasury over $50 billion in foregone tax revenue each year.[21] The Internal Revenue Service (IRS) regulations approved on June 22, 1959, establish a definition of "charitable," for the purposes of 501(c)(3) status, as follows:

> The term "charitable" is used in section 501(c)(3) in its generally accepted legal sense and is, therefore, not to be construed as limited by the separate enumeration in section 501(c)(3) of other tax-exempt purposes which may fall within the broad outlines of "charity" as developed by judicial decisions. Such term includes: relief of the poor and distressed or of the underprivileged; advancement of religion; advancement of education or science; erection or maintenance of public buildings, monuments or works; lessening of the burdens of government; and promotion of social welfare by organizations designed to accomplish any of the above purposes, or (i) to lessen neighborhood tensions; (ii) to eliminate prejudice and discrimination; (iii) to defend human and civil rights secured by law; or (iv) to combat community deterioration and juvenile delinquency.[22]

In theory, such a definition could provide at least some very general standards by which to evaluate nonprofits. But commenting on this definition and its interpretation by the IRS, Marion Fremont-Smith concludes that "overall, the Service has been liberal in its interpretations of the definition of charity, expanding the category of public purposes to meet changing societal needs."[23] In practice, this means that some organizations fit much more comfortably within the enumerated categories (and with commonsense understandings of what constitutes a "charitable" purpose) than others.[24]

There are at least two ways in which we might be suspicious about whether an organization ought to qualify as charitable (or a donation as tax-deductible). On the one hand, we might think that an organization's purpose is malign or its activities harmful in ways that make it unworthy of public recognition or subsidy. We might worry, for example, that the Sons of Confederate Veterans, a 501(c)(3) charitable organization, uses its advantageous tax position to promote a misleading version of the history of the U.S. Civil War and Reconstruction. In other cases—say, that of the National Duck Stamp Collectors Society—we might think that public money is better (or more appropriately) spent elsewhere, without having any objection at all to an organization's aims. In both cases, determinations of what should count as charitable are controversial and contested. People on each side of the abortion debate routinely grumble about the tax-exempt status of groups on the other: depending on one's views, one is likely to resent subsidizing either Planned Parenthood or the American Life League or subsidizing them to the same degree. But the determination about whether an organization qualifies for 501(c)(3) status is binary: as far as the IRS is concerned, there is no such thing as being a little bit charitable.

The broad eligibility of nonprofits for an advantageous tax status is accompanied by weak oversight. Reich, Dorn, and Sutton find that "obtaining recognition by the IRS as a public charity is an embarrassingly easy thing to do": the IRS approves many thousands of organizations for 501(c)(3) status every year and rejects very few (in 2008, it rejected only 2.17 percent, or 1,211 of the 56,190 applications processed).[25] Monitoring of established nonprofits is minimal. Indeed, according to Fremont-Smith, qualifying for exemption from federal taxes is the closest most nonprofits must come to accounting for their ambitions and activities: "Governments require no accountings of the methods by which nonprofit organizations pursue their missions nor make any attempt to assure that charitable assets are used effectively or efficiently."[26] More recently, IRS screening and oversight of small charities in particular have further eroded,[27] partly in response to continuing political fallout from a 2013 scandal in which conservatives accused the IRS of targeting Tea Party organizations for additional scrutiny.[28]

While nonprofits' privileged tax status and the lack of public oversight (both in the acquisition of nonprofit status and after the fact) represent dramatic forms of institutional deference to philanthropy, they are not the only or even the principal forms of deference that will most occupy my attention in the chapters to follow. Worries about deference do not depend on a tax-deduction mechanism for subsidizing philanthropy (for reasons that I explain in more detail in chapter 3) or even on allegations of lax oversight.

Liberal democracies also show institutional deference to philanthropy in creating mechanisms for the enforcement of philanthropists' wishes over time. Many, including the United States, allow for the creation of institutional entities that facilitate the long-term operation of philanthropic influence: the private grant-making foundation, permitted to exist in perpetuity and carry out the charitable plans of its creators even after they die, is an important example. But even without creating their own charitable institutions, donors enjoy protection for their wishes beyond what applies in ordinary contractual relationships. The law on charitable gifts and bequests is content neutral but aims at the protection of the donor's intent. Major gifts often come with terms, conditions, and restrictions on approved uses of the gift, and these can be notoriously difficult to modify. The principal obligation of trustees is to ensure that the donor's charitable plan is carried out to the fullest extent possible. State attorneys general are charged with monitoring charities and enforcing donors' wishes. In general, the only way legally to use a restricted gift for purposes other than those originally set forth by the donor is to show that accomplishing the donor's charitable plan has become impossible (either because it has already been accomplished, as in the case of an eradicated disease, or because the goal is otherwise obsolete, as in the case of a donation to preserve a now-extinct species) or illegal. In such cases, provided that it can be shown that the donor had a "general charitable intent" beyond the specific purpose outlined in the gift, courts may grant relief under the doctrine of *cy pres* (from the French *cy pres comme possible*, or "as near as possible"). Under *cy pres*, a charitable gift may be used for a different purpose than originally specified so long as it approximates the donor's original charitable plan as closely as possible (by, say, fighting a similar disease or preserving the habitat of a related species). As Iris Goodwin puts it, "the *cy pres* doctrine harbors no criterion by which to evaluate the continued social efficacy of a nondiscriminatory restricted gift short of showing that it has ceased to exist," and the concepts of impossibility or impracticability (the standards for *cy pres* relief) generally do not provide relief even "where there is a significant opportunity cost to the charity because a mission has become dated or even anachronistic in the ordinary sense of these words."[29]

Legal deference to donor intent has been upheld even when the donor's charitable purpose becomes not merely obsolete but socially obnoxious. In a famous case, Senator A. O. Bacon of Georgia left property to the city of Macon to be used as a park—for white people only. Bacon's 1911 will specifically states his conviction that "the two races (white and negro) should be forever separate."[30] More than fifty years after Bacon's death, the city was faced with a dilemma: it could no longer run the park for white people only and so sought *cy pres* relief to remove the racial restriction. The Georgia courts and, eventually, the Supreme Court of the United States refused: "Segregation was 'an essential and inseparable part of the testator's plan.' His charitable intent was not 'general,' but 'specific'; and since it could not be carried out, the park land would revert to Senator Bacon's heirs."[31] The land was sold and is now occupied in part by an office park.

Other emblems of durable philanthropic influence are more idiosyncratic and less contested. For over thirty years, since a famous art heist carried off works including three Rembrandts, a Vermeer, and a Manet, empty frames have hung in the Dutch Room of Boston's Isabella Stewart Gardner Museum.[32] Isabella Stewart Gardner's 1924 will left land and an art collection "in trust as a Museum for the education and enjoyment of the public forever," but the will also specified that "no works of art shall be placed therein for exhibition other than such as I, or the Isabella Stewart Gardner Museum in the Fenway, Incorporated, own or have contracted for at my death."[33] Gardner's will provides that if at any time the trustees place new artworks for exhibition or "change the general disposition or arrangement of any articles which shall have been placed in the first, second, and third stories of said Museum at my death, except in the kitchen and adjoining bedrooms on the first floor," then "the said land, Museum, pictures, statuary, works of art and bric-a-brac, furniture, books and papers, and the said shares and the said trust fund" would pass to Harvard College to be sold.[34] The empty frames hanging today are a visible reminder not only of the theft but also of the museum's (legally enforceable) deference to the wishes of its founder.

At first we might seek to explain the treatment of such bequests as part of a more general deference to the wishes of a deceased person in disposing of her property. This explanation will be particularly tempting to those who credit (or blame) the United States for an exceptional regard for private property rights. But the rights of donors making charitable bequests receive an unusual degree of protection. If a bequest is deemed to have a charitable purpose, the donor's authority exceeds what is granted for noncharitable bequests. Unsurprisingly, American law prevents the creation of trusts for the support of illegal activities; it also places limitations on trusts that are merely capricious. For example, when Leona Helmsley died in 2007, she left $12 million to be held in trust for her lapdog, Trouble. In 2008, a judge deemed that this amount exceeded what was necessary to care for a dog and reduced Trouble's inheritance to a modest $2 million.[35] But had Helmsley created a charitable trust narrowly devoted to the care of Maltese dogs residing in her neighborhood—even if this number were negligible—it would have been much more difficult to divert the money.[36] The law does not undertake assessments of caprice in the case of charitable bequests: at issue is whether a bequest qualifies as charitable at all, but (once again) this is an all-or-nothing question. If it *is* found to be charitable, the full range of protections and benefits apply.[37]

These protections and benefits represent political choices. Philanthropy is, as Rob Reich argues, an "artifact of the state."[38] The state determines what counts as a charitable purpose or bequest, and it accords these special legal protection and tax advantages. These forms of special treatment require justification and cannot be explained simply by a more general respect for property rights. The right to property does not entail that some uses of property or types of organizations be granted preferential treatment through the tax code. And a supposed natural right to have one's (former) property used according to one's stipulations after it has been given away and even long after one's death would be, at the very least, controversial. Whatever one's views are about the *moral* rights of property holders, the legal rights of charitable donors are creations of the state. Arguments appealing to property rights push us either to apply consistent standards to state regulation of commercial and charitable transactions or to explain why different normative standards apply to the regulation of philanthropy as distinct from other uses of private property. Why should someone who wants to tell Leona Helmsley the maximum acceptable amount to spend on a dog be reluctant to tell (say) Andrew Carnegie which institutions are worthy of support?

In the next section, I consider some candidate reasons for defining certain uses of private resources as charitable or philanthropic and according such uses social or institutional deference.

The Sources of Deference

Notwithstanding the kinds of criticism and scrutiny already mentioned, the default presumption remains that philanthropy is, at least standardly, a good thing. Of course, most people recognize the potential for corruption, mismanagement, or grift. If I do not spend much time discussing these problems, it is not because examples have been in short supply in recent years. David Fahrenthold's Pulitzer Prize–winning investigative reporting on the Donald J. Trump Foundation for the *Washington Post* uncovered corruption and self-dealing and (along with an investigation by New York's attorney general) led to the foundation's dissolution in 2019. And in the summer of 2020, amid national protests following the murder of George Floyd by Minneapolis police, a nonprofit calling itself the Black

Lives Matter Foundation raised some $4 million before it became widely reported that the organization lacked any apparent affiliation with the #BlackLivesMatter movement (the foundation's stated mission was "to help bring the police and the community closer together").[39] But such cases are generally understood to be aberrations. I want to stress that democratic criticisms of philanthropy apply to much harder cases and to many kinds of philanthropy that most observers would intuitively classify as "good." Before elaborating those lines of criticism, then, it will be useful to examine the reasons behind the commonsense endorsement of (most) philanthropy.[40]

In what follows, I divide the reasons for valuing philanthropy by focus: on philanthropy's importance for its beneficiaries, for givers themselves, or for society as a whole. These categories are not exhaustive or watertight; they simply help to organize my inquiry into the different and potentially competing values that we might prioritize in the evaluation and regulation of philanthropy. As I will argue, none of our diverse reasons for valuing (some) philanthropy provides a justification for subsidizing or weakly regulating the sector as a whole.

The Beneficiaries: What Philanthropy Provides
(and States or Markets Don't)

Philanthropy can do good: this is the broadest and most obvious reason for endorsing it. Philanthropic donations can enhance the welfare of recipients (or of the people served by recipient organizations). By providing goods that are not supplied (or are undersupplied) by states and markets, philanthropy can complement those other sectors and act as a hedge against their fallibility. Philanthropy also can help to drive changes in the behavior of other actors—for example, by calling attention to or attempting to correct injustices. In the case of both service-delivery and advocacy philanthropy, there are therefore good reasons to worry about what beneficiaries and the broader community would lose if philanthropic activity declined.

Most strikingly, perhaps, philanthropy can play an important mitigating or remedial role when government policy is unjust or illegitimate. In the Jim Crow era, state governments in the southern United States blocked public investment in schools and higher education for Black students. Private philanthropy, notably by Julius Rosenwald and the Rosenwald Fund, attempted to address that gap. Between 1913 and 1948 (when, unusually for a private foundation, the Rosenwald Fund spent itself out of existence), Rosenwald's private wealth built over 5,000 schools in the rural South. W. E. B. Du Bois was by no means an uncritical champion of northern philanthropists: he frequently criticized their compromises with the white South and their discomfort with Black leadership;[41] he also stressed the unrealized potential of publicly funded and Black-led institutions during the early Reconstruction years.[42] But he nevertheless praises Rosenwald in a memorial notice in *The Crisis*, stressing the context of public and democratic abdication: "The South accepted his gift effusively, and never even to this day has apparently recognized the failure of democracy which permitted an individual of a despised race [Rosenwald was Jewish] to do for the sovereign states of a great nation that which they had neither the decency nor justice to do for themselves."[43] Rosenwald's philanthropic efforts are an example of philanthropy seeking both to counter and to correct a public injustice. By tying his grants for schools to a modicum of public investment, Rosenwald attempted to encourage the reform of state policy and to create a precedent for investment in Black children's education. Du Bois focused on the importance of this dissenting and catalytic role in his tribute to Rosenwald: "He was a great man. But he was no mere philanthropist. He was, rather, the subtle stinging critic of our racial democracy."[44]

Parallel claims are made on behalf of advocacy philanthropy—for example, philanthropic funding of NAACP litigation in the civil rights era and contemporary movements for marriage equality and immigration reform. Philanthropy can help promote the protection of minority rights and the interests of people who are underserved by electoral institutions. And philanthropic service delivery (e.g., in the health and education sectors) can likewise help to offset the failures of state and market provision. The appropriate attitude to take to philanthropy in contexts of state or market failure is a complicated question. As I argue in the following chapter, liberal egalitarians will generally think that there is a moral remainder when justice-required goods are supplied through discretionary philanthropy. Similarly, we might worry about nonprofit provision "letting government off the hook." But in cases where an important need is unmet by states and markets, few people object to nonprofit provision as such. We might regret that some people should need to have recourse to charitable homeless shelters while still endorsing shelters' good effects and the efforts of the people who contribute to running them.

So philanthropy can be an important stopgap in situations where government is unable or unwilling to meet the requirements of justice. But philanthropy can also play a complementary and not just a remedial role vis-à-vis the state. Its capacity to do good is not limited to areas where government has failed to recognize and protect people's rights or to provide benefits and services to which they are entitled. Consider the Hole in the Wall Gang Camp, a 501(c)(3) charity founded by the actor Paul Newman.[45] Since 1988, the charity has run a free residential summer camp in Connecticut for children with serious medical conditions. Most people will agree that such a charity is doing good even if it is not doing something just, something obligatory, or something that ought to be done by the state. In such cases, there may be no moral remainder at all when a charity provides the service. We might think that government will not be able or competent to provide some services or, more positively, that some projects will better be pursued by nonprofits. Even people who think it highly desirable that recreational opportunities be offered to sick children might believe that services will be better conceived and managed by dedicated nonprofits than by state agents or bureaucrats. Arguments about philanthropy doing good also need not rely on strong claims about charities making optimal use of their resources. Some might doubt whether programs that save no lives and cure no diseases represent the best use of charitable donations. And there is likewise room for debate over whether such services ought to be publicly subsidized. But even people who would prefer to see both public and private funds spent elsewhere can acknowledge that these charities meet genuine human needs and significantly benefit the people whom they serve. At worst, they are a low priority in the universe of misspent funds.

Citizens also disagree about what government should provide and how. In liberal democracies, these questions are subject to democratic decision-making that will inevitably leave some people disappointed, and market provision may not always fill the gap. Philanthropic donations can widen the circle of people whose preferences are satisfied. Economic theories of nonprofit organizations often emphasize philanthropy's role in supplying (or supplementing) public goods that are expected to be underprovided by both states and markets.[46] Burton Weisbrod focuses on the role of nonprofits in "providing collective goods where consumer demand is heterogeneous."[47] Governments can provide public goods where there are collective action problems (or individual incentives not to contribute), but they will generally only do so up to the level that would satisfy the median voter. For "undersatisfied demanders" of collective goods, nonprofits and philanthropy can meet residual demand and act as "mini governments."[48] Importantly, philanthropy here acts to add options for people unsatisfied with those provided by the state, not to restrict or remove options that would otherwise exist.[49]

Even when it duplicates public or for-profit services, we might value philanthropy for its ability to give individuals options and to contribute to a desirable pluralism in services offered. A system where government holds a monopoly over a given service (essential or nonessential) may be less likely to register and respond to information about the preferences of service recipients: it allows only for the exercise of "voice," whereas philanthropic provision can add the option of "exit."[50] When donors and nonprofits are involved in the funding and delivery of welfare and other services, individuals may be better able to express their preferences (with the option of "exit" and sometimes without the requirement of ability to pay) and to make informed choices between the alternatives available to them (say, by being able to choose between a secular public education for their children or a private religious one). On this account, again, philanthropic provision is a matter of adding to the list of available choices, not of removing any choices from people.[51] (Some authors also suggest that we have a pro tanto reason to prefer nonprofit provision to government provision because the former involves no coercion.)[52] Choice-based reasons for supporting philanthropy are often part of a more general disposition to favor extensive private service provision,[53] but they need not be rooted in antigovernmentalism: they can rather derive from a more general commitment to the value of pluralism in the provision of public goods.

Some have argued that philanthropy's insulation from political accountability allows it to function as society's "risk capital"[54] and that large philanthropic institutions enjoy a comparative advantage related to their long time horizons. Innovation, dynamism, and an entrepreneurial approach to long-term social goals are often cited as the defining virtues of the philanthropic sector and especially of the large American foundations.[55] Reich proposes two standards according to which foundations, understood as elite institutions, may nonetheless be "not merely consistent with democracy but supportive of it": pluralism (foundations act as a salutary counterweight to government orthodoxy by funding and promoting a diverse range of public goods) and discovery (foundations can be drivers of innovation and experimentation, given their unaccountability and long time horizons).[56] To some extent, family foundations, like the Rockefeller, Ford, and Gates Foundations, have delivered on these promises— for example, by pursuing research agendas on food security and infectious diseases that were far more ambitious and transformative than parallel government efforts.[57] We might think that such innovation will be less likely if government assumes all responsibility for the cultivation of knowledge and for long-term visions of social progress. Philanthropy lets us try out new ideas and new ways of meeting needs, allowing us to decide in a more informed way about what government should do; we can interpret many philanthropic innovations as "auditioning" for eventual public approval or uptake.[58]

The reasons canvassed here—considerations of justice; of goods and benefits beyond justice; of choice, pluralism, and innovation—yield one set of rationales for according philanthropy special deference: perhaps governments and citizens judge these forms of deference to philanthropy to be necessary or efficient for extracting public benefits. Rationales pointing to public benefits need not deny the permissibility of the state's regulating philanthropy differently. Indeed, they at least imply that governments *ought* to regulate philanthropy differently if it turns out that these forms of deference are *not* necessary or efficient in extracting public benefits.[59]

Other arguments for deference to philanthropy are less contingent on an assessment of its effects; they argue instead that we have reason to treat philanthropy differently from other transactions based on the giver's motivations and the nature of her actions.

The Givers: Charity versus Consumption

Arguments for according broad latitude to private philanthropy need not discriminate between philanthropy and (other) consumption goods: libertarians, as well as many liberals, will say that, having paid one's taxes, one is entitled to spend one's money (and time) on any legal pursuit that one likes. This argument could support the enforcement of contracts between donors and recipients, but it would be less likely to support any state subsidy of philanthropy (e.g., through tax exemptions or deductions). If philanthropy deserves respect only as a consensual use of private property, then we should treat it like any other. However, some defenses of philanthropy either deny that it is rightly characterized as consumption at all or claim that philanthropy is morally better or more important than ordinary consumption spending.

The view that philanthropy is distinct from personal consumption is reflected in the structure of state incentivization of philanthropy in many countries, including in the United States. When Americans claim tax deductions for charitable contributions, they subtract the value of their donations from their taxable income.[60] The tax deductibility of donations to nonprofits can be defended on instrumental grounds, as a desirable encouragement or subsidy of philanthropic contributions. But it can also be defended on noninstrumental grounds as the correct way of assessing a person's taxable income.[61] As Reich puts it, the claim here is that "deductibility is *intrinsic* to the tax system": the standard definition of taxable income includes personal consumption and wealth accumulation, but on this view, charitable donations are neither.[62] There is widespread acceptance of the idea that charity represents a choice to forgo consumption (or is even analogous to paying taxes: consider Mitt Romney's claim during the 2012 presidential election campaign that "every year, I've paid at least 13 percent [of income in taxes], and if you add, in addition, the amount that goes to charity, why the number gets well above 20 percent").[63] Bill Gates, reflecting on Thomas Piketty's *Capital in the Twenty-First Century*, writes that Piketty "doesn't adequately differentiate among different kinds of capital with different social utility."[64] Instead of Piketty's proposal for a progressive tax on capital, Gates would prefer a progressive tax on consumption, a point he makes by distinguishing between three different kinds of wealthy people: "One investing in companies, one in philanthropy, and one in a lavish lifestyle. There's nothing wrong with the last guy, but I think he should pay more taxes than the others."[65] Philanthropy in particular, Gates thinks, deserves more space than Piketty gives it as a potential solution to inequality, since it "not only produces direct benefits for society, it also reduces dynastic wealth."[66]

Intuitive distinctions between charity and consumption may prevent us from registering concentrations of wealth and power in the charitable sphere. Warren Buffett has a famously restrained conception of appropriate inheritance. In an oft-quoted formulation, Buffett "believes in giving his children 'enough so that they feel they could do anything, but not so much that they could do nothing.' That means, in his judgment, 'a few hundred thousand each.'"[67] But in 2006, Buffett gave each of his three children $1 billion. This would likely have attracted some suspicion of hypocrisy had Buffett not specified that the billions of dollars involved were to be directed to his children's charitable foundations. Buffett was not trying to give them additional income: he was giving them influence. With the stroke of a pen, Buffett was able instantly to make each of his children a significant player in the philanthropic sector; suddenly, they could advance their own favored causes and influence other organizations. Gates may be right to say that philanthropy sometimes reduces dynastic wealth, but it can also shore up dynastic power in ways that the charity-consumption distinction obscures.[68]

In everyday language, arguments contrasting philanthropy with consumption work better for some categories of philanthropy than others. The claim that donors have selflessly relinquished money they might otherwise have spent on yachts often merits further scrutiny (notably in the case of the many yacht clubs registered as public charities). Some philanthropy is quite easily conceived as consumption: the donor gives money to a nonprofit organization (largely) because she enjoys or expects some benefit from it, as in the case of opera patrons. But even donations that primarily serve others can bring the donor indirect or intangible benefits. (As Thomas Hobbes once explained of his own charity to an elderly beggar: "I was in paine to apprehend the miserable condition of the old man; and now my Almes, giving him some reliefe, doth also ease me.")[69] Attempting to single out a subset of philanthropy as nonconsumption looks unpromising.[70]

Historically, many assessments of philanthropy (including, but not limited to, religious traditions of almsgiving) have focused on the morality and motivations of the giver, contrasting egoistic consumption as well as (some) self-serving donations with altruistic or duty-based giving. One difficulty lies in the inscrutability of donors' motives. If deference is owed only to selfless giving, we need to distinguish genuinely altruistic gifts from others, and this faces obvious difficulties (and not only in the case of donors like Hobbes). But even if donors' motives were transparent to observers, the political and public policy implications of the distinction between selfish and selfless giving would be unclear. The mere fact that an action is morally praiseworthy does not provide the state with sufficient reason to promote that action through its policies (any more than the mere fact that an action is selfish or otherwise morally blameworthy gives the state sufficient reason to legislate against it). Assessments of the relative moral value of different motivations for giving—insofar as these are taken to have implications for government *policy*—sit uneasily with liberal commitments to toleration, antipaternalism, and respect for privacy.

A different argument fares better from a liberal point of view. If acts of giving and volunteering help individuals develop and express their conceptions of justice and of what is valuable or meaningful in life, then perhaps government should encourage philanthropy for reasons that do not assume a general government interest in promoting virtuous behavior.

The point is not that philanthropy counts as foregone consumption or that it is necessarily morally superior to (other forms of) consumption spending. Rather, philanthropy may have special ethical importance in the lives of givers and volunteers. I agree that philanthropic giving and volunteering is valuable to givers as a way of expressing and enacting moral and political commitments. But the same could be said of political contributions and even of extravagant consumption spending: pointing to how much a person cares about a particular use of money, or even the degree to which *her* interests would be advanced by such spending, does not carry us far toward the specification of the appropriate regulatory structure. As in the cases of consumption and campaign spending, a presumption in favor of expressive and economic liberty might be outweighed when we consider effects on public outcomes and democratic equality.[71]

The Community: Civic and Associational Externalities

We have just been considering philanthropy's value as an expression of the giver's ethical priorities or conception of the good. A related but less individualistic strand of argument instead emphasizes philanthropy's civic benefits for participants and positive externalities for communities. As with the values of pluralism and innovation, these can be expressed both as direct benefits to participants in philanthropic transactions and as benefits to society as a whole.

On civic arguments for philanthropy, the value of the nonprofit sector does not depend on whether the projects to which citizens devote their time and money are particularly ethically exalted[72] or on the material results of their activities. There is another kind of benefit that philanthropy provides to citizens and society, one that cannot be measured in terms of project effectiveness or individual morality. Rather, the benefits are (at least in part) social or civic. By cooperating with other citizens on their own initiative, donors and volunteers help to build "social capital": the "features of social organization such as networks, norms, and social trust that facilitate coordination and cooperation for mutual benefit."[73] We might regard an active civil society as good in itself. But we might also see it as a key precondition for a functioning democracy: voluntary participation in civil society helps to train people in the virtues we want democratic citizens to have.

Surveying the role of voluntary associations in American civil life, Alexis de Tocqueville claims that the "art of associating" is crucial for promoting the "morals and intelligence of a democratic people"; for combating democratic societies' tendency toward individualism and atomism; and as a bulwark against creeping government despotism.[74] John Stuart Mill borrows this point from Tocqueville and classes "philanthropic enterprises by voluntary associations" among other participatory institutions and practices "as parts of national education; as being, in truth, the peculiar training of a citizen, the practical part of the political education of a free people, taking them out of the narrow circle of personal and family selfishness, and accustoming them to the comprehension of joint interests, the management of joint concerns."[75] Such civic arguments for philanthropy do not depend on claims that voluntary provision will do a better or more efficient job of providing goods and services than government could. Associational activity is rather to be valued for its educative potential and its positive social and political externalities. Participants learn to feel ownership over public projects and empowered to affect the direction of their communities, and even nonparticipants can benefit from the reservoirs of trust and reciprocity that associational activity helps to supply.[76] The relationship between the strength of public institutions and the vibrancy of the philanthropic sector is positive sum: in a virtuous circle, active and engaged members of civil society contribute indirectly to strengthening democracy.

There are legitimate doubts about the degree to which philanthropy exhibits the virtues or delivers the benefits claimed for it, and I engage these questions in more detail in later chapters. But we must, I think, acknowledge that philanthropy does good—in ways large and small, marginal and transformative—for the well-being of beneficiaries, for the moral development of givers and participants, and for the shared life of a community. How to evaluate and weigh the good that philanthropy does, and what forms of regulation follow from it, are more difficult questions.

Disaggregating Deference

Our reasons for valuing philanthropy may emphasize what it does for beneficiaries, for donors themselves, or for society at large. These reasons are not unassailable; some may be stronger than others, none apply to all of the transactions and practices that might be grouped under the label "philanthropic," and most offer indeterminate guidance on many of the most important political questions surrounding philanthropy (e.g., the appropriate rules of engagement between donors, nonprofits, and government regulators). But they raise considerations that should hold some weight in normative evaluations of philanthropy and political arguments around it.[77]

However, reflecting on candidate reasons for extending special treatment to philanthropy also helps us to see how *under*explained many existing forms of deference are. While the reasons just canvassed typically single out some forms of philanthropy (though not always the same forms of philanthropy) as dramatically more valuable than others, existing regulations and even social attitudes often fail to make similar distinctions.

For example, benefit-focused arguments for philanthropy are much better positioned to explain some incentive mechanisms for giving than others. Perhaps tax deductions for philanthropic contributions are meant to encourage socially beneficial gifts. If so, this might call into question the scope of the incentive: Are all the 501(c)(3) charities that are currently eligible to receive tax-deductible contributions contributing greater social value than government might produce with the lost tax revenue? Even if we think that the answer to this question rests on controversial value judgments of a kind that public policy ought to avoid, related questions need not. Donor-advised funds (DAFs), increasingly popular vehicles for philanthropic contributions, permit donors to take advantage of tax incentives for donations that may not actually be *spent* for many years. As critics of DAFs point out, these legal creations are difficult to justify by pointing to the production of public benefits: they make it easier to make tax-deductible contributions without producing any benefits at all, at least in the short term, and they do not appear to stimulate additional giving in proportion to the lost tax revenue.[78] Similarly, the low mandatory payout requirements for private foundations seem more likely to facilitate the consolidation of philanthropic power than the timely disbursal of benefits.[79] One might accept that foundations can play a valuable role in democracies but nonetheless argue that this role should be time limited—for example, by increasing foundations' mandatory annual payout such that their endowments would be spent down.[80]

If we consider, instead, pluralism and choice-based rationales for philanthropy, we again find cases that fit awkwardly to the model. Defenses of philanthropy that draw distinctions between government, market, and nonprofit spheres of competency and legitimacy have further work to do in explaining why they approve (if they do) of the proliferation of mixed forms of service delivery. In recent years, the lines between the public and private sectors have blurred, and novel arrangements involve government collaboration and contracting with both for-profit and nonprofit service providers. This has been particularly true in the United States since the welfare reforms of the mid-1990s, which introduced "charitable choice" legislation authorizing governments to contract with charitable (including religious) providers for welfare and health services.[81] Perhaps such programs combine the best of both public and philanthropic provision, bringing choice and efficiency to public services and resources and legitimacy to nonprofits. But it is equally possible that these mixed arrangements will combine the worst, rather than the best, of public and private provision: we might, for example, sacrifice accountability without appreciable gains in choice or efficiency.

Associational arguments also present striking examples of mismatches between the theory and practice of deference. Many arguments about the civic and social benefits of philanthropy apply better to time than to money.[82] Such arguments may have difficulty justifying the tax subsidies of philanthropy in their most prevalent form, where people who give their money are eligible to claim deductions, but there is no comparable mechanism to subsidize or incentivize time spent volunteering. Civic arguments might give us reason to extend preferential treatment to volunteers over donors; it is difficult to see how they could justify the inverse. To the extent that civic arguments give a defense of the philanthropic sector, they appear to have a subset of that sector in mind. This becomes consequential when reasoning that seems paradigmatically to point to the benefits of citizens volunteering their *time* (for example, the civic and associational arguments surveyed earlier) is deployed in defense of the weak regulation or tax deductibility of philanthropic *money*.

We should be wary of synecdochical reasoning—of leaping from fairly specific reasons for endorsing *some* philanthropy to undifferentiated deference to everything currently grouped under the label "philanthropic." The shape of the nonprofit sector is not self-evident, and attempts to offer an all-purpose defense of philanthropy suffer from underspecification. Any time a reason is invoked for supporting philanthropy or for insulating it from government taxation and regulation, we should keep in mind the kinds of philanthropy that this particular reason would protect. None of the reasons canvassed here apply (and certainly not with equal force) to all of the individuals, groups, and institutions that comprise the "nonprofit sector." Little or no actual philanthropy can be equally well defended with reference to all possible reasons for supporting philanthropy.

Moreover, our diverse reasons for valuing philanthropy might sometimes point in different directions on questions of regulation and management. We do not yet know the relative weight of the pro-philanthropy rationales explored in this chapter, and we should be alert to the possibility of trade-offs between them.

I have been referring to reasons for *valuing* philanthropy rather than *justifications* for incentivizing or weakly regulating it. This distinction is often obscured in discussions of philanthropy. But identifying benefits that philanthropy can provide does not resolve the question of the appropriate governance of philanthropy (or even the appropriate attitudes to take toward it, all things considered) any more than identifying benefits that aristocratic elites can provide resolves the question of the appropriate distribution of wealth. A justification for the role of philanthropy in a liberal democracy, if it is not to operate simply as a rationalization, must consider not only our reasons for valuing philanthropy but also competing values: liberal, egalitarian, and democratic.

Conclusion

The time is right to reevaluate the regulation of philanthropy and our attitudes toward it. This book does so by focusing on philanthropy's compatibility with democracy and with relationships of social and political equality. Identifying forms of deference that lack adequate explanation or justification helps us to recognize aristocratic or oligarchic tendencies in (what pass as) ordinary features of contemporary democratic practice.

There is more than one route to a critique of "other people's altruism." Sometimes backseat donors complain that money could be spent on better purposes or in more efficient ways. Sometimes criticism is rooted in a fear of robber barons bearing gifts—in an aversion to dirty money or a suspicion of impure motives. But there is a distinctively democratic criticism to be made of philanthropy, one that is too often neglected but which this book pursues: some people's altruism puts other people under their power. Even genuine altruism can operate through and reinforce social and political relationships that are inimical to democracy. In the next chapter, I begin to develop this criticism and consider alternative ways of interpreting the demands of democratic equality as they relate to philanthropy.

CHAPTER TWO

Equality and Philanthropic Relationships

Charity and philanthropy sit uncomfortably with ideals of equality, in at least two distinct ways. Giving often occurs against a backdrop of economic inequalities: it may be made possible by surplus wealth and made urgent by serious deprivation. Egalitarians may therefore view some philanthropy as an objectionable effect of unjust inequality—for example, when opportunities to practice philanthropy arise from unjust allocations of resources, or when people depend on private benevolence for goods to which they are entitled as a matter of justice. There is also a second way that philanthropy can violate egalitarian principles: by creating or reinforcing objectionably hierarchical social and political relationships.

To the extent that it has considered philanthropy, liberal egalitarian political theory has used the first of these two frames. For liberal egalitarians in the Rawlsian tradition, transcending the injustices that can be associated with charity requires putting in place just social institutions to maintain a fair distribution of resources and opportunities. In a just society, philanthropy would either become superfluous or focus on providing goods that public institutions need not or ought not supply. Liberal egalitarians have exacting conceptions of what would be necessary to secure people's standing as equals, but those conceptions are defined mainly in relation to public rather than private power. The problems with charity relations are largely derivative of problems with unjust social institutions, and so the theoretical interest of philanthropy itself is secondary to the problem of specifying fully just social institutions.

In the first section of this chapter, I show the limitations of such an approach. Rather than understanding philanthropy as a secondary distributive mechanism (e.g., for approximating the just distributions that institutions fail to achieve or for supplying some goods that liberal states ought not to), we should attend to philanthropy's first-order significance for shaping social and political relationships in egalitarian or inegalitarian ways.

In the second section of this chapter, I reconstruct (with a view to reviving) a long-standing tradition of social theorizing about philanthropy. By contrast with contemporary liberal egalitarians, earlier theorists paid far greater attention to the kinds of social and political relationships that philanthropy promotes or subverts. Both egalitarians and proponents of hierarchy recognized that philanthropy's social and political significance far outstripped its impact on distributive shares.

In the third section, I give special attention to John Stuart Mill's and Jane Addams's critiques of philanthropy, both of which combine a relational perspective with egalitarian commitments. Mill and Addams both treat philanthropy as part of a system of subordinating relationships. In criticizing familiar models of charity, their concern is not primarily to impugn the intentions of donors or (only) to improve philanthropy's distributional outcomes. Rather, they seek to replace hierarchical and paternalistic relationships with democratic and egalitarian ones.

To egalitarians today, it might seem that we are past the need to talk of rehabilitating philanthropy: our task should be to imagine and construct just *political* institutions. But recovering a relational perspective on philanthropy does not require us to concede the inevitability (much less the desirability) of relying on voluntary giving to meet important social needs. The important insight to be gained from relational egalitarian perspectives is that charity can compromise equality in ways that are not reducible to the injustice of background institutions and their distributional effects—for example, by encouraging relationships of personal dependence, domination, and paternalism.[1] This insight makes philanthropy and its regulation a more important site of egalitarian and inegalitarian political action than we often recognize.

Voluntary Giving and Distributive Egalitarianism

Charity or philanthropy is not a major concern in most contemporary liberal egalitarian theories of justice.[2] This is not because liberal egalitarian theorists idealize philanthropy or assign it a first-best role in discharging obligations of distributive justice. It is unrealistic to think that we could maintain a just distribution exclusively through voluntary transfers; and, in any case, it would be unreasonable to expect individuals to arrange all of their choices with a view to promoting an overall pattern of social justice. Therefore, most liberal egalitarian theory in the Rawlsian tradition focuses on principles of equal liberty and distributive justice as they apply to the institutions of the "basic structure" of society and to the ways that major social institutions distribute rights, opportunities, benefits, and burdens.[3]

However, liberal egalitarian theory does furnish principles from which one can attempt to derive guidance for voluntary giving and political responses to it. There are two main routes available. First, liberal egalitarian principles can distinguish between appropriate and inappropriate roles for philanthropy.[4] It is objectionable when things that are owed to recipients as a matter of justice are supplied (exclusively) through discretionary charity rather than guaranteed by political entitlements. (This point holds whatever one's view of distributive justice, but theories that take an expansive view of what social justice requires have correspondingly greater occasion to deplore the misapplication of the "charitable" label.) In practice, this often leads to the conclusion that the state should fund the supply of important social goods like education, health care, and welfare services through coercive rather than voluntary redistribution.[5]

But justice does not require the state to supply all kinds of goods; it may not even permit the state to supply goods of some kinds. For example, some liberals object to state funding of religious and other cultural goods, whose public provision or subsidy is thought to implicate the state in favoritism, moral or aesthetic perfectionism, or both. The doctrine of liberal neutrality holds that the state must be neutral between citizens' comprehensive moral and religious doctrines and between their "conceptions of the good."[6] In an oft-cited formulation, Ronald Dworkin argues that "liberalism takes, as its constitutive political morality," a theory of equality that "supposes that political decisions must be, so far as is possible, independent of any particular conception of the good life, or of what gives value to life."[7] Given the variety in conceptions of the good, "the government does not treat [citizens] as equals if it prefers one conception to another, either because the officials believe that one is intrinsically superior, or because one is held by the more numerous or more powerful group."[8] Arguably, accepting neutrality as a constraint on government action presents serious obstacles to (for example) state funding for the arts: it is not the business of the state to tell people what art is worth looking at or to subsidize the expensive tastes of consumers of high culture.[9] Nevertheless, we might think it desirable that *someone* fund museums, operas, and symphonies, both for the sake of the people who already have tastes for these goods and so that opportunities to discover and cultivate such tastes are broadly available. Philanthropy might help provide opportunities to access cultural goods while freeing up public spending for goods whose public provision or egalitarian distribution is required by justice.[10] So just as there are some goods that philanthropy ought not to supply, there may be goods that philanthropy is *better* positioned to supply than the state.[11]

This proposed division of labor between public institutions and private philanthropy may be attractive in ideal theory, but it is less clear how its prescriptions apply outside it.[12] When the institutions of the basic structure are less than just, should philanthropy limit itself to the role that it would appropriately play under just institutions and fund (say) cathedrals and art installations? Or does the absence of just institutions change the moral situation so that philanthropists ought to engage in (and political communities ought to tolerate) kinds of giving that, in ideal theory, would represent an overstepping of the just institutional division of labor? While an ideal theory of philanthropy might be of some theoretical interest, we should not assume that its conclusions are portable to nonideal theory, where both the institutions of the basic structure and the background distribution of wealth may be unjust in ways that complicate ideal-theoretic conclusions.[13]

There is a second way that liberal egalitarian principles can guide voluntary giving in nonideal theory: donors can give in ways that respond to and attempt to correct distributive injustices. Voluntary giving on its own cannot achieve justice: justice is a virtue of social institutions, not of states of affairs, and so determinations of justice turn on the social outcomes that institutions guarantee and not on the outcomes that happen to come about (e.g., through market or charitable transfers). Justice is not *equivalent* to a particular distribution of goods, resources, or opportunities—but many egalitarians think that justice does *require* some such pattern of distribution. This pattern ought to be secured and maintained by the institutions of a just basic structure. But when institutions fail to perform that role, perhaps philanthropists can identify the outcomes that would result under just institutions and aim to approximate them as closely as possible. The Rosenwald Fund's work[14] building schools for Black children in the southern United States shows how important philanthropy can be in partially offsetting the effects of public institutions that distribute resources and opportunities unjustly.

Liberal egalitarians will resist the idea that voluntary giving can fully compensate for unjust institutions. Donors have neither sufficient money nor adequate information to secure and maintain a just pattern of distribution for society as a whole. But, for individuals contemplating donations, concerns like these will rarely serve as reasons for not giving; they are, rather, reasons for judging a society unjust if it relies too heavily on voluntary giving to meet its social needs. One could acknowledge the insufficiency of voluntary giving while still seeing it as a valuable second-best option in the context of unjust institutions. Perhaps, following Rosenwald, donors should give so as to make outcomes more just rather than giving as they would if institutions were *already* just.[15] Philanthropy can serve as a remedial virtue for individuals when social institutions are vicious.[16]

So liberal egalitarian principles of distributive justice can be invoked both to recommend upholding the institutional division of labor by focusing philanthropy on non-justice-required goods and to encourage philanthropists to supply the justice-required goods that are underprovided by states. But the problem is not only one of indeterminate advice to donors about where to give.

Liberal egalitarian views focused on distributive obligations also obscure important ethical and political issues that go beyond the obvious allocative question. When some people voluntarily contribute private resources to benefit other people or the public at large, whose judgments about how best to use those resources should be authoritative? How should democrats evaluate the influence that philanthropists exercise in public life? Can philanthropists wrong their beneficiaries in important ways, even when benefiting them in distributive terms? These questions are especially likely to be ignored if we suppose either that philanthropy is funding non-justice-required goods or that it is remedying public injustices; in either case, the advantages of philanthropic action may seem to dwarf the democratic and relational risks.

Distributive egalitarianism has the advantage of keeping an exacting ideal of social justice in view: it urges us not to concede too much to the status quo or to let the state off the hook. But it struggles to gain critical purchase on philanthropy *itself*.[17] From the perspective of distributive egalitarian ideal theory, when we see people relying on philanthropic gifts for things that should be theirs by right; when philanthropy gives the rich an outsized role in the provision and direction of public goods; or even when we see givers attaching exploitative or paternalizing conditions to their assistance, the fault is with the way that social institutions distribute wealth and other important resources, and that is where we should direct our critical attention. Provided that recipients have a right to refuse gifts they do not want or whose conditions they deem unacceptable, it is difficult to see how voluntary giving can make recipients worse off than unjust institutions have already made them.

In the remainder of this chapter, I argue that evaluating philanthropy in relation to an ideal of just institutions (and a just institutional division of labor, and a just distributive pattern) is not the only or most important way of deriving guidance in nonideal theory. Social theorists have long argued that voluntary giving—like other modes of distributing goods—can have important effects beyond its immediate distributive consequences. In particular, it can affect (for better or worse, and on different conceptions of what counts as better or worse) the ways that members of a society relate to each other, both socially and politically. These perspectives can help us think more clearly about how philanthropy might promote a society in which people relate as equals. Adopting a relational egalitarian perspective on philanthropy does not require abandoning ambitious distributive egalitarian ideals, but it discourages defining philanthropic obligations too narrowly in relation either to an institutional division of labor or to an overall social pattern of distributive justice.

Social Theories of Voluntary Giving

A broader approach to social and political theorizing helps to reveal very different standards for evaluating voluntary giving. Many contemporary egalitarians may struggle to articulate how philanthropy could make things worse than unjust institutions already have. But for many earlier thinkers it would have seemed perfectly obvious that indiscriminate charity could be worse than no giving at all, even holding constant the background social institutions. This can be true even on distributive conceptions—for example, if one believes that distributive justice involves each person receiving things in proportion to her moral worth, then government and charitable aid are equally capable of upsetting the desirable pattern. (Hence the strong emphasis on distinguishing deserving from undeserving recipients in the history of both public and private poor relief.) But worries about voluntary giving need not refer only to the distributive consequences of gifts. Past theorists and practitioners saw philanthropy as an important site of, and influence on, relationships between individuals and social groups.[18]

Charity and philanthropy have often been understood as particularly important in underscoring the differences between rich and poor members of society and in structuring attitudes toward class hierarchy. Paul Veyne makes this point in relation to ancient Greece and Rome: in a classic study, he argues that large-scale civic giving for public works and festivals functioned as a marker of the elevated status of the rich.[19] Writing about nineteenth-century America, Tocqueville similarly suggests that the rich pursue philanthropy in part as a way of maintaining their social distance from other citizens.[20] But charity can also be a more intimate site for enacting alternative conceptions of class relationships (whether paternalistic or solidaristic). On many nineteenth-century accounts, charity was a particularly important way for both the poor and their benefactors to learn their respective places in the social and political hierarchy. In his history of Progressive Era class relations in New York City, David Huyssen describes Josephine Shaw Lowell's Charity Organization Society of New York as exemplifying "prescriptive class relations" in which "bourgeois individuals or groups attempt to prescribe or choreograph the behavior of the poor and working class with a minimum of violence."[21] On the other hand, he identifies settlement house movements as cases of cooperative class relations, with wealthy individuals "listening to or allying themselves with labor-dependent citizens (or noncitizens) on collaborative terms."[22] Voluntary giving could exemplify different normative conceptions of social relationships, but historically, the idea that one important function of philanthropy was to promote social and political relationships of *some* kind was taken as obvious.

Authors such as Tocqueville point to effects on social relationships as a principal reason for preferring philanthropic to public provision of poor relief. Writing of English responses to pauperism, he praised individual almsgiving over public relief, partly on the grounds that private charity "established valuable ties between the rich and the poor. The deed itself involves the giver in the fate of the one whose poverty he has chosen to alleviate. The latter, supported by aid which he had no right to demand and which he may have had no hope to getting, feels inspired by gratitude. A moral tie is established between those two classes whose interests and passions so often conspire to separate them from each other."[23]

With public poor relief, by contrast, the rich man "sees the poor man only as a greedy stranger invited to share his wealth. The poor man, on the other hand, feels no gratitude for a benefit that no one can refuse him and that could not satisfy him in any case."[24] Similarly, Herbert Spencer argues against public relief (funded through compulsory taxation) on the grounds that such a practice would crowd out altruism and morally valuable relationships. Spencer laments that "the payment of poor rates will supplant the exercise of real benevolence," leading to a "dormant condition" of "nobler feelings" and, inevitably, to "a depreciation of the national character." He also claims that it will leave the poor no better off: "while there is a public provision for poverty, there will be no incentive to the exercise of benevolence on the part of the rich, and no stimulus to prudence and economy on the part of the poor."[25]

We do not need to endorse these authors' views of moral psychology or their policy conclusions to agree that, when evaluating alternative modes of distribution, we should take account of more than their immediate distributive consequences. Here, a comparison to philosophical treatments of markets is illuminating. Philosophers concerned about the ethical implications of markets and marketization have argued that, for better or for worse, the ways that goods are supplied and distributed (e.g., through publicly guaranteed entitlements versus through market exchange) can change the social meanings of goods as well as social relationships.[26] The issues at stake in debates around marketization have always been both empirical and normative: How does selling a good affect its quality, supply, and distribution; the social meanings ascribed to the good; and relationships between people in society?

For both intrinsic and nonintrinsic reasons, the social meanings and relational effects associated with voluntary giving are often thought preferable to those associated with market exchange. Richard Titmuss's classic study of blood donation and the "gift relationship"[27] is a touchstone for this view. Comparing the blood donation regimes of the United Kingdom, where paid donations were prohibited, and the United States, which permitted some measure of commercialization, Titmuss found that rates at which people gave blood actually declined in the United States following the introduction of payment. He hypothesized that commercialization had changed the meaning of blood donations. For some givers, what was once an expression of generosity and solidarity was recast as a somewhat tawdry transaction (whether or not they were themselves motivated to seek payment for giving blood). Counterintuitively, permitting paid donations seemed to negatively affect both the quality and quantity of the blood supply. Here, then, is a candidate case of a good that ought to be supplied philanthropically, whether because of the first-order importance of the relational effects of commercialization or merely because of the instrumental importance of social meanings and relational effects in conditioning the supply of the good.[28]

Titmuss is usually cited as support for arguments against commodification and the *market* provision of certain services,[29] but Michael Walzer suggests that parallel arguments could apply against government provision: he takes it that voluntary blood donations are preferable not only to market provision but also to a blood "tax."[30] Even setting aside objections from bodily integrity, we should hesitate to replace voluntary blood donations with coerced contributions, since, in doing so, we would close off important opportunities for people to act virtuously and to express (as well as foster) social solidarity. Walzer argues that the superiority of the gift relation extends beyond blood to other social welfare services, at least where the capacity to contribute is broadly distributed: "There is an argument to be made, very much like Titmuss's argument about blood, that private giving should be encouraged. The act of giving is good in itself; it builds a sense of solidarity and communal competence."[31] The argument shares important premises with Tocqueville's and Spencer's: in comparison with public provision (relying on coerced redistribution), private philanthropy promotes intrinsically as well as instrumentally valuable social relationships.

But critics of Titmuss note that the social effects of gift relations might not be unambiguously positive. In addition to his better-known finding about blood donation, Titmuss's U.S.-U.K. comparison contrasts the incidence of malpractice suits in the United States with the relative unimportance of such suits in Great Britain. On the basis of this difference, Titmuss suggests that the commercialization of medicine promotes more antagonistic relationships between doctors and patients (and, implicitly, that commercialization can be criticized on these grounds). Kenneth Arrow identifies a reactionary impulse in Titmuss's critique of the commodification of medicine.[32] For Arrow, Titmuss's criticisms of malpractice suits idealize a world where patients receive care as a gift—gratefully and without hostility—and "where doctors and hospitals are protected from the consequences of their errors, at least as far as legal proceedings are concerned."[33] Titmuss, Arrow thinks, neglects the central issue of whether the malpractice suits under consideration are *justified*: if there is indeed (as Arrow thinks the evidence suggests) "a lot of malpractice in the United States," then to discourage suits "would simply be a way of denying compensation to legitimate victims for the costs imposed upon them, and of minimizing a method of exerting pressure on doctors who perform badly."[34] Indeed, Titmuss himself acknowledges that in the U.K. system "the scales are weighted in favor of the doctor" and fails to specify methods other than litigation by which patients may press their claims. For Arrow, "what is disturbing, in this case as in many others, is that an appeal against the marketplace and its coldness has a way of slipping into a defense of privilege."[35]

This is not to say that only markets can protect the vulnerable and hold the powerful to account, nor that they are generally the best means of doing so. But the gift relationship, to the extent that it suggests unquestioning (or at least nonlitigious) gratitude as the appropriate response to goods and services received, may well do worse even than markets with respect to promoting egalitarian social relations and the forms of accountability that support them. This point complicates the contrast between (benign) altruism and self-interest or profit seeking, and it is often overlooked. For example, Peter Singer and Michael Sandel both defend Titmuss against Arrow and attack the latter's characterization of altruism as a "scarce resource" in need of conservation.[36] But neither addresses the egalitarian dimensions of Arrow's critique of Titmuss: Arrow's point was not only that we should avoid overreliance on altruism for fear of using it up; he also calls attention to *whose* altruism we rely on when we prefer the gift relationship to other mechanisms of distribution.

Contrary to arguments that the relational effects of giving are a reason to *prefer* philanthropic to state or market provision of some goods, we should consider whether they might be a reason to reject it. Arrow's perspective has deep roots in classical political economy. Consider Adam Smith's dictum that "it is not from the benevolence of the butcher, the brewer, or the baker that we expect our dinner, but from their regard to their own interest."[37] Why should this be a good thing, for the person wanting her dinner? On Debra Satz's reading, the point is not only that self-interest makes the supply of a good more reliable; Smith is also making an emancipatory relational claim on behalf of markets, since "the motivation of self-interest that fuels a market differs from those motivations involved in the exercise of an arrogant and personal power."[38] Buyer and seller may not be the most morally exalted roles in which individuals encounter each other, but they are far from being the most degrading.

If markets are capable of crowding out some desirable sentiments and values, they may also be capable of crowding out some relational vices.

Distributive egalitarians can share the worry about domination or personal dependence and (as noted in the previous section) regard many kinds of gifts and donations as inadequate substitutes for state-guaranteed entitlements. At the same time, many will see charitable provision as morally preferable to *market* distribution of a justice-required good. Both charitable and market transactions occur without recipients having a guaranteed entitlement to the relevant good, but market exchanges may seem more likely to produce outcomes that reflect or exacerbate distributive inequalities. Obviously, if one cannot effectively claim an entitlement to something, it is at least *in one way* better to receive it for free than for a price.

But it may be only in one way better. Our all-things-considered judgment should depend on social as well as distributive factors.[39] Receiving something as a gift may do more than simply "subtract" the element of monetary price from what is otherwise an ordinary market transaction. It can occasion changes in how the transactors understand their relationship. Just as it may be disrespectful to redescribe as a charitable gift something to which a person is entitled by right, it can be offensive to redescribe market exchanges as acts of charity (e.g., by hiring someone to perform work for an agreed fee but later announcing—or even implying—that the work was unnecessary and the wage offered out of pity). From the point of view of effects on relationships, gifts are not necessarily a strict improvement on exchanges. Insofar as receiving something from the benevolence of the giver is (sometimes) undesirable, receiving something as a gift rather than purchasing it might be preferable from the point of view of cost while at the same time being offensive or injurious to the recipient's self-respect.

This can be true even when one person is genuinely attempting altruistically to benefit another rather than relabeling self-interested behavior as altruism after the fact. People with disabilities, for example, sometimes express offense and frustration at sincere offers of help (or spontaneous attempts to help—for example, by opening doors), even while recognizing the good intentions that often motivate these gestures.[40] Notably, this can be true even of people who need some service and would have no objection to paying for it. Unilateral attempts at help can be patronizing in cases where help that comes in response to a request for a service, or an offer of payment for a good, would not be. A great deal depends on who identifies and articulates the need and who defines the strategy for responding to it.

These relational considerations are not reasons to reject philanthropy wholesale. The meanings that we attach to different modes of distributing goods and services (e.g., ideas about what counts as insulting or demeaning) are contingent; sometimes, they can and should be revised.[41] Moreover, as I stressed in the previous chapter, philanthropy is not a unitary category: it encompasses a wide range of purposes, practices, and norms, which can be expected to produce different social and relational effects. Both of these points are consistent with my central claim that, in order to assess the relationship between voluntary giving and equality, we need to look not only at its effects on distributive holdings but also at its effects on relationships. Even when the transfer of goods proceeds according to a desirable distributive pattern, giving can be managed in ways that are disrespectful of recipients or beneficiaries and that can contribute to inegalitarian relations over time. Charitable donations, like market transactions, can transform the ways that members of society relate to important social goods and to each other. The challenge is to design gifts and voluntary assistance so that they are supportive rather than subversive of recipients' entitlements, autonomy, and equal social standing.

Of course, it is important not to assume the permanent necessity of meeting important needs through philanthropy. A relational perspective need not lead to (what liberal egalitarians would consider) political quietism and low expectations for social institutions.[42] What is wanted are perspectives that balance concern for the justice of social institutions with a recognition of the importance of philanthropy's relational effects. To that end, in the next section, I reconstruct John Stuart Mill's and Jane Addams's analyses of charity's bearing on social and political relationships. Both authors embed critiques of existing models of charity in a progressive vision, according to which democratic and egalitarian social relationships will and should replace relationships of discretionary benevolence. They therefore criticize philanthropy to the extent that it reproduces subordinating social relations. For these authors, paternalistic social and political relations are grounds for criticism, not only of unjust background institutions but also of philanthropy as a social and political practice.

Mill and Addams on Philanthropy and Subordination

John Stuart Mill wrote against the grain of Victorian enthusiasm for private charity. In *Principles of Political Economy*, when arguing for state-guaranteed aid to even the able-bodied poor, Mill stresses not only the inadequacy but also the ineptitude of most private aid and worries about its tendency to encourage dependence.[43] In *The Subjection of Women*, he refers to women's increased philanthropic activity as a *drawback* of their expanding sphere of public participation:

> The great and continually increasing mass of unenlightened and short-sighted benevolence, which, taking the care of people's lives out of their own hands, and relieving them from the disagreeable consequences of their own acts, saps the very foundations of the self-respect, self-help, and self-control which are the essential conditions both of individual prosperity and of social virtue— this waste of resources and of benevolent feelings in doing harm instead of good, is immensely swelled by women's contributions, and stimulated by their influence.[44]

This is a remarkable indictment considering its author and its context: in his most important feminist treatise, Mill suggests that women exercise what public influence they have in harmful ways. The puzzle dissipates once we realize that women's subjection and their misguided charitable efforts are, for Mill, closely related. Mill's criticism of Victorian women's philanthropy has two main strands. First, he argues that women's subjection—including their educational and occupational limitations and the prevailing ideal of feminine virtue—seriously compromises the competence and utility of aid. Second, he argues that women's zeal for charity is a product of their internalization of a damaging patriarchal ideal:

> A woman born to the present lot of women, and content with it, how should she appreciate the value of self-dependence? She is not self-dependent; she is not taught self-dependence; her destiny is to receive everything from others, and why should what is good enough for her be bad for the poor? Her familiar notions of good are of blessings descending from a superior. She forgets that she is not free, and that the poor are.[45]

Mill thinks that, rather than promoting justice, philanthropy reflects and reproduces subordinating social relations. To avoid caricaturing Mill's view, it is important to note that the particular evil he stresses is dependence on *private* benevolence: Mill defends entitlements to a legally guaranteed subsistence, but he seems to think that the charity relationship is distinctively destructive of the autonomy and equality of recipients.

Jane Addams founded Chicago's Hull House in 1889; she became the most famous face of the American settlement house movement, as well as one of the most prominent reformers of the Progressive Era. Addams read *The Subjection of Women*, and it made an impression on her.[46] In her speeches and writings, she quotes the following line: "There is nothing, after disease, indigence, and guilt, so fatal to the pleasurable enjoyment of life as the want of a worthy outlet for the active faculties."[47] Mill's critique of charity occupies a relatively small part of *Subjection*: he concentrates most of what he has to say about it into two long paragraphs,[48] and so it is possible that Addams simply took little notice of that thread. However, this possibility is made somewhat less likely by the fact that the "active faculties" passage she quotes on multiple occasions is drawn from one of those two paragraphs. How much of the critique did she absorb? Addams's work on behalf of Chicago's poor and working communities might look like either a repudiation or a misinterpretation of Mill's advice: his point is precisely that charity is *un*worthy as an outlet for active faculties and is more likely to do harm than good.

In fact, Addams shares Mill's rhetorical ambivalence about charity: she famously wrote that she was "always sorry to have Hull House regarded as philanthropy."[49] Addams interprets the settlement house's work of providing services in working-class and immigrant neighborhoods as importantly distinct from charity or philanthropy. While acknowledging that Hull House did have "several distinct charitable departments," she objects to what she criticizes as a tendency to confound "the problems of the working class" with those of "the inefficient, the idle, and distressed":

> Working people live in the same streets with those in need of charity, but they themselves, so long as they have health and good wages, require and want none of it. As one of their number has said, they require only that their aspirations be recognized and stimulated, and the means of attaining them put at their disposal. Hull House makes a constant effort to secure these means for its neighbors, but to call that effort philanthropy is to use the word unfairly and to underestimate the duties of good citizenship.[50]

Whether or not through any direct influence, Mill and Addams converge on several points. First, they agree that avoiding misguided and counterproductive aid requires givers' direct involvement and contact with beneficiaries rather than sentimental donating from a distance.[51] Addams continually stresses the residential component of the settlement house, where volunteers live among the community they seek to benefit, as an important condition of its efficacy. Beyond this prescription for active involvement, Mill and Addams share a deeper ambivalence about philanthropy (and resistance to characterizing their preferred models of aid as charity). They both point to pervasive category mistakes that people make when theorizing or practicing charity: for Addams, this involves confusing the needs of the working class with those of "the inefficient, the idle, and the distressed" or "those in need of charity"; for Mill, the philanthropic woman "forgets that she is not free and that the poor are."[52] The idea that free and independent people do not or should not need charity might sound like victim blaming or a specious excuse for withholding benefits. But Mill and Addams both argue for expanded government aid to the poor and see value in some forms of private aid as well. To make sense of their critiques of charity or philanthropy, we need to understand them as criticizing not the distribution of benefits to a particular population but rather a form of social relation: charity or philanthropy, they think, is the wrong way of *relating* to free and independent people.

Mill and Addams share a broadly optimistic conception of social progress: society is moving toward democratic, egalitarian social relations characterized by reciprocity and mutual respect. In the context of such a conception of progress, they converge on a specific critique of philanthropy: philanthropy represents an archaic social relation, poorly adapted to changing social and political circumstances in the second half of the nineteenth century. It is not uncommon to hear the virtues associated with philanthropy described as feudal or aristocratic ones. Mill and Addams both invoke this connotation and mean something particular by it. Philanthropy is a feudal relation in the sense that it is hierarchical and paternalistic: it asks the poor and working classes to trust others to define their interests and act on their behalf. Addams makes this point through an extended analogy between the Pullman Strike and *King Lear*. Each drama, she thinks, features a man convinced of his own generosity and goodness—a man who attributes his misfortunes to the ingratitude of those who owe him deference.[53]

George Pullman was the owner of the Pullman Car Company, which manufactured railcars on the South Side of Chicago. He had designed the company town (also named Pullman) as a model community, where most of his factory workers lived. According to historian Almont Lindsey, Pullman insisted upon "a planned community with beautiful houses and lovely streets, parks, and public buildings," but "his motive was not entirely philanthropic. . . . Desirous of avoiding labor difficulties, Pullman believed that paternalism wisely administered would lull the restless yearnings of the laborer."[54] It did not. In 1894, layoffs and salary reductions led to a wildcat strike and to conflict (sometimes violent) that engulfed Chicago and spread to other cities. Pullman refused arbitration, just as he had previously refused to allow a union presence in the factory or town. On Addams's reading, Pullman had "assumed that he himself knew the needs of his men, and so far from wishing them to express their needs he denied to them the simple rights of trade organization."[55] In exchange for the benefits he conferred, he had expected the "almost feudal virtue of personal gratitude"[56] and had been bitterly disappointed. It is in this sense that Pullman "lived out within himself the tragedy of King Lear": "The shock of disaster upon egotism is apt to produce self-pity."[57]

Addams uses Pullman's errors (or her stylized interpretation of them) to stand in for the errors of philanthropic industrialists in general: "Lack of perception is the besetting danger of the egoist. . . . But, doubtless, philanthropists are more exposed to this danger than any other class of people" because "their efforts are overestimated" and "easily idealized."[58] On Addams's interpretation, Pullman's principal failing was his inability to imagine the perspective or take seriously the agency of the people he was trying to benefit. Like Lear, who loves Cordelia but is unable to see her refusal to flatter as a kind of integrity, Pullman is accustomed to deference and blind to the reasons animating his subordinates: He "could not see the situation from the social standpoint."[59] He wanted to be "'good to people,' rather than 'with them.'"[60] In this he is emblematic of a broader philanthropic error:

> It is so easy for the good and powerful to think that they can rise by following the dictates of conscience by pursuing their own ideals, leaving those ideals unconnected with the consent of their fellow-men. The president of the Pullman company thought out within his own mind a beautiful town. He had power with which to build this town, but he did not appeal to nor obtain the consent of the men who were living in it.[61]

In a literal sense, of course, the inhabitants of Pullman *did* have a choice as to whether or not to live there, and so it is clear that Addams means something more exacting when she urges philanthropists to connect their ideals to "the consent of their fellow-men."[62] This demand for respectful engagement cannot be satisfied simply by providing the option to refuse benefits or by engaging in community "consultation" (a favored practice of philanthropists today). Addams asks for a more radical redistribution of control, one that would grant previously subordinated groups the authority and the means to define and pursue their own interests—and this, she thinks, is what philanthropy resists.

Addams characterizes the philanthropic attitude as part of a broader (and obsolete) "individual ethics," which she opposes to democratic "social ethics": philanthropy, like feudal and patriarchal power, is part of a *system* of subordinating social relations whose time has passed. Mill makes his own version of this point (including the analogy to patriarchal power) in his critique of a conception of social relations that he refers to as the "theory of dependence and protection":

> According to [the theory of dependence and protection], the lot of the poor, in all things which affect them collectively, should be regulated *for* them, not *by* them. They should not be required or encouraged to think for themselves. . . . It is supposed to be the duty of the higher classes to think for them, and to take the responsibility of their lot. . . . This function, it is contended, the higher classes should prepare themselves to perform conscientiously, and their whole demeanour should impress the poor with a reliance on it, in order that, while yielding passive and active obedience to the rules prescribed for them, they may resign themselves in all other respects to a trustful *insouciance*, and repose under the shadow of their protectors. The relations between rich and poor, according to this theory (a theory also applied to the relation between men and women) should be only partly authoritative; it should be amiable, moral, and sentimental: affectionate tutelage on the one side, respectful and grateful deference on the other. The rich should be *in loco parentis* to the poor, guiding and restraining them like children.[63]

The problem with this theory is not only its vulnerability to abuse but its inappropriateness to a society of equals. Mill concedes that this model of social relations has some nostalgic appeal: "there is something naturally attractive in a form of society abounding in strong personal attachments and disinterested self-devotion. Of such feelings it must be admitted that the relation of protector and protected has hitherto been the richest source."[64] However, he argues that "these virtues and sentiments . . . belong emphatically to a rude and imperfect state of the social union" and are now obsolete: "the assumption of the part of protector, and of the power which belongs to it, without any of the necessities which justify it, must engender feelings opposite to loyalty."[65] Models of social or political interaction that reinforce the theory of dependence and protection, and the sentiments underlying it, set the wrong moral example.[66]

By exploring the similarities between philanthropy and other archaic, hierarchical relations, Mill and Addams help to explain how recipients might experience even well-intentioned, consensual, and all-things-considered beneficial charitable transfers as subordinating. They measure progress not only in terms of distributive outcomes but also in terms of the egalitarianism and reciprocity of social relations. Money could be flowing in the right direction while at the same time bolstering objectionably hierarchical relations. The politically regressive aspects of philanthropy can be more difficult to see in the abstract than when we look at the history of philanthropy as Mill and Addams do: as a history of attempts at once to increase poor people's welfare and to affirm elite control.

Mill and Addams share a pragmatic interest in the moral lessons that we draw from our experience of relationships with other people, and they agree that those lessons are likely to be good or bad to the extent that the relationships are egalitarian or hierarchical. They therefore criticize modes of interaction that legitimize paternalistic and patriarchal relations and valorize interactions that model equality and reciprocity.[67] This shifts the priorities of voluntary action. For both Mill and Addams, replacing philanthropy with nonsubordinating relations is a democratic imperative and part of what Addams calls "the duties of good citizenship."[68] Addams writes of the need to "extend democracy beyond its political expression,"[69] and this objective figures importantly in her vision of a social settlement as "an experimental effort to aid in the solution of the social and industrial problems which are engendered by the modern conditions of life in a great city."[70] As an experiment in democracy, the social settlement meant giving up on strict attempts to control the objectives and outcomes of social progress. In part, Addams and her counterparts in the British settlement house movement were reacting to the first wave of "scientific philanthropy," in which groups like the Charity Organization Societies attempted to make aid more effective through the strict specification and enforcement of conditions on assistance.[71]

Addams's positive model of assistance calls for reversing the flow of deference between benefactor and beneficiaries. In a rebuke to philanthropists who assert a prerogative to do good efficiently by their own lights, she articulates an experimental social ethic:

> The one thing to be dreaded in the Settlement is that it lose its flexibility, its power of quick adaptation, its readiness to change its methods as its environment may demand. It must be open to conviction and must have a deep and abiding sense of tolerance. It must be hospitable and ready for experiment. . . .

It must be grounded in a philosophy whose foundation is on the solidarity of the human race, a philosophy which will not waver when the race happens to be represented by a drunken woman or an idiot boy. Its residents must be emptied of all conceit of opinion and all self-assertion, and ready to arouse and interpret the public opinion of their neighborhood. They must be content to live quietly side by side with their neighbors until they grow into a sense of relationship and mutual interests.[72]

She defends such an approach partly on epistemic grounds: the settlement house resident cannot know the needs and desires of a community without close and ongoing communication with its members, and to assume that she did would preclude forms of learning crucial to the settlement's success. But duties of respect are not reducible to their anticipated instrumental value—hence their stringency, militating against philanthropic arrogance even toward "a drunken woman or an idiot boy." In striving to explain "the gist of the Settlement movement" to her neighbors, Addams stresses the need "to make clear its reciprocity."[73]

What reciprocity entails is not articulated in advance as a matter of theory; rather, it is worked out through practice and concrete relationships. However, some themes emerge with applicability beyond the social settlement. One is the importance, for democratic ethics, of antipaternalism and of refraining from imposing one's own values and priorities on others. In practice, this requires an experimental approach and an open agenda that creates space for people to identify and articulate their own needs and desires. For Addams this meant, among other things, allowing Hull House's educational and social programming (e.g., language classes, reading clubs) and the services provided through the settlement house (e.g., child care and an open-use kitchen) to be driven by the expressed interests and needs of its neighbors. Addams denied that philanthropists are better placed than their intended beneficiaries (whether individuals, families, or communities) to define either the ends to be pursued or the best strategies for attaining them.

As Addams recognized (and reminds us), there is a tension between achieving highly specific objectives and respecting egalitarian relations; the persistent temptation for philanthropists is to discount the latter aim in pursuit of the former. Addams argues for responsiveness, reciprocity, and an ethical and political obligation to forgo the pursuit of predetermined philanthropic objectives. Voluntary action should be oriented by conceptions of progress and equality but not toward a fixed endpoint: the latter would be too rigid to allow broad and reciprocal participation in defining the goals of progress. Reflecting on the Pullman story, she argues that aspiring reformers must learn to restrain "archaic" forms of "personal ambition" in favor of pursuing "lateral progress":

> The man who insists upon consent, who moves with the people, is bound to consult the feasible right as well as the absolute right. He is often obliged to attain only Mr. Lincoln's "best possible," and often have the sickening sense of compromising with his best convictions. He has to move along with those whom he rules toward a goal that neither he nor they see very clearly till they come to it. He has to discover what people really want, and to "provide the channels in which the growing moral force of their lives shall flow." What he does attain, however, is not the result of his individual striving, as a solitary mountain climber beyond the sight of the valley multitude, but it is underpinned and upheld by the sentiments and aspirations of many others. Progress has been slower perpendicularly, but incomparably greater because lateral. . . .[74]

Neither Mill nor Addams is under the illusion that philanthropists will find it easy to restrain their exercise of power. Addams's reference to "the sickening sense of compromising with [one's] best convictions" recognizes that her ideal is a difficult and demanding one: it asks philanthropists to forgo not only gratuitous self-aggrandizement but also exercises of power motivated by deeply held moral principles and which might produce valuable outcomes. Indeed, Addams argues that Lear and Pullman deserve our compassion too; they are in the grip of an archaic understanding of social relations, and their blindness and disappointments are to that degree inevitable. There is a tragic element here for individuals who want to be good: the moral debt that unjust institutions create cannot be resolved through unilateral distributive action. There is not a single act of spending that cancels it, because the responsibility is collective, political, and democratic. The "duties of good citizenship" go beyond individual distributive obligations. Voluntary giving is important not only for its relationship to distributive justice but also for its effects on relationships: whatever its provenance or (other) effects, philanthropy can increase the control of the rich over the poor, or it can affirm the entitlement and competence of beneficiaries to control their own lives. Mill and Addams could agree that egalitarian relations require (for their full realization) just social institutions. But pursuing just institutions does not obviate the need to practice relating as equals in the here and now.

Relational Equality and Philanthropy Today

Mill's and Addams's critiques have particular (and sometimes idiosyncratic) understandings of philanthropy in mind, and we should not be too literal in looking to them for advice on contemporary dilemmas. Philanthropy today is less personalized than the interactions that Mill and Addams describe: face-to-face contact between donor and recipient is rarer, and donors often give to institutions rather than to identifiable people. Moreover, philanthropy is less often (or at least less obviously) cross-class than it was in Mill's and Addams's time: donations to organizations that directly serve poor people make up a relatively small share of contemporary philanthropic giving.[75] Finally, many of the functions that Mill and Addams describe philanthropy performing are widely (but also controversially) considered the purview of the welfare state. We might therefore think that the task of providing respectful assistance belongs to the state more than to philanthropists.

But Mill's and Addams's central question remains relevant: What kinds of social and political relationships does philanthropy (or philanthropy of different kinds) promote? Whether philanthropy is personal or impersonal; whether or not it benefits poor people; whether or not it impinges on actual or appropriate state functions: in each case, we can ask about the conceptions of desirable social relationships that underpin philanthropic action. Do philanthropy and its regulation endorse prescriptive social relations, with some groups deferring to other people's conceptions of what would be good for them? Does philanthropy reinforce patriarchal or paternalistic relations, or egalitarian, democratic, cooperative ones? Philanthropy can transform relationships in detrimental ways, even while conferring material benefits. We can criticize patronage relations as subordinating even if we think they produce good outcomes in some cases.[76]

The kind of holistic ethical and political assessment that this requires provides indeterminate guidance about *which* particular goods philanthropy should promote or supply but more determinate guidance about *how* it should promote or supply them. A focus on relational equality calls attention to the ways that donors may use their gifts to gain objectionable forms of unequal influence in public life and over the lives of their intended beneficiaries. At whatever scale philanthropy operates—whether it seeks to benefit particular individuals or the community writ large—the intended beneficiaries of voluntary giving have a claim to be involved in the definition of what their good consists in, rather than deferring to the philanthropist's conception of their best interests. Unilateral and paternalistic models of philanthropy are not appropriate for a society where people live together as equals.

Mill and Addams help us to see how philanthropy can reinforce inequality in ways not reducible to the injustice of background institutions—and that might complicate strategies for pursuing justice. This is the most important way that their perspectives can complement and enrich the theories of both voluntary giving and of justice that are currently on offer. Unjust institutions create economic and political inequalities that may be independent of the will of any philanthropist. But philanthropists nevertheless face choices about whether and how to exploit their superior power and resources. And political institutions, as well as public attitudes, affect how philanthropists exercise their power over beneficiaries and in public life. Recognizing the ways that philanthropy can compromise relational equality can be useful in generating ethical advice for donors. But more importantly, it can inform collective, political responses to philanthropy.

Addams tells us what a democratic ethic for philanthropy came to mean at Hull House. What should it mean for philanthropy and its governance today? The next two chapters develop complementary aspects of a relational egalitarian ideal. Chapter 3 focuses on democracy's "political expression" and on philanthropy's potential to usurp or subvert citizens' shared authority over matters of common concern. Chapter 4 focuses on relationships of superiority and inferiority more generally and on philanthropy's potential to paternalize its intended beneficiaries. Once these strands of the argument are developed, we will be in a better position to ask whether and how philanthropy might be made compatible with a democratic society of equals.

CHAPTER THREE

Plutocratic Philanthropy

Democracies, unlike oligarchies or plutocracies, do not reserve political influence or authority for the rich: instead, democratic citizens enjoy equal political status and are supposed to share authority over their common life. But since democracies nevertheless contain rich people, democrats naturally worry about the ways this formal principle might be violated in practice.

The challenge of achieving political equality in the face of economic inequality raises both empirical questions about how economic elites are able to translate money into influence and normative questions about the kinds of elite influence that count as objectionably undemocratic. A growing political science literature considers whether the United States is, for all practical purposes, ruled by an oligarchy. Authors in this literature have presented evidence that, in the decisions of elected representatives, the views of the very rich count disproportionately more than the views of the middle class, and that the views of the poor count for almost nothing.[1] Whatever one thinks about economic inequality as a moral concern, the democratic worry here is obvious: there cannot be a fair adjudication between political ideologies and policy preferences if only the preferences of the very wealthy count. And the democratic concerns will be sharpened if the policy preferences of the wealthy differ systematically from those of their fellow citizens: if, for example, the very wealthy are "much more favorable toward cutting social welfare programs" and more likely to "oppose government action to redistribute income or wealth."[2] Worries about elite influence likewise gain salience from evidence that economic inequality itself is growing and that wealth is increasingly concentrated at the very top of the income distribution—in the hands of the "1 percent" or, indeed, the "0.1 percent."[3] There is increasing recognition that confronting inequality requires attention to the role of the rich as well as to the plight of the poor.[4]

On the other hand, and in contrast to the much broader conceptions of democracy advanced by authors like Mill and Addams, the new oligarchy literature has so far taken a relatively narrow view of the democratic worries that economic inequality raises. It has focused on the direct political influence of the superrich and has paid comparatively little attention to the influence of money outside electoral politics and formal political institutions. (For representative examples, consider Larry Bartels's claim that "one of the most basic principles of democracy is the notion that every citizen's preferences should count equally *in the realm of politics and government*" and Lawrence Lessig's claim that "the idea that in a democracy you should be able to trade your wealth into more influence *over what the government does* is just wrong.")[5] This restricted scope makes sense if the concern about democracy is a concern about preventing the corruption of particular institutions or sites of decision-making. But if the worry is that the rich will use their money and influence to gain control over important public outcomes or aspects of common life, that concern applies beyond familiar cases such as campaign finance.

The oligarchy literature has also focused primarily on the self-interested use of private money by the rich and on cases where the rich seem to be trying to benefit themselves at the expense of their fellow citizens. For example, in an article on democracy and the policy preferences of wealthy Americans, the authors write that "the implications of unequal political influence depend heavily upon exactly what wealthy Americans actually want government to do. . . . If the wealthy have very distinctive preferences *that conflict with the interests of other citizens*, their disproportionate influence would seem to create a serious problem for the working of democracy."[6] Again this risks underestimating the scope of democratic concern, unless one's definition of democracy focuses exclusively on the quality of outcomes or the degree to which the substantive interests of the majority of people are served. Elites who used their disproportionate influence to secure economic or political benefits would of course be open to democratic objections, but so might elites who wielded their unequal influence for what they perceived to be (or really was) the common good.

In this chapter, I show how the concerns underlying the oligarchy critique extend to philanthropy as an exercise of plutocratic power. I propose amendments to both the scope and the grounds of the oligarchy critique as it has been developed so far. I argue that we should extend our understanding of the kinds of private spending that can result in undemocratic forms of elite control to include philanthropy as well as familiar forms of political influence. But in the course of making that argument, I also aim to clarify why private power and elite control matter for democracy. The problem is not (or not only) bad outcomes or selfishly motivated donors but rather the rich usurping control over a society's common life and matters of common concern.

This identification of the key democratic principle at stake should inform the kinds of democratic remedies we propose. In the case of philanthropy specifically, the threat to democratic equality arises from the conjunction of three factors: economic inequality, acceptance of an extensive public role for philanthropy, and laws and attitudes that privilege the wishes of donors (discussed in chapter 1). This, in turn, gives democratic publics a range of ways to address elite philanthropic influence: they can seek more redistributive taxation (whether to reduce the scope for philanthropic influence or for independent reasons), they can prohibit philanthropy in some issue areas, and they can attempt to redistribute control over philanthropic funds from donors to recipients or to the general public. I give particular attention to the latter possibility. We need not think that it would be possible or desirable to equalize influence over all social outcomes, but democracy does commit us to the erosion of legal and policy mechanisms that privilege, magnify, and enforce the influence of the rich.

The first section of the chapter sketches a picture of elite political spending and elite philanthropy as relevantly similar: both are ways for the rich to use their money to influence social and political outcomes. It also specifies what is distinctive about elite philanthropy, compared to donations by ordinary citizens: the degree of influence and the sustained control that wealthy donors are able to exercise through their gifts. The second section argues that such elite philanthropic influence can be undemocratic. The third section examines the limitations of some existing responses to elite philanthropy. The fourth section considers what democratizing philanthropy would mean and how we might pursue this goal, identifying some strategies for eroding elite influence that do not require (or assume) fully just political institutions.

How Does a Billionaire Give?

In this section, I make two related claims: that we tend to overestimate the differences between elite political spending and elite philanthropy and that we tend to underestimate the differences between elite philanthropy and charitable donations by ordinary citizens.

We are used to evaluating philanthropy from an ethical rather than a political perspective. Generally, ethical perspectives on giving posit standards by which we can evaluate whether someone is meeting her moral obligations, and they treat the giving behavior of the very rich as distinctive only in its scale. Peter Singer, for example, argues for a famously demanding individual obligation to give one's money away for the relief of global poverty and the suffering that it causes. Writing in the popular press, he has asked: "What Should a Billionaire Give—and What Should You?"[7] In answer, he proposes a sliding scale for personal donations to fight global poverty. This scale is presented as the working out of a universal moral obligation: giving by the wealthy will of course differ in dollar amount and so in practical significance, but Singer does not treat it as different in kind. Similarly, Liam Murphy uses the case of a billionaire to make the more general point that "it is not always best, from the point of view of justice, to devote one's efforts to making institutions, considered in themselves, just."[8] He asks,

> What is the best thing a just American billionaire can do with the fraction of his fortune he doesn't really need? Donate it to the Democratic Party? Run for president or found a "third" party? Set up a political action committee to pressure members of Congress to pursue a more just welfare policy? Or might it be better for him to donate the money directly to inner-city hospitals or schools around the country (with adequate oversight, of course)?[9]

On this view, it will often be the case that billionaires—like the rest of us—"should do what they can directly, rather than through the reform of institutions."[10]

Of course, an American billionaire (just or unjust) might pursue both strategies simultaneously. The commonsense idea that people are self-interested in their campaign contributions while altruistic or public spirited in their philanthropic donations probably captures quite poorly the ways in which people think about their own giving. Donors may instead view political influence and philanthropic spending continuously, as a complementary set of strategies for using wealth to bring about outcomes that they value. The donor who contributes to electoral campaigns to support her selfish interests but is wholly disinterested in her philanthropic donations not only has a strangely bifurcated moral psychology; she also has a limited or obsolete strategy for realizing her preferred ends. The

Philanthropy Roundtable, a conservative advocacy organization, has published a "Wise Giver's Guide to Influencing Public Policy," which advises prospective donors that "it is now common for savvy philanthropists to supplement their charitable giving with some correlated donations that aim to adjust the law and rules of governance, to inform public opinion, or to influence or change occupants of public offices."[11] The guide goes on to list the range of instruments that a savvy donor might deploy in a coordinated effort at social change: a private foundation, 501(c)(3) public charities, 501(c)(4) social welfare organizations, political action committees (PACs), independent-expenditure PACs ("Super PACs") and, of course, one's personal checkbook.[12] The U.S. tax code acknowledges different purposes and sets out different rules for different kinds of organization (with, for example, limitations on the political activities of tax-exempt nonprofits), but a donor can use a diverse portfolio of giving instruments to promote a common set of objectives.

This point receives the most attention from critics worried about the coordinated political influence of the self-interested rich.[13] Brothers Charles and (the late) David Koch have become notorious for spearheading a consortium of wealthy donors seeking to push the Republican Party to the right, to influence state as well as federal elections, and to promote rightward ideological change more broadly. This has involved not only campaign and PAC or Super PAC contributions but also extensive donations to 501(c)(3) organizations. The latter include donations to universities and think tanks, as well as to a group that stretches the IRS's limitations on lobbying and overt political activities by 501(c)(3) organizations: the American Legislative Exchange Council (ALEC).[14] ALEC, though officially a "nonpartisan, voluntary membership organization of state legislators dedicated to the principles of limited government, free markets, and federalism,"[15] uses its library of model bills (and the tax-deductible donations that it receives) to promote business-friendly and antiunion legislation at the state level. One objection is that this is philanthropy in tax status only: rather than giving for the *public* good, donors are using tax-deductible gifts to engage in political advocacy that will maximize their own profits while harming other people's interests (e.g., by weakening unions or blocking environmental legislation). Arguably, this objection undersells the ideological motivations of at least some members of the Koch network and donors to ALEC. But, more importantly, the objection elides the distinction between what might be substantively harmful about Koch and ALEC activities and what might be *undemocratic* about them. Framing the problem in terms of donors' selfish motives or the substance of their policy agendas risks obscuring a more general democratic objection to important forms of elite influence.

The Kochs and other villains of the new oligarchy literature are not alone in noticing that money can affect public outcomes in a wide range of ways. Today, the choice to seek influence via political institutions or outside them can reasonably be based on an estimation of where money will most efficiently help to bring about the desired outcomes. The new playbook for elite influence applies whatever a donor's motivations or objectives may be. Instrumental rationality, rather than egoism, predicts that donors will attempt to pull multiple levers in seeking to influence social or political outcomes.[16] Indeed, each of the available strategies for using money to affect political and social change may be *self*-described as philanthropic (note that the Philanthropy Roundtable presents efforts at political influence as a "supplement" to charity rather than the inverse). Consider, for example, Mark Zuckerberg's explanation of his and Priscilla Chan's intention to donate 99 percent of their (enormous) fortune through the vehicle of a limited liability corporation:

> The Chan Zuckerberg Initiative is structured as an LLC rather than a traditional foundation. This enables us to pursue our mission by funding non-profit organizations, making private investments and participating in policy debates—in each case with the goal of generating a positive impact in areas of great need. . . . What's most important to us is the flexibility to give to the organizations that will do the best work—regardless of how they're structured.[17]

That is, the flexibility to pursue complementary strategies for exercising influence (or "generating a positive impact"), without running afoul of the IRS's limitations on political activities for foundations, was, in Zuckerberg's view, worth forgoing the tax benefits of setting up the Chan Zuckerberg Initiative as a traditional foundation.

Viewing philanthropic and political spending as continuous fits neatly with what some scholars call the "hydraulic" problem in campaign finance reform. The expectation underlying the literature on elite political influence is that (at least some) rich people value particular social or political outcomes and will try to use their money to help bring about those outcomes: people give to political campaigns or make independent expenditures because they think that those ways of giving will influence the relevant outcomes.[18] But this problem is not specific to any particular legal framework or set of available instruments: "If money has the outcome-determining effects on the electoral process that reformers have identified, then moneyed political interests will continue trying to use money to influence outcomes whatever the regulatory regime."[19] Samuel Issacharoff and Pamela S. Karlan use the image of campaign finance "hydraulics" to capture the idea that "outcome-determining" money has to go somewhere. They make this point to caution skepticism about the ability of any set of campaign finance regulations wholly to eliminate the problem of elite influence. But the point extends also to elite philanthropy. Pursuing *some* kinds of outcomes requires (or suggests as overwhelmingly the most efficient strategy) making contributions to or around political campaigns. But we can expect money to flow into charities and nonprofits where that seems a better or more efficient way of bringing about the outcomes that the rich care about or where other channels of influence are blocked.

Once we start to think about philanthropy politically, and not just ethically, one particular feature comes to the foreground: for the very rich, philanthropy allows for powerful forms of influence that may be obscured when we use billionaires as examples in more general ethical and psychological arguments. Consider John D. Rockefeller Sr.'s claim that the wealthy donate from a more universal human impulse "to do things which give satisfaction to someone besides themselves"; in this, he thinks, "the very rich are just like the rest of us."[20] This is an eyebrow-raising use of the first-person plural from the richest American ever, whose heir once occupied his own tax bracket. But whether true or false as an account of donors' motivations, Rockefeller's claim obscures important differences between elite and ordinary philanthropy. For billionaires, philanthropy is not just an expression of altruism or moral commitment and a potential contribution to the public good. Compared with ordinary donors, elite philanthropists hold greater sway over recipient organizations and enjoy more sustained control over how money is spent.

The basic point that organizations have the greatest incentive to please those in a position to make the largest donations is familiar enough. Nonprofit organizations have an automatic interest in appealing to the wealthy—in conforming to their wishes and even in trying to anticipate those wishes in the hopes of securing contributions. But the wealthy also have more formalized mechanisms of influence. Large donations typically come with conditions or restrictions on their use—conditions that ordinary donors are rarely in a position to demand. Iris Goodwin's survey of the *Chronicle of Philanthropy*'s regular column reporting on major gifts suggests that "a major gift (in excess of $1 million) that is unrestricted is an exceptional occurrence" and "an unrestricted gift in excess of $10 million often appears to be sufficiently noteworthy to justify mention in the table of contents of the issue."[21] Conditions on large gifts are very difficult for recipient organizations to overturn, even with the passage of time: as discussed in chapter 1, the law on charitable gifts and trusts protects donor intent and does not permit balancing the plans of donors against those of recipients or against considerations of broader social utility. The rich can take advantage of this (superficially neutral) form of deference in ways that ordinary donors generally cannot.

Compared with ordinary donors, then, the very wealthy can influence the behavior of recipient organizations in more significant, sustained, and structured ways. This is especially true where they manage giving through their own institutions, of which the private foundation is the most important. There are over 110,000 private foundations in the United States,[22] and these account for approximately 17 percent of total philanthropic giving.[23] While not the largest source of philanthropic dollars,[24] private foundations pose the problem of plutocratic philanthropy in an especially salient way. They represent significant accumulations of wealth and exert a gravitational pull on the nonprofit sector: hence Dwight Macdonald's memorable description of the Ford Foundation as "a large body of money entirely surrounded by people who want some."[25] Charities, nonprofits, social movement actors, and in some cases individuals (including academics!) compete for foundation grants and have incentives to adapt their activities to foundation priorities. And since foundations are permitted to exist in perpetuity, they can preserve and transmit influence across decades. It is in the strength and durability of the influence that they can achieve philanthropically that the rich are not "like the rest of us": unlike ordinary citizens, the very rich can donate their money while retaining control of how it is spent.

The continuities between political and philanthropic influence are particularly easy to see in the case of policy advocacy. The movements for welfare reform at the state and federal levels[26] and the efforts of liberal elites to promote action on climate change[27] provide two examples of donors deploying philanthropic as well as campaign contributions in attempts to shape the outcomes of political decisions. But, as I argue in the following section, even philanthropy that is less easily assimilated to political spending can represent the exercise of elite control over social outcomes. This gives people committed to the value of democracy reason to worry about elite philanthropy.

This focus on control distinguishes the democratic critique of elite philanthropy from substantive arguments about its motives, goals, and social
impact. As I noted above, the most obvious way of critiquing elite philanthropy is to interpret it as covertly self-interested. Individual donors
may seek direct benefits or enhanced social status through their giving.[28]
Robber barons might use donations to provide ethical cover for their
business activities or to engage in reputation laundering. Perhaps, too,
philanthropy serves the interests of the rich as a class—either by winning
policies and funding programs that primarily benefit elites themselves or,
in the long run, by helping to legitimize economic inequality and an elite-
dominated political system.[29] Scholars of social movements such as Erica
Kohl-Arenas and Megan Ming Francis have argued that foundations and
other donors have influenced movement leaders to moderate their demands and pursue less radical agendas for poor people's empowerment or
for racial justice.[30] And Rob Reich points out that philanthropy in general
is not significantly redistributive.[31]

These empirical arguments are important for understanding how philanthropic influence is exercised and for informing all-things-considered
judgements about how it should be addressed. However, my democratic
objections to elite philanthropy and its governance do not depend on any
particular view about the substance of elite philanthropic activity: it is not
necessary to show that donor influence produces bad outcomes or frus-
trates just causes to sustain the claim that it is undemocratic.[32]

Moreover, to say that elite philanthropic influence is undemocratic
does not necessarily entail a negative moral judgment of the elites who
exercise that influence. A democratic (as opposed to an ethical) theory of
philanthropy will reserve much of its criticism for government and public
officials, who may be guilty of wrongfully outsourcing important public
responsibilities to private actors[33] and who create the structures through
which philanthropic influence and conditionality can operate. In general,
elite donors are not breaking any laws; if elite philanthropy *is* an undemocratic form of influence, the relevant ethical question is whether (or
when) it can be morally justifiable to exercise legal but unfair or undemocratic forms of influence. I do not assume that the answer is "never"—
for example, it may sometimes be morally appropriate to try to exercise
undemocratic power as a counterweight to other political injustices. (Indeed, at the level of personal morality, it may sometimes be appropriate
to exercise *illegal* powers in order to prevent or correct sufficiently serious
injustices.) My focus in this chapter is on the structural and democratic

problems with elite influence, and the attitudes that democratic citizens should take toward that influence, not on the moral evaluation of donors.

Finally, to call elite philanthropy or its regulation undemocratic is not to say that elite philanthropy cannot bring about good results or produce real social benefits such as innovation and discovery.[34] It is rather to deny that there is anything democratic about the way that those benefits are brought about or that the direct benefits always outweigh the democratic costs.

Elite Philanthropic Influence as Undemocratic

Philanthropy can be an important vehicle of elite influence, and this gives democrats reason to worry about it. But to make the case that elite philanthropy is undemocratic, it is not enough to show that its motivations and effects can overlap with those of political contributions. To evaluate whether or not a form of influence is undemocratic, we need a general principle about what democracy requires.

First, a terminological clarification. The terms *democratic* and *nondemocratic* can describe decision-making in a range of contexts (including, for example, associations and workplaces as well as public institutions). On most views, democratic decision-making is not normatively required or even desirable in all the contexts where it might conceivably be implemented. I therefore reserve the term *undemocratic* for objectionably nondemocratic influences on decisions and social outcomes; the term tracks views about the appropriate form and scope of democratic decision-making. Two major questions for normative democratic theory bear on the identification of a form of influence as undemocratic: the degree to which opportunities for influence ought to be equalized and the scope of outcomes that should be subject to democratic norms and procedures.

My answer to the first question does not claim that democracy commits us to equalizing the substantive political or social influence of all citizens. The argument proceeds from the more modest claim that it is undemocratic if outcomes of common concern—including both formal political decisions and the social outcomes over which those decisions ought to be authoritative—are overwhelmingly responsive to the preferences of the rich and not dependent on the preferences of ordinary citizens. We can concede or leave open the possibility that democracy permits some degrees or kinds of inequalities in influence while preserving at least a prima facie democratic objection to the outsized influence of the rich.

Assumptions about the restricted scope of democratic principles are a greater obstacle for democratic criticisms of elite philanthropy. People committed to the value of democracy are less likely to argue in defense of oligarchic influence than they are to doubt that philanthropy counts as an exercise of oligarchic political influence (except, perhaps, in cases where philanthropy "crosses the line" into politics, as observers have claimed of the ALEC and Koch cases). But I will argue that this response relies on an overly narrow view of when and how philanthropy might usurp democratic authority and threaten democratic equality. No plausible principle of democratic control can restrict itself to limiting elite influence over electoral outcomes: even staple worries raised by the oligarchy critique, about the ability of the rich to influence legislators' decisions through campaign contributions and lobbying, point to elite influence over decisions made outside of elections. A principle requiring only (formal or informal) equality of opportunity to influence *electoral* outcomes would therefore fail to capture common intuitions about when and how democratic authority matters. Too much of a focus on equalizing either formal or substantive influence at any particular procedural stage can be misleading. More broadly, democracy requires a commitment to reducing or constraining some kinds of inequalities in influence over some set of social *outcomes*.

The general democratic principle that I will appeal to is this: it is presumptively objectionable if outcomes of common concern and important aspects of a society's common life are subject to the control of the very rich.[35] While there is room for debate about what we ought to count as outcomes of common concern, that set is not composed solely of elections: it extends *at least* to the set of outcomes that citizens reasonably expect election results directly to influence. I will argue that it also extends further to include aspects of common life that should be controlled *neither* by majoritarian procedures nor by the rich. But even on the narrower and less controversial claim, elections are not the only outcomes over which we should aim to reduce or constrain the influence of the rich. Even the more minimal standard of democracy is violated by some philanthropic influence.

This is a midlevel democratic principle, compatible with different views about the normative grounding of democracy. In line with other authors, I understand democracy to be an important part of a broader relational ideal: democracy is the political manifestation of respect for people's status as equals, and it is instrumentally important to people's ability to interact as equals in social life.[36] As James Lindley Wilson argues, political equality both constitutes one important kind of equal relation and promotes egalitarian social relations more broadly.[37] Unaccountable private control over decisions that affect people in common would fail to respect people as political equals and would predictably erode relations of social equality over time. However, the general anti-oligarchic principle that I am appealing to here does not require a social or relational egalitarian account of democracy's value. Something like it is widely accepted as a core democratic commitment, though there is of course disagreement over how to flesh it out and about *why* violations of the principle are objectionable. I believe that some such principle underlies much of the oligarchy critique, even though it often remains implicit. Criticisms of elite influence are often couched instead in the language of corruption: that is, it is thought to be corrupt (not necessarily quid pro quo corruption, but a kind of improper influence or "institutional corruption") if elected officials' decisions are determined by fundraising incentives rather than the interests or express wishes of their constituents.[38] But this way of putting the problem begs the question as to why it is important that some decisions be made through uncorrupted democratic processes in the first place.

The midlevel democratic principle I am using—that outcomes of common concern ought not to be subject to the control of the very rich[39]—explains our intuitions in familiar cases of political corruption. When it comes to decisions on laws and government policies, which are presumptively of common concern to all citizens, the rich should not have outsized influence. But the principle also applies to social *outcomes* that are presumptively of common concern, whether or not law and policy directly control them or allocate control over them. The principle establishes a general presumption in favor of democratizing philanthropy because, almost by definition, philanthropy (as opposed to private consumption) aims to affect social outcomes that are of common concern to some class of people.

To illustrate how the principle can guide our evaluation of philanthropy, I now turn to some examples of elite influence in the domain of education. I choose the educational sector because it represents an area where elite influence is concentrated and salient. Schools and higher education have long been areas of focus for elite donors in the United States. However, philanthropic involvement in U.S. kindergarten through twelfth grade (K–12) education has attracted increased attention in recent years due to high-profile gifts such as Mark Zuckerberg's $100 million donation to the Newark school system in 2010 and to the longer-term involvement of major philanthropists like Bill and Melinda Gates and the late Eli Broad. Observers have raised democratic concerns about the major philanthropists' convergence on similar agendas for education reform and their increased willingness to engage in aggressive conditionality and overt policy advocacy.[40] Education reform is fraught with substantive controversy, but we can examine the structure of philanthropic involvement while remaining neutral on the appropriate education policy for the United States (or for specific states and districts).

Some concerns about foundation involvement in education reform focus on donor influence over elected officials. These concerns can be expressed in the familiar language of political corruption and oligarchic influence, with critics claiming that "foundations set the policy agenda not only for school districts, but also for states and even the U.S. Department of Education."[41] This framing presents the issue as one of money's influence over elected officials; it leaves open the question of whether other avenues of influence are more democratically acceptable. But in view of the new playbook of coordinated political and philanthropic influence (described in the previous section), we should consider the different ways that a billionaire school reformer with strong preferences about K–12 education policy might try to influence the outcomes of interest to him.

He could try to bring about an outcome he wants through political spending: he might try to buy influence over elected officials through campaign contributions in the ways oligarchy critics often worry about. (Of course, it could be considerably cheaper to buy such influence over local officials; money goes further in school-board elections than in federal election campaigns.) Suppose that a billionaire school reformer were to offer a large campaign contribution to a public official, contingent on that official adopting the reformer's preferred policy agenda. If the incentive were made explicit, we would have a recognizable case of quid pro quo corruption. If the linkage between the campaign contribution and the official's policy stance were made more subtle, we would instead have a case of what Dennis Thompson and Lawrence Lessig call "institutional corruption." On Thompson's definition, this involves "the improper use of public office for private purposes" in ways which violate "principles that promote the distinctive purposes of the institution."[42] On Lessig's definition, "Institutional corruption is manifest when there is a systemic and strategic influence which is legal, or even currently ethical, that undermines the institution's effectiveness by diverting it from its purpose or weakening its ability to achieve its purpose," including by undermining "either the public's trust in that institution or the institution's inherent trustworthiness."[43] In our case of the campaign contribution, rather than pursuing the distinctive purposes associated with her public role, the official is motivated by private gain to promote the donor's priorities. Such a case would count as undemocratic even on a more minimal democratic principle than the one I am defending—one that merely held it to be undemocratic for rich people to exert outsized, direct influence on law and policy by extending financial incentives to elected officials.

Now change the example so that the financial incentive extended for the policy change is no longer a campaign contribution but rather an offer to make resources available for public use—again, contingent on the adoption of a particular policy course. This is not a fanciful case: for philanthropists aiming to achieve public impacts, the goal is generally to "leverage" their resources in order to steer the (much larger) resources of the public.[44] For example, the Gates Foundation has in the past offered to fund consultants to prepare the lengthy proposals required for U.S. states applying for federal education grant money. The offer was available to any state that could demonstrate that it was adopting the foundation's preferred reforms, such as setting higher bars for teacher tenure.[45] Does this second hypothetical case differ significantly from the first, obviously undemocratic one of influencing a corrupt official? It depends on the degree to which our concern in the first example was the official's motivation (her concern for private gain), as opposed to the distorting effects of the donor's influence on the official's work. In the second case, it may be easier to believe that the parties involved are acting from public-spirited motivations (although note that the donor, at least, might equally be acting from altruistic motives in the corruption case). But in the case of the philanthropic offer, just as in the more familiar case of institutional corruption, what is democratically objectionable is that a decision being made by public officials is made *because* someone was rich and able to pay to have his preferred policy adopted (in a particularly naked and obvious way). The donation does not divert the institution from its purpose in the sense of orienting officials to the pursuit of private *gain*, but it does permit the private determination of public policy priorities. The philanthropic donation, like the campaign contribution, short circuits the democratic and administrative processes through which we expect the relevant decisions to be made.

As the previous example shows, even if we appeal only to the widely accepted principle that rich people's buying power should not directly influence the decision-making of public officials, some philanthropy will count as undemocratic. But the real concern should not only be *whom* rich elites influence but also whether matters of common concern are being shaped in ways compatible with people's status as equal citizens. After all, if the concern were only with preventing the corruption of public officials, then the problem could be solved by making schools private (as some philanthropists would in fact prefer). What really drives worries about philanthropic influence in this area is the fear that education outcomes and the organization of schools—vitally important matters of common concern—are becoming increasingly subject to the preferences and influence of the rich.

If that is indeed the worry, then democrats should not restrict their attention to top-down forms of influence over high-level elected officials and bureaucrats. The argument that elite philanthropic influence is undemocratic extends to at least some donations that bypass formal political institutions. In addition to donating to various levels of government, education-oriented foundations often offer conditional gifts to schools and educational nonprofits. Public, private, and charter schools accepting grants from major patrons such as the Gates, Broad, and Walton foundations have been required to restructure themselves in accordance with their donors' views on best practices. This has often meant breaking large schools into smaller ones, along with adopting an emphasis on testing and merit pay for teachers.[46] Conditional and restricted giving is something that elite donors do a great deal of (and that we could presumably expect them to do more of if leveraging influence over elected officials became more difficult).

When elite influence operates using philanthropic instruments, we are less likely to register it as corruption; when elite influence does not change laws or public policy, we are less likely to perceive a democratic concern. But notice that from the point of view of parents and community members, the usurpation of control that has occurred here looks identical to the earlier cases of institutional corruption: either way, the outcome is that public schools—institutions that ostensibly deliver democratically determined public policy—in fact deliver the policy preferences of rich donors.[47] Citizens can reasonably complain that their shared authority over educational policy has been compromised not by any outsized influence over an election outcome or formal policy but by the reorientation of effective control to private actors. The wealthy do not need to corrupt a political process when they are able to bypass it altogether. A narrow focus on political influence obscures some ways that philanthropy can subject ordinary citizens to undemocratic forms of elite control.

Notice, too, that restricted gifts result in more than just influence in the sense of rich donors providing considerations for or against something. Where such gifts are accepted, the donor's preferences actually come to determine the outcome of interest. The decisions of school administrators and principals reflect those preferences, and conditionality permits them to be enforced over time. As we have moved from considering cases of political corruption to cases of philanthropic policy influence and, finally, to the case of restricted gifts, the "corruption" of public officials looks less extreme; however, the concentrated and direct control of the rich over educational outcomes arguably tightens. In that sense, some gifts might actually be worse from a democratic point of view than campaign donations with the diffuse expectation of influence, since they may not be mediated or countered by influence of other kinds. Whether or not we want to go that far, the democratic worry is that philanthropy can progressively remove (or further insulate) important decisions about outcomes of common concern from democratic control, even if gifts are accepted by democratically authorized actors at some decision point.[48] In doing so, it threatens to erode political equality over time by shrinking the set of decisions which citizens are able to participate as equals in influencing. The cumulative effect is a kind of informal privatization, or usurpation of policy authority by rich donors.

From this worry about philanthropic privatization, one might draw the conclusion that public schools need to be rigorously insulated from accepting or being influenced by philanthropic donations, but that philanthropic influence over private schools would be unproblematic from a democratic point of view. From this it may appear that the democratic worries about elite philanthropy are parasitic on other intuitions: people who think that education should be entirely publicly funded and democratically controlled will object to elite educational philanthropy, while people who are open to at least some private provision and control of education may not. A similar division of intuitions might occur regarding health care, and these intuitions will vary in part with context: the unusual salience of philanthropy in the United States reflects a wider acceptance of the private provision of public goods than we find in other countries. Considering these dependencies, we might think that elite philanthropy raises democratic concerns only when something is appropriately a public function or joint social institution, one over which democratic government authority should be preserved.

But again, this risks missing the point about the importance of the outcomes that philanthropy influences and the question of how authority over those outcomes should be shared. Elite philanthropy can be a concern even in cases where the institutions and decisions that it influences are not and need not be publicly operated. The class of cases where democrats should worry about elite control is broader than the class of decisions that should be under formal or direct democratic control. Indeed, the very reasons that justify shielding some institutions from direct democratic control, such as a concern for pluralism and the protection of distinctive institutional purposes, can give us reason to worry about outsized philanthropic influence over those institutions. Where some kinds of insulation from democratic control may be consistent with respect for citizens' status as equals and with their shared authority over matters of common concern, private philanthropic influence over the same institutions can be democratically troubling.

Consider donations to universities. There is disagreement—and variation between countries—over the question of whether postsecondary education should be public or private. Today, both public and private universities encounter donors who seek to make restricted gifts: some cases have been controversial and broadly condemned (e.g., donor demands for control over faculty hiring)[49] and others are widely accepted (e.g., naming rights for buildings and departments). Democratic objections to donor influence over (even private) universities need not rely on the claim that all universities should be publicly operated or directly democratically controlled. Universities and other research institutions have distinctive purposes, relative to which fundraising incentives can be distorting. (This is most widely recognized in the case of medical and pharmaceutical research, where the problem of institutional corruption and the influence of for-profit corporations have long attracted attention.) Of course, relative to distinct institutional purposes, direct *democratic* control might be distorting as well. There are some institutions that we recognize as affecting outcomes of common concern but which we might want to shield from democratic decision-making and short-term political considerations. But to say that an institution should be insulated from direct democratic control need not mean that there is no objection to that institution's being controlled by the preferences of the rich. Even if one accepts the legitimacy of private university education, one might recognize the undesirability of a system where higher education becomes overly dependent on and responsive to the preferences of the wealthy. This situation raises democratic concerns, especially in its aggregate effects. (A parallel argument might be made about concentrated ownership of large media outlets.)

What counts as a social outcome of common concern and, to what degree, is contested and itself a matter to be resolved through democratic processes.[50] Not everything is a plausible candidate: where outcomes do not have significant unchosen effects on other people, elite control of a decision may be nondemocratic without being undemocratic (and even without raising democratic concerns).[51] The general theoretical point is that the democratic worry about elite philanthropy does not reduce to the question of whether or not our established democratic machinery for making decisions should be deployed in some area or not. We should care both about unequal influence over formally collective decisions and about unequal influence over outcomes that are of common concern to some group of people. This can be true even when bringing the relevant outcomes within the jurisdiction of formalized democratic decision-making procedures is not a sensible solution. The question is not only which outcomes should be public or private but also which distributions of influence are appropriate for free and equal citizens sharing authority over important aspects of their common life. The underlying democratic issue is not about money intervening on *public* institutions but the degree to which matters of common concern are under the control of the rich.

This identification of the key democratic issue can help us to evaluate the merits of alternative reform proposals. In the following section, I survey some existing treatments of elite philanthropy by democratic theorists and show their limited ability to address the key problem of elite control over matters of common concern.

Boundary Policing and Nonideal Theory

While debates about elite philanthropy often concentrate on the substance (good or bad) of what wealthy philanthropists do, some authors have mounted structural or procedural criticisms. Often, these arguments call for the insulation of the public or political "sphere" from the effects of economic inequality. In this section, I argue that approaches focused on policing the boundary between public and private arenas are inadequate for understanding the democratic challenge that elite philanthropy poses and for addressing the practical dilemmas that confront us. The democratic problem is elite control over outcomes of common concern, whether that occurs through philanthropy or through other channels of influence. Existing solutions fail to address those other channels and the hydraulics of elite control. I examine two versions of the boundary-policing response to elite philanthropy: the first focuses on the fair distribution of political influence and the second on the fair allocation of public money.

Acceptable and Unacceptable Spheres of Influence

A common response to the problem of elite influence in general is to insist on the fair distribution of electoral influence, coupled with a more rigorous insulation of public or political institutions from private money. This insistence characterizes much of the literature on campaign finance reform, and it often seeks ways of reconciling economic inequality with political equality. In his criticisms of U.S. congressional fundraising and lobbying practices, Lawrence Lessig's main target is not economic inequality but the conversion of wealth into political access and influence: "the idea that in a democracy you should be able to trade your wealth into more influence over what the government does is just wrong."[52] The important thing is to police the boundaries between private money and public officials and to insulate the political sphere from the influence of money.[53]

Some insulationist arguments suggest that if we were able to secure the equal (or otherwise fair) distribution of political influence, philanthropic influence over nonpolitical organizations and institutions (however defined) would be unobjectionable or even salutary from the point of view of democracy. For example, Ryan Pevnick argues that philanthropy has a positive role to play in the support of cultural goods since, unlike the state, "philanthropists have no responsibility to remain neutral between competing conceptions of the good life," so that "their contributions to the cultural framework of society do not raise concerns related to perfectionism."[54] As I argued in chapter 2, such recommendations about philanthropy's appropriate scope and focus may be attractive in ideal theory; however, they travel poorly to actually existing democracies. The problem is not only that citizens' other needs (e.g., for education and health care) may seem more urgent than their needs for the goods that philanthropy might ideally be charged with supplying: it is also that the institutional division of labor (whatever it is) and the public outcomes that it helps to produce may lack democratic legitimacy.

There are good reasons to accept the normative *priority* of equalizing influence over political decision-making, even if one denies the normative *sufficiency* of formal equality of opportunity to influence government. Niko Kolodny gives a good statement of the rationale for this priority from the point of view of a relational egalitarian conception of democracy's authority: "If we do have equal influence over political decisions, and those decisions have final authority over nonpolitical decisions, then that itself contributes to moderating the threat of social inequality posed by unequal influence over nonpolitical decisions."[55] Residual hierarchies would be less threatening in a society that secured equal opportunity to influence political decisions, since in such a society "whatever hierarchy there may be is ultimately regulated or authorized from a standpoint of equality."[56] But the weaker we think the connection is between ordinary citizens' preferences and political decision-making, the weaker becomes the claim that political decisions can play the role of meaningfully authorizing or mitigating lower-level inequalities. No authorization from the standpoint of equality exists; instead, even the wealthy donor who pursues genuinely desirable goals does so by exploiting a superior power that lacks democratic legitimation.

Democratic deficits in a society's political institutions put countervailing pressures on political theories of philanthropy and on insulationist arguments in particular. To the degree that we doubt that responsive democratic institutions are successfully regulating lower-level inequalities, we may have additional reason to scrutinize the wealthy's exercise of power through philanthropy, since we cannot reasonably interpret this power as having been delegated or authorized by their fellow citizens. On the other hand, the more that public institutions suffer from defects in their democratic legitimacy, the less we may trust them to regulate and restrict philanthropy for democratic purposes. There is a risk of simply shoring up one kind of undemocratic control against others.

If we imagine ideally democratic institutions, then any philanthropic influence that distorts or usurps their decisions will look undemocratic. But for actually existing societies, the claim that philanthropy is distorting democratic decisions is often more complicated. To the degree that the background distribution of influence over political decision-making is not fully democratic, it becomes more difficult to assess the net democratic impact of some philanthropic influence.

For these reasons, solutions that insist on a public monopoly over the supply of collective goods should be troubling even to people who would endorse exclusively public provision in ideal theory, since it is not clear what effects such moves to block philanthropy would have on the overall distribution of control over the outcomes of interest. In the case of public schools, for example, it is by no means clear that blocking philanthropic donations would, on its own, achieve a more equal or democratic distribution of control, given other relevant and potentially undemocratic inequalities in influence. For example, some scholars cast doubt on the democratic credentials of local school boards, given the significant demographic disparities between voters in school-board elections and the students who attend public schools.[57] Under such circumstances, blocking philanthropic donations without making other changes to the distribution of influence over decision-making could stabilize or intensify undemocratic control of other kinds (and may seem especially objectionable given that the effects of inadequate public funding are also distributed unequally). Likewise, in the case of advocacy philanthropy in areas like climate policy, restricting (only) elite philanthropic influence without addressing industry influence over elected officials might amount to unilateral disarmament rather than the assertion of democratic control. Elite philanthropy remains a nondemocratic form of influence, but it may also act as a countervailing force to other, more powerful undemocratic influences. If we are considering piecemeal solutions to implement in the real world, we need to consider the broader ecosystem of influence.

In examining problems of elite control, we rightly accord priority to political institutions, since those are the institutions charged with regulating distributions of resources and of power more generally (including in the nonprofit sector). But we should also attempt to democratize influence in other ways and in other institutional settings. This is especially the case if political institutions themselves are inadequately responsive to most citizens and responsive instead to the same rich elites who are in a position to exercise influence philanthropically. In the final section of this chapter, I make some suggestions about how we might weaken the undemocratic power of elite patronage without relying too heavily on imperfectly democratic political institutions and without sacrificing other important values.

Fair Allocations of Public Money

Insofar as political theorists have turned their attention to the problem of elite philanthropy, they have focused much of their criticism on the tax treatment of charitable donations. This has produced arguments about the misuse of *public* rather than private money. Critics have noted that the American tax-deduction mechanism for supporting philanthropy, which allows taxpayers to subtract charitable donations from their reported pretax income, unjustly favors wealthy citizens. In the first place, the deduction is ordinarily only available to people who complete an itemized tax return, who are generally wealthier than those who choose to take the standard deduction.[58] Given progressive income taxation, people in higher tax brackets also see their gifts "subsidized" by the deduction at correspondingly higher rates. (For example, by deducting a $100 donation, a donor who pays the top tax rate of 37 percent would effectively receive $37 in tax relief, while a donor in a lower tax bracket might only receive $24.) These disparities provide plausible reasons to think that the tax deduction in its current form is inconsistent with the fair and equal treatment of citizens and that the mechanism ought to be abolished or significantly reformed. However, we should be more skeptical of the idea that reforming this tax mechanism would overcome the tension between elite philanthropy and democracy.

Attempts to isolate the charitable tax deduction for criticism rely on a characterization of the deduction as a "public subsidy" in the form of "foregone tax revenue" (to the tune of $50 billion per year). On this interpretation, "providing tax-deductions for philanthropy allows donors to decide where public funds are directed."[59] By distributing this opportunity to direct "public funds" in ways that skew in favor of the wealthy, the tax-deduction mechanism facilitates "the market's pollution of political equality" and "the straightforward conversion of unequal economic means into unequal political power."[60] For Pevnick, the chief recommendation of the voucher system that he proposes as an alternative to the deduction mechanism is that the wealthy would no longer have a disproportionate ability to direct *public* revenue or *public* resources. We would instead distribute vouchers redeemable for nonprofit support, in equal shares; holding constant the current level of "foregone tax revenue," this would allocate about $225 worth of nonprofit support to each voting-age citizen. Citizens would remain free to contribute to nonprofits from their private funds in addition to using their vouchers. A voucher system, Pevnick thinks, "overcomes the tension between political equality and economic inequality that haunts deductions and credits."[61]

Shorn of idealizing assumptions, such domain-specific evaluations of the tax code can be misleading. Many tax and policy mechanisms inflate the incomes of wealthy people, providing them with fungible money that they may spend, invest, or attempt to convert into public influence. If we do not assume that a society's tax code and overall distribution of wealth are otherwise just, it becomes difficult to isolate the charitable tax deduction as uniquely problematic. Pevnick claims that the market pollutes political equality when the rich are allowed disproportionate control over the direction of foregone tax revenue or public resources. But if we consider that tax policy (and public policy generally) might unjustly favor the rich in other ways, it is difficult to see what we are to count as foregone tax revenue—that is, as the money that the rich should not be allowed disproportionately to direct to their preferred projects and that must instead be allocated equally among citizens.[62] If the charitable tax deduction is not the only source of allocative unfairness in the U.S. tax code, it would be claiming too much to suggest that reforming the deduction would overcome "the tension between economic inequality and political equality": that tension is deeper and, in the case of philanthropy, more difficult to fix than criticisms focused on the charitable tax deduction might suggest.

Moreover, reforming the deduction mechanism is insufficient insofar as we are worried about not only the fairness of subsidizing elite giving but also the consequences of elite influence. Without a subsidy for their giving, the wealthy would need to pay the "full dollar amount" for their influence, but they would retain greater buying power in the nonprofit sector (even if they scaled back their donations in amounts corresponding to the lost tax incentive). Changing only the incentive mechanism for philanthropy would not significantly affect the ability of wealthy people to exercise influence over recipient organizations or to leverage influence over public institutions and officials. For it is not only the deduction mechanism that gives wealthy citizens a greater ability to see their preferences realized through the activities of nonprofits and policy-delivery bodies; their money itself gives them that, in conjunction with policies permitting a wide scope for philanthropic activities and laws privileging donor intent. That the current mechanism for incentivizing philanthropy favors the wealthy is sufficient grounds for thinking that the mechanism is inconsistent with a commitment to equality, and nothing here speaks against a reform of the charitable tax deduction. But it is not the only or even the dominant explanation for a nonprofit sector that "generates policy outcomes that are not equally responsive to all citizens" and is instead "responsive to the needs, interests, and preferences of a small portion of the citizenry."[63] The nonprofit sector's responsiveness to elite preferences and the ability of the wealthy to shape policy outcomes would survive a reform or elimination of the subsidy. Strategies for democratizing philanthropy must address the practical exercise of elite influence and not only (one of) the tax mechanisms supporting it.

Democratizing Philanthropy

The previous section surveyed some existing approaches to the democratic concerns that elite philanthropy raises. These approaches share a focus on drawing and defending boundaries between what is (appropriately) public and what is (appropriately) private; the ambition is to secure equality in public, political decision-making and insulate that sphere from the influence of money. In my view, these strategies are of limited help in addressing elite philanthropy today: they operate at a level of idealization (about democratic institutions or background distributions of resources) that make them difficult to apply in existing democratic societies. In addition, they often treat elite control as an inextricable feature of elite philanthropy and fail to note the features of law, policy, and public attitudes that facilitate that control.

Deference to donor control may seem like a natural and universal feature of philanthropic giving, to the point where it is tempting to treat it as a fixed point in discussions of philanthropy (in contrast, say, to the scale of philanthropy in the United States, which is widely recognized as exceptional). But many of the instruments by which elite philanthropists enjoy durable influence are the contingent creations of laws and policies that give special deference to charitable purposes. For example, as discussed in chapter 1, trust law shows more deference to a testator's wishes when those wishes aim at public rather than merely private benefits; from a democratic point of view, this gets it backward. Democrats should look for ways to erode and challenge the structures through which elites have outsized influence or control, even where those structures are themselves traceable to other background injustices. We should direct our attention to oligarchic outliers in our societies—arrangements that intentionally or predictably amplify the influence and authority of the rich over other citizens, whether through formally public institutions or within institutions whose distinctive public purposes might be usurped by the influence of the rich. To treat donor control as an oligarchic outlier in this sense, we do not need a fully developed conception of what equal political influence would involve and whether it is realizable. Instead, we need closer attention to the places where law, policy, and public attitudes operate to encourage or deter the exercise of elite power through patronage. This project is compatible with seeking more just distributions of wealth and of political influence, but it need not and should not wait for their achievement.

Like other aspects of deference, donor control varies and depends significantly on institutional choices and public attitudes. Consider one strategy for governing elite munificence in the Greek cities of the Roman Empire in the first through third centuries AD. Records of proclamations and of inscriptions on public buildings and monuments suggest an explosion of elite giving to the cities. The neologism coined to describe the practice is "euergetism," from the Greek word *euergetes* (benefactor), which appears in many of the inscriptions. On some accounts, elite provision of "bread and circuses" functioned as a marker of the elevated status of the rich.[64] But Arjan Zuiderhoek stresses that elite giving was, in fact, a negotiated process in which nonelite members of the demos wielded more agency than we might have expected:

> [I]t was only when the civic community . . . had accepted a certain contribution as constituting a public gift that it would qualify as an act of civic euergetism and generate the appropriate honours. Donors proposed gifts, but were in fact dependent on the outcome of the power games involving themselves, their peers and the demos, which were set in train by their proposals. Making a public donation did not automatically turn you into an *euergetes*; only public acceptance of your gift and the granting of the appropriate honours could do that.[65]

Zuiderhoek attributes the importance of these delicate negotiations to the rise in economic inequality and the increasing political oligarchization in Asia Minor, beginning in the late first century AD. If unrest was to be avoided, he suggests, nonelites needed frequent public recognition of their status and importance as citizens; their entitlement to receive (or reject) elite gifts marked them out as special and—in one sense—still the political equals of elites.[66]

The ideal of elite giving as a negotiated process between political equals provides us with an interesting alternative perspective on elite philanthropy and on the question of who appropriately exercises agency in philanthropic relationships. Ancient models requiring popular uptake of elite gifts recognize that the range of options for regulating philanthropy is much wider than a choice between, on the one hand, blocking patronage or redirecting it to private consumption and, on the other, unlimited deference to elites. Governments and democratic publics can instead permit or encourage giving but on terms that cede less control to the donor. We need not imagine that this will always involve an overweening state enforcing uniform policies against the efforts of philanthropic innovators.

It could rather be a matter of empowering both public and private recipients of philanthropic gifts (universities, hospitals, school boards) relative to donors. We should think creatively about what institutional mechanisms (whether laws, tax incentives, or uses of administrative discretion) might elicit giving while weakening the presumption that elites should control gifts.

In this spirit, legal scholars have recommended increasing trustees' ability to flexibly repurpose gifts beyond what *cy pres* permits by reducing or eliminating the legal enforcement of dead hand control.[67] This strategy would avoid both perpetual enforcement of the original donor's intent and excessive reliance on courts to determine appropriate charitable purposes. Instead, it would place "ultimate decisions about changing the use of charitable assets in the hands of living trustees" and create loci of control independent of both government and donor.[68] While potentially valuable in addressing the long-term impact of donor conditionality, this would not significantly diminish or democratize the power of living donors.

Beyond weakening the legal protection or enforcement of donor control, we should also create a structure of tax incentives less favorable to it. For example, rather than abandoning the charitable tax deduction, we might instead make it available only for unrestricted gifts or general support grants. Objections to eliminating the charitable tax deduction often argue that charitable giving is elastic and responsive to tax incentives. While this is usually presented as a danger and a reason not to tamper with existing regulations, from a democratic point of view it represents an opportunity: if true, this would give us another instrument to influence elite giving, in ways that do not raise significant concerns about respect for property rights. This would mean using the tax deduction as a tool for democratic control rather than only as an allocative mechanism; it would represent an attempt to shape the giving behavior of the rich by providing an incentive against exercising one kind of power over recipients.

These suggestions are not meant to be exhaustive or (individually or collectively) a democratic panacea. Creating disincentives for restricted gifts would not solve the problem of elites exercising undemocratic power over social outcomes. Given the hydraulic problem discussed above and the preference of some donors for continued control over money directed to public purposes, many donors' decisions about where and how to give might not be changed by altering tax incentives. Moreover, as long as donors can direct (unrestricted) gifts to specific charities, their preferences will continue to make a significant difference to social outcomes of democratic concern. Weakening donor control and promoting public norms less favorable to it would nevertheless be a step in the right direction and focus our attention in the right place. Attempting to weaken the influence of elite donors over outcomes of common concern would express a commitment to democratic equality and bring philanthropic regulation more closely in line with democratic principles, without sacrificing any value of comparable importance. It targets not the freedom to give, but the entitlement to control. It represents a way of eroding elite control in one area while respecting a pluralist distribution of influence over public goods. Compared with the option of blocking donations that affect outcomes that are appropriately subject to collective decision-making, this strategy is less likely to have the perverse result of magnifying elite control in other ways (e.g., by giving monopoly power to public institutions over which citizens do not enjoy equal influence). Whatever the merits of insulationist strategies in ideal theory, we have good reason to worry about their effects when the background distribution of political influence is unequal and to seek more pluralist ways of challenging elite control.

We should also doubt the efficacy of any purely institutional solution. To the degree that social deference to philanthropy is high, institutional innovations are unlikely to make much headway in redistributing control. While weakening legal deference to donors and creating tax incentives for redistributing control could help, institutions competing for fundraising will retain incentives to defer to donors' wishes. Philanthropy therefore raises important questions of public and institutional ethics at multiple levels; we can ask what fostering a more democratic philanthropic ethic would look like, on the part of different institutional actors. For philanthropists themselves, it would mean acting against the grain of recent decades of philanthropic advice and declining to assert control over grantees. An interesting example is Resource Generation (RG), an organization of young donors committed to giving in ways that divest themselves not only of their inherited wealth but also of the power that comes with it.[69] But democratization cannot happen only as a function of the choices of donors. Recipient organizations and public observers also shape attitudes around giving. Avoiding the concentrated and entrenched control of donors would likely require a certain amount of ingratitude—or at least a willingness to risk that interpretation—on the part of grantees. This can be not only financially dangerous but also personally uncomfortable, given the sincere gratitude that generous gifts often inspire. We are probably still more comfortable telling philanthropists to restrain their exercise of power than we are telling recipients, or permitting ourselves, to be ungrateful. But accepting or rejecting a gift can be as important a political act as making one.

The strategies canvassed here for minimizing elite influence would not require controversial restrictions of donor property rights; at most, they would bring the treatment of charitable property more closely in line with property of other kinds and remove legal and tax advantages currently extended to charitable gifts. A different kind of objection to these proposed changes is consequentialist in nature: that reductions in the scope for donor control would lead to significantly decreased donations. Perhaps the rich will be unwilling to give unless they are assured of continued control over how money is spent. It is worth highlighting the assumptions on which this objection rests. Many nonwealthy people donate money—to churches, charities, or school fundraisers—without expecting sustained control over how their money is spent. People in general seem able to adjust their expectations of control to the opportunities afforded them. To the extent that we think that the rich would be unable to do the same, we may be attributing to elites a moral psychology that should give us pause regarding their fitness to make decisions on the public's behalf. In any case, the relevant consequentialist question is, How much institutional and attitudinal deference to elite philanthropists is required to elicit the benefits that we judge important to secure? Important social benefits might be worth some trade-offs in democratic control, while unimportant ones might not. But even where important social benefits are at stake, we should seek, in the first place, to *register* the democratic trade-offs and, second, to question whether those trade-offs are *necessary* to secure the benefits we want. Pointing to gaps in public funding helps explain acceptance of elite control, but it does not render it democratic.

The United States is not unique in attempting to harness private money for the public good. Premodern societies with limited powers of taxation depended to a much greater extent on the contributions of rich citizens for the provision of public benefits. Sometimes this meant coercing "gifts";[70] elsewhere, cities extracted public contributions from their wealthiest citizens through the conferral of public honors. The distinctive compromise of the latter model of civic giving was, at least in theory, to allow elites public honors for their gifts while expanding popular control of the gifts themselves. In this respect, they represent a salutary corrective to even our most exacting ethical theories of giving; the point is not how much ethical credit givers are due, but how much effective policy control the public is to allow them. To say that we want to permit elite philanthropy, even in publicly important areas like education, is not yet an answer to the question of how control over philanthropic gifts is to be distributed between donors, recipients, and the public at large. In the ancient case, perhaps the hyperbolic displays of public gratitude should be less surprising than the degree of vetting that elite gifts received; perhaps it is our own deference to philanthropic plutocrats that stands in need of explanation.

Conclusion

Elite philanthropists wield an influence that is concentrated, entrenched, and consequential for ordinary citizens. I have argued that that influence can be undemocratic, even when it is exercised not through a political process but through the gaps in one: the common problem underlying concerns about both elite political influence and elite philanthropy is increases in elite control over matters of common concern. This problem can and should be addressed partly through measures aimed at more equitable distributions of political influence and public resources. But there is also a democratic case for targeting more directly the mechanisms that amplify elite philanthropic influence. The aim should not be to concentrate all control over the provision of public goods in the hands of imperfectly democratic public institutions and officials. But pluralism in the provision of public goods does not require—in fact, it may well be compromised by—excessive deference to donor control. The fact that philanthropic money is capable of doing much good does not answer the democratic question of how giving should be governed. In particular, it leaves open the question of how control over philanthropic money is to be distributed between giver, recipient, and the wider public.

The democratic perspective developed here has implications that will strike many people as unattractive: it suggests that it *is* sometimes better to deter elite philanthropy (e.g., by reducing the attractiveness of donating) than to allow giving to proceed on objectionably hierarchical terms. This may seem perverse. Distributive egalitarians in particular may have trouble resisting the intuition that, so long as we do have rich people, it is better—morally better, and better for the community—for them to spend their money on anything but consumption. This intuition is not universal; consumption spending has sometimes been celebrated as a desirable alternative to more politically threatening uses of private wealth. For example, Hume and Smith argue that luxury spending played a civilizing role in England's political history: as England's barons redirected their spending from patronage to the private consumption of luxuries, their political power gradually eroded.[71] We often have good ethical reasons to think better of a person who spends on charity rather than on personal consumption. But this does not mean that philanthropic buying power is less consequential than consumption spending when our concern is to diagnose social and political inequalities. Indeed, the literature on unequal political influence ought to have prepared us for the thought that consumption spending may not be the most *democratically* troubling behavior of the very rich.

In that sense, plutocratic philanthropy presses us to think about our complaint against plutocratic power more generally. Most of the recent political science literature frames oligarchic influence as objectionable because (and to the extent that) it is self-interested or self-serving. As I have argued with specific reference to elite philanthropy, that perspective is too narrow. The outsized influence of the rich is undemocratic even if that influence is aristocratic rather than oligarchic in character—if the claim is merely that the rich are entitled to shape public life for the common good.

These are, at root, familiar democratic questions about who should exercise authority in particular policy domains and over important aspects of a society's common life. They apply with particular force to the subset of philanthropy that is pursued by economic elites, that is directed at public and communal institutions, and that creates significant externalities for members of society not immediately party to the philanthropic transactions. Of course, this does not describe all kinds of philanthropy—and, as I have suggested, elite philanthropy itself could be reformed in ways that would mitigate the democratic worries. However, the democratic concerns that I have outlined in this chapter ought not to exhaust egalitarian concerns about philanthropy. While political equality is a vitally important component of an egalitarian ideal, such an ideal has other dimensions as well. In the following chapter, I develop a second strand of criticism of philanthropy, which can apply even in circumstances where large-scale democratic concerns may seem insignificant: that philanthropy can be objectionable where paternalistic.

CHAPTER FOUR

Philanthropic Paternalism

Philanthropy is patronizing—literally so, in the neutral sense of providing aid or support, and more controversially so, in the negative sense of condescending. It is the latter sense that I take up in this chapter. In addition to undermining political equality in the sense of shared influence over matters of common concern, philanthropy can subvert relations of social equality in a second way: by paternalizing the people whom it affects.

A commitment to relational equality, properly understood, requires us to avoid objectionable forms of paternalism: free and equal citizens ought not to relate to each other as parents to children. This claim is in line with a long tradition of liberal argument, although its application is sometimes restricted—wrongly, I believe—to state and public officials. In this chapter, I argue that philanthropy too can create or reinforce objectionably paternalistic relationships.

I begin by sketching what I mean by philanthropic paternalism before addressing a potential problem with this classification: standard definitions of paternalism generally draw our attention to cases of coercive interference with individual liberty or autonomy, paradigmatically (though not necessarily) by the state. On such a definition, it might be difficult to see how philanthropy—usually understood as providing *additional* options to recipients or to the public—can count as paternalistic. But a closer consideration of philanthropy helps us to better understand the character and wrongness of paternalism in general. Standard accounts err in assuming that coercion or interference with autonomous choice is the key factor either in constituting paternalism or in making it objectionable. I defend an alternative account that focuses on paternalism's insulting expressive content and its relational context and effects. Paternalism is presumptively objectionable because it is disrespectful of its targets and subversive of egalitarian social relations. Analyzing philanthropic practice helps us see that objectionable paternalism can occur even in the absence of coercive interference with autonomy. It also leaves us better positioned to understand the importance of antipaternalism for democracy by revealing how closely tied objections to paternalism are to a concern for respecting and promoting people's status as equals.

I will argue that paternalistic models of philanthropy fail to show respect for people and can in the process exacerbate objectionable inequalities of social standing. This claim, if correct, has several implications: it gives philanthropists reasons to avoid paternalistic models of giving, gives beneficiaries a significant moral complaint against philanthropists who pursue paternalistic giving (even if those philanthropists benefit them in distributive terms), and gives third parties reason to criticize paternalistic philanthropy and attempt to mitigate its effects.

Paternalism and Its Philanthropic Expressions

In some ways, the claim that philanthropy can be paternalizing is perfectly ordinary and familiar.[1] Charles Dickens satirizes philanthropic paternalism without using the term in *Bleak House*, portraying a class of charitable ladies distinguished for their "rapacious benevolence"[2]— among them, the formidable Mrs. Pardiggle, who insists that "the only one infallible course was her course of pouncing upon the poor and applying benevolence to them like a strait-waistcoat."[3] "Everyday" acceptance of the idea of philanthropic paternalism uses paternalism as a synonym for a range of personality traits—arrogance, self-importance, conceit, condescension—that we associate with badly motivated or graceless givers. This is especially true of the amorphous subset of philanthropy called "charity"; here the pejorative sense of the word is so familiar that many celebrated philanthropists are eager to disclaim "charity" as a label for their efforts.[4]

But the charge of paternalism that is being made or anticipated in philanthropic cases is often vague. I therefore begin with a preliminary account of paternalism and its philanthropic expressions. Important elements of my account of paternalism and of what makes it objectionable will require more specification and defense later in the chapter. Yet even the preliminary account will help us to understand and gain analytic leverage on familiar complaints about philanthropy.

I use the term *paternalism* to refer to behaviors and policies that both (1) attempt to restrict, manipulate, influence, or circumvent an agent's choices or behavior and (2) express the judgment that the agent's ability to choose or act well on her own behalf is deficient or inferior to that of the paternalist in some relevant respect or domain. This definition is influenced by recent philosophical work on paternalism,[5] but both of its elements remain controversial: the first, because many definitions of paternalism require that a paternalizer *coerce* or remove choices rather than shaping them in other ways;[6] the second, because many definitions (including some that accept the possibility of noncoercive paternalism) understand paternalism to be distinguished by the *intention* of the paternalist to benefit the person paternalized, rather than the judgment expressed by the paternalistic policy or behavior.[7] I defend both elements in more detail below.

Why might paternalism so defined be presumptively morally objectionable as a way of treating one's social or political equal? The answer cannot be "because it is coercive" (since it may not be) or "because it blocks the paternalized from making their own choices" (since it may not). The answer, I argue, is that paternalistic exercises of power or influence are both disrespectful of others' status as equals and contribute (instrumentally and constitutively) to inegalitarian social relations over time. Relating as equals requires recognizing, and acting in accordance with, people's equal entitlement to respect for their choices about how to pursue their own good; it requires recognizing that, at least within some domains, others are entitled to the same kinds of authority over their lives as I claim over my own. Paternalism's insulting expressive content and relational effects are what distinguish paternalism from (nonpaternalist) coercion and from other exercises of power such as exploitation. These forms of influence may be deeply objectionable for other reasons, but they do not necessarily express the same insulting judgment about a person's competence to manage her own life for herself. The insult expressed by paternalistic behavior explains why it can be objectionable even when it confers genuine benefits (e.g., by promoting the welfare of the paternalized). I do not claim that paternalism's negative moral weight is decisive; it should factor importantly in all-things-considered judgments about whether and when paternalistic behavior or policies can be justified, but other moral considerations will also affect such judgments.

Philosophers such as Seana Shiffrin, Jonathan Quong, and Nicolas Cornell have developed sophisticated objections to paternalism that turn (partly or entirely) on the wrongness of insulting or failing to respect people.[8] But none discusses paternalism in philanthropic contexts. This tracks the broader paternalism literature's bimodal focus on government paternalism (as expressed in law and policy) and interpersonal, dyadic paternalism (toy cases of agent A's myriad paternalistic interventions on long-suffering agent B). As I will show, philanthropic paternalism represents a useful intermediate level of analysis from which to consider paternalism more generally. A consideration of philanthropic paternalism reveals the strengths of accounts of paternalism that focus on insult and disrespect; it also reveals the necessity of embedding such accounts in a conception of morally appropriate social and political relations.

This understanding of paternalism—hinging on the expression of an insulting judgment and on disrespect rather than coercion—helps make sense of our intuitive reactions to paradigm cases of charitable condescension. Consider the following remarks by Victorian social reformer Octavia Hill on her efforts to help her tenants manage their difficulties in paying their rent:

> The fluctuations of work cause to respectable tenants the main difficulties in paying their rent. I have tried to help them in two ways. First, by inducing them to save: this they have done steadily, and each autumn has found them with a small fund accumulated, which has enabled them to meet the difficulties of the time when families are out of town. In the second place, I have done what I could to employ my tenants in slack seasons. I carefully set aside any work they can do for times of scarcity, and I try so to equalize in this small circle the irregularity of work, which must be more or less pernicious, and which the childishness of the poor makes doubly so. They have strangely little power of looking forward; a result is to them as nothing if it will not be perceptible till next quarter![9]

Disregard, for now, the question of whether Hill's "inducing" her poor tenants to save is paternalistic, since this might depend on the specifics of how she induces them. Focus instead on her practice of rationing the employment that she offers. Rather than hire her tenants to perform work for her as the need arises, she waits for "times of scarcity" when her tenants are underemployed and (she anticipates) without adequate savings because of their incapacity for deferred gratification. There is nothing essentially paternalistic about hiring people to work in times of scarcity (whether or not it is the best available option for helping people). What makes Hill's practice paternalistic is the same feature that will make her account of it sound insulting and objectionable to many contemporary readers: her disrespect for poor people and their "childishness," expressed in her judgment that decisions about when to work, save, and spend are best left to her. *She* must ration odd jobs and anticipate the future needs of her tenants, because they are unable to do so.

In chapter 2, I showed how earlier theorists linked normative arguments about philanthropy to normative conceptions of social and political relations. I made the point that a *relational* theory of philanthropy need not be a relational *egalitarian* theory of philanthropy: one might argue that the most morally appropriate social relations are hierarchical. Defenses of hierarchy often have recourse to paternalist justifications; they claim that social and political inferiors, as well as superiors, benefit from hierarchical relations. Often, the claim is that the weak morals, intelligence, or willpower of some people will prevent them from recognizing and taking the actions that would be in their own best interest. Hill's hierarchical picture of morally appropriate social relations had critics even in its own time: recall Mill's attack on the "theory of dependence and protection," a theory that hums through Hill's writing. (Just after the passage cited above, she notes of the poor that "another beautiful trait in their character is their trust; it has been quite marvelous to find how great and how ready this is. In no single case have I met with suspicion or with anything but entire confidence.")[10] Paternalism became a political concern not (or not only) because of an increased tendency to value individual liberty or autonomy but because of increased recognition that many of the inequalities in status and (presumed) competence that were traditionally used to license paternalism were unfounded and unjust. It is because social hierarchies are not presumptively justified that paternalism is presumptively suspect. Early critics like Mill and Addams recognized that philanthropic paternalism is objectionable when and because it insults and subverts other people's status as the donor's moral, social, and political equals.

The expression of disrespect that characterizes paternalism—the explicit or implied judgment that an agent is deficient or inferior in her ability to choose or act well on her own behalf—can manifest in different aspects of philanthropy. Taking some examples of philanthropic practices in turn, we can recognize paternalism in donors' choices about what kinds of benefits to provide (and when), in the terms on which they offer benefits, and even in decisions *against* giving to some people or groups.

Decisions about what benefits to provide and when are, of course, shaped by many nonpaternalist factors: most obviously, by the giver's resources and available options for giving. But often donors' decisions about what benefits to provide are also shaped by negative judgments about the recipients' ability to use open-ended gifts or resources wisely. A preoccupation with the uses to which poor people would put any assistance provided them is pervasive in Western charitable practice. We often find it invoked as a rationale for offering in-kind relief instead of cash and for the careful monitoring of beneficiaries. By the nineteenth century, whether the defects of the poor were described in terms of immorality or incompetence, the conclusion was the same: "Since recipients of relief could not be trusted to spend money wisely or morally, charity officials would guide their expenditures or, better still, decide themselves what the poor needed" and provide it through in-kind relief.[11] In-kind aid need not be paternalistic if a nonpaternalist justification is available to explain why a benefit is being provided in kind (e.g., because the giver has access to a resource like food or clothing but not to cash, or because giving in kind is required to make an important benefit available at all, e.g., for a particular medicine not readily available for sale). But absent such justifications, in-kind giving often expresses a lack of respect for beneficiaries' (paradigmatically, poor people's) ability and entitlement to make their own choices about what would improve their lives. (Libertarians make a similar point in reference to some welfare state programs, though usually without extending the same criticism to philanthropy.)[12]

In the history of charitable enterprises, poor people's susceptibility to shortsighted or immoral spending was not always taken as fixed. Philanthropy has sometimes been structured as a tutorial relationship between the poor and their benefactors. Among the late Victorians, "there was a strong consensus that the primary objective of any enterprise or reform was that it contribute to the moral improvement of the poor."[13] The American Charity Organization Societies likewise took seriously their responsibility to distribute assistance in ways that would conduce to the improvement of beneficiaries. Middle- and upper-class women volunteered as "friendly visitors" to the houses of poor beneficiaries, where they would dispense moral and practical advice in addition to (and as a condition for receiving) material aid.[14] A manual from the time, authored by the general secretary of the Baltimore Charity Organization Society, describes the deep satisfaction "in teaching the slatternly, irresponsible mother the pleasure of a cleanly, well-ordered home; in helping a man who has lost his sense of responsibility toward wife and children to regain it."[15] In this case, paternalism, and the relevant negative judgment about beneficiaries, is expressed in the practice of making the receipt of benefits conditional on consent into tutelary social relations.

Negative appraisals of the maturity, competence, and willpower of one's prospective beneficiaries can also undergird decisions about where and how *not* to give, and they have shaped large-scale philanthropic enterprises as well as personalized acts of charity. Andrew Carnegie, for example, writes in his "Gospel of Wealth" that "one of the serious obstacles to the improvement of our race is indiscriminate charity. It were better for mankind that the millions of the rich were thrown into the sea than so spent as to encourage the slothful, the drunken, the unworthy."[16] The "true reformer" is "as careful and anxious not to aid the unworthy as he is to aid the worthy, and, perhaps, even more so, for in almsgiving more injury is probably done by rewarding vice than by relieving virtue."[17] Given the grim likelihood that money given unconditionally will be misspent, what is required are models of charity in which "the millionaire will be but a trustee for the poor, intrusted for a season with a great part of the increased wealth of the community, but administering it for the community far better than it could or would have done for itself."[18] What Carnegie prescribes is a paternalistic social relation, to be enacted through and sustained by elite philanthropy.

These nineteenth-century stories may seem distant from our own concerns. The story of the rise of "scientific philanthropy" is often told as one of progress away from antiquated and ineffective models of almsgiving: business titans brought principles of efficiency honed in capitalist enterprise to the management of philanthropic resources, with the result that private welfare, educational, and cultural efforts were increasingly systematized.[19] Similar stories of increased efficiency and performance are told about contemporary "strategic philanthropy" (where these values are likewise traced to increased oversight and control by the philanthropist).[20] We might have expected the systematization and depersonalization of philanthropy to mitigate the problem of paternalism—for example, by reducing the pressure on individual supplicants to convince censorious benefactors of their worthiness. But there is another side to the story. Scientific philanthropy also traces its origins to a paternalistic complaint with traditional models of charity and almsgiving: that traditional almsgiving permits the giver too little control over how his money is spent. Oliver Zunz suggests that, in the late nineteenth century, the new rich and the progressive social reformers whom they sometimes funded agreed on an important point: "the large newly-available philanthropic resources should not go directly to the poor."[21] What was wanted were ways to benefit the poor without enabling poor choices. Where once a philanthropist's options might have been limited to offering and refusing aid according to the merit of each prospective recipient, the possibility of philanthropic paternalism began to expand beyond individual, personalized interactions. The effort to systematize private welfare was intimately linked with a paternalistic impulse to remove spending decisions from the control of poor people and instead to vest decision-making power in their benefactors—their "trustees."

This impulse survives in contemporary philanthropy and in ways that extend beyond the paradigm poverty-relief case that I have focused on so far. We are now more likely to find philanthropists defending a preference for sustained control over grant money in technocratic terms rather than in Carnegie's openly contemptuous ones. But judgments about the relative competence of donors, recipient organizations, and beneficiaries continue to play a central role in structuring philanthropic relationships. A recent report by the Center for Effective Philanthropy notes the gulf between the very high value that nonprofits place on the receipt of multiyear general operating support (GOS) or unrestricted grants compared with the relative dearth of such grants from donors. While the report is unable to account for donors' choices against providing multiyear GOS grants, it finds that nonprofit leaders most often attribute those choices to "a lack of trust in nonprofits and a desire to maintain control."[22] Philanthropic paternalism is not only about a tradition of tropes stigmatizing the poor or other social groups. At its heart, philanthropic paternalism is about affirming donor control over the benefits to be provided—not merely as an entitlement accruing to wealth or property but because donors know better than the people they are trying to benefit.

But Is It Paternalism?

The critique of philanthropy as paternalistic, though familiar in public discourse, is relatively rare in philosophy. The omission follows not only from a general neglect of philanthropy but from influential philosophical accounts of paternalism, many of which stipulate that paternalism necessarily involves coercion, violations of liberty or autonomy, or defects in the consent of the person (putatively) paternalized. In this section, I consider the implications of accepting this narrower conception of paternalism; using examples from philanthropic practice, I argue that the narrower conception fails to capture paternalism's distinctive moral importance.

Standard definitions of paternalism turn on the concept of interfering with an agent "for her own good." The classic antipaternalist statement is Mill's harm principle: "That the only purpose for which power can be rightfully exercised over any member of a civilized community, against his will, is to prevent harm to others. His own good, either physical or moral, is not sufficient warrant."[23] Later authors have often positioned themselves as amending or clarifying Mill's formula. Gerald Dworkin, in an influential account, defines paternalism as meaning roughly "the interference with a person's liberty of action justified by reasons referring exclusively to the welfare, good, happiness, needs, interests, or values of the person being coerced."[24] Joel Feinberg likewise focuses on paternalism as a (permissible or impermissible) justification for coercion.[25] These definitions focus on the infringement of liberties, or opportunities for autonomous choice, that (in the absence of the paternalistic intervention) the person being paternalized would otherwise enjoy.

Such standard accounts make it difficult to see how philanthropy can count as paternalistic. Typically, philanthropy is understood to be a matter of providing (intended) beneficiaries with additional options, not of restricting their choices. And how can *expanding* the choice set be paternalistic? The intended recipient is free to refuse the good or service offered. Indeed, to the extent that government blocks or constrains philanthropic transactions between citizens, it will be government and not the philanthropist that acts paternalistically (even if that paternalism might be justified, all things considered).

On this account, examples of philanthropic behavior that we might unreflectively call paternalistic will be acquitted once we recognize that they are not properly described as cases of interference. Given the option to refuse aid, beneficiaries are at worst "opting in" to (what would otherwise be) paternalistic restrictions—something that Feinberg, for example, is careful to distinguish from genuine paternalism. He distinguishes a class of cases of "persons voluntarily relinquishing liberties for other benefits"; he suggests that there are "examples of persons who voluntarily 'put themselves under the protection of rules' that deprive them and others too of liberties, when those liberties are unrewarding and burdensome."[26] He gives the example of undergraduate students choosing between residences with and without curfew rules. While it would be paternalism to force the curfew rules on a student "for his own good," it is not paternalism "to *permit* him to live under the governance of coercive rules when he freely chooses to do so, and the other alternative is kept open to him. In fact, it would be paternalism to deny a person the liberty of trading liberties for other benefits."[27]

Prospective recipients of philanthropic gifts are not often as happily situated as Feinberg's hypothetical student, who opts in to restrictions (perhaps as a welcome precommitment device) in the context of a choice between two available and otherwise equally good options. (The parallel case would be if the prospective recipient of a philanthropic gift were offered a choice between two donations of identical value, one with conditions attached and the other without.) Rather than choosing between options that are similar but for the conditions attached, recipients must often choose between a conditioned gift and no gift at all. But Feinberg's basic point can nevertheless be adapted to exonerate rules and conditions attached to philanthropic gifts from the charge of paternalism.

Consider the example of a religious nonprofit that wishes to save the souls of its clients; it might require them to pray before they are able to access the service provided. (This is not a purely hypothetical case: an Indiana food bank briefly lost its eligibility to receive free food items from the federal Emergency Food Assistance Program (TEFAP) because of a policy under which its volunteers asked recipients to pray with them before distributing food.)[28] If we focus on coercive interference with liberty or autonomy, it might seem that the nonprofit cannot be guilty of paternalism, since beneficiaries have the option of forgoing the service (even if their reserve option is significantly less desirable than the one in Feinberg's example). Depending on how great the need for the service is, the nonprofit's actions could be described as exploitive or manipulative. But, for litigating the charge of paternalism, the crucial point is that the nonprofit's clients remain free to opt out of the (putatively) paternalistic relationship.

Now, defenders of coercion-centric accounts might argue that, if philanthropy appears to be paternalistic, it is only when and because it really *is* coercive. People may be desperate for the goods that donors or organizations offer and lack acceptable alternative ways of obtaining them. If that is the case, then perhaps it is false to say that recipients are free to opt out of the paternalistic arrangement. One's position here will depend on one's understanding of coercion. Liberals and libertarians often hold that coercion requires not only that the putatively coerced lack an acceptable alternative but also that the putative coercer threaten to make the coerced worse off relative to some baseline.[29] On such a view, philanthropic offers may not qualify as coercive even if beneficiaries are desperate and lack acceptable alternatives to acquiescing to donor conditions.

Another way to defend the claim that philanthropy is paternalistic—even (or only) on standard, narrow definitions of paternalism—is to claim that some philanthropic action infringes on beneficiaries' rights. Standard accounts require that the paternalist interfere with the paternalized, but this can occur whenever a paternalizer violates rights or fails to respect just claims (even if it is not the case that the paternalized is coerced or left without acceptable alternative to acquiescing). Philanthropic "gifts" may consist of goods to which people are entitled as a matter of justice. If, for example, the people who rely on religious food banks are owed access to adequate food, then withholding access to food or imposing conditions on its distribution looks especially unjust. One difficulty with this argument is that (if we set aside the complicating factor of government support for many religious nonprofits) it seems implausible to claim that the food bank's visitors are owed access to food *by that food bank* or its employees. If desperate clients are treated unjustly when they are offered or accept private aid under conditions that they find repugnant, it is the *state* that is responsible: robust public service provision would remove any bite that the nonprofit's conditions might otherwise have. Even if they are owed a subsistence, it is not clear that the food bank's clients are having their rights violated by *philanthropists*—especially if philanthropists are trying, however imperfectly, to compensate for the effects of background injustice.

Of course, pointing to defects in the justice of social institutions does not make moot the question of whether other actors are acting wrongly against that backdrop. We could adjust the argument to say that, even if it is the state and not philanthropists that bears primary responsibility for background injustice, the unjust deprivation of community members creates defects in their consent, of a kind that could support the charge of paternalism. If a nonprofit is exploiting its clients' lack of an acceptable alternative (i.e., to using a food bank), then perhaps the recipients' acceptance of that nonprofit's conditions (i.e., their consent to pray) cannot be regarded as genuine. (Recall the claim of the apothecary in *Romeo and Juliet*: "My poverty but not my will consents.") In circumstances of serious deprivation or background injustice, philanthropists may really be in a position to coerce prospective recipients or to exploit recipients' paucity of available options in ways that are so unfair that recipients' consent loses its moral force.[30] (On the other hand, even if recipients themselves could credibly claim this, for governments or other third parties to make the same claim *for* them might itself look paternalistic.) Furthermore, in the context of large-scale and institutional philanthropy (e.g., of the kinds considered in the previous chapter), beneficiaries may have their options shaped or restricted by conditions to which they do not individually consent or opt in. Even on narrow definitions of paternalism that require coercion, interference, or defects in consent, it is thus likely that *some* philanthropic activity will count as paternalistic.

I raise this possibility without insisting or focusing on it. This is for two reasons. First, I assume that even if some kinds of philanthropy count as coercive for the reasons described above, others will not: often, philanthropy really does expand the choice set for people who have acceptable alternatives. Second, and more fundamentally, a charge of paternalism need not rely on claims about coercion by the paternalizer or defects in the consent of the person paternalized.[31] While worries about violations of liberty or autonomy may play a role in our reactions to some cases of philanthropic paternalism, objectionable paternalism can arise even without them.

To the extent that standard definitions of paternalism focus on coercive interference with individual liberty, they are too narrow to capture what should interest us about paternalism. Paternalism need not be coercive; it can also inhere in noncoercive attempts to structure or influence choices.[32] This possibility is implicit even in some traditional accounts of paternalism: the harm principle begins by asking the purposes for which *power can rightfully be exercised.* The first step is to recognize that exercises of power need not take the form of coercion. Exercising power over someone can instead involve shaping her choices, manipulating her incentives,[33] or exploiting one's own superior bargaining position. To restrict our normative evaluations of power's exercise to coercion impoverishes our understanding of what paternalism is and of why we should reject it. Precisely because it gives donors wide scope for exercising power in noncoercive ways, the case of philanthropy helps us to see that objections to paternalism can be grounded in something other than paternalism's supposed violation of liberty.

For some readers, intuitive reactions to the cases of philanthropic paternalism already described may be sufficient to support my claim that paternalism's moral significance does not reduce to concerns about coercion. Recall Hill's practice of rationing the work that she offers to her tenants. Here, there is no question of her coercing people, since (as far as we know) she attaches no conditions at all to her offers of employment. (Even if her tenants are desperate for work, when it does become available, they do not seem to be *paternalistically* coerced: Coerced to do what?) Hill's expressed goal is to prevent her tenants from running out of money due to their own short-sighted spending, but to accomplish this, she simply waits to offer employment until such time as she thinks they need it. Assuming that she does not owe them the money (i.e., without requiring them to work), she is acting within her rights—presumably there is no standing obligation to hire workers for odd jobs the minute such jobs become available or can be created. Nevertheless, Hill's tenants have (at least) a prima facie complaint that her treatment of them is paternalistic, *even if* they do not have an independent claim on the work or money that she offers. The way that she exercises her power (regarding whom to hire and when) both expresses an insulting judgment about her tenants' ability rationally to govern their own lives and promotes a subordinating relationship. Her behavior is paternalistic independently of whether it is coercive.

For those not yet persuaded—perhaps because of a sense that an objection to coercion might be driving their intuitions in the poverty-relief cases—consider the following example. Suppose that a philanthropist wishes to fund scholarships for university students, subject to conditions on their behavior while at the university. To adapt Feinberg's example, perhaps the terms of the scholarship require that the students live in a residence with curfew rules; perhaps the students are also prohibited from attending parties where alcohol is served or from entertaining friends and romantic partners in their rooms. Stipulate that the students are not entitled to this money and have acceptable alternatives to the arrangement. Nevertheless, a philanthropist who imposed these kinds of conditions on the behavior of her beneficiaries would be acting in an objectionably paternalistic way by expressing disrespect for the ability of her beneficiaries to make their own choices about how to conduct themselves and by exercising her power (in the form of financial incentives) in an attempt to control their behavior.

I have argued (and elaborate in the next section) that paternalism is objectionable because of its disrespect for and subversion of people's status as equals; this can occur without coercion, liberty infringements, or autonomy violations. But even if we take the concern about paternalism to be fundamentally a concern for the liberty or autonomy of the paternalized, a focus on coercion or rights infringement provides too narrow a perspective. Actions that are not coercive or do not infringe rights in the moment (i.e., because the person targeted by them consents to them) can have the aim and effect of constricting a person's future liberty and autonomy. Something like this dynamic is at work in the university scholarship case just described: although it is true that the donor's beneficiaries consent to the conditions at one point in time, the paternalistic conditions significantly raise the costs of some choices later in time. This diachronic element is important in understanding the significance of paternalism. Paternalism often involves the attempt to put in place an unequal and asymmetrical *relationship*, even if this attempt involves the paternalized's consent into such a relation for the sake of a valued benefit. The case of philanthropy, where paternalism standardly operates through incentives rather than through coercion, helps us to see that paternalism is not only about one-off acts of interference or liberty restriction but also about relationships of power and control that endure over time.

Insulting Expression

The distinctive moral weight of paternalism comes not from coercion, interference, the removal of options, or limitations on individual autonomy but from the exercise of power in ways that express an insulting judgment about someone's capacity to choose or act well on her own behalf. This conjunction of power and expressed superiority of judgment is characteristic of paternalism. Exercises of power that avoid negative expressions about an agent's competence to choose or act on her own behalf may be objectionable for a wide range of reasons but are not generally insulting in the way that paternalistic exercises of power are. And, conversely, negative appraisals of an agent's competence that do not have the aim or effect of influencing her decisions, actions, or options may be insulting, but they are not subject to the same kinds of moral and political objections as (even similar) judgments that attach to an exercise of power.[34]

I have already given some examples, from different aspects of philanthropic practice, to show that negative appraisals of an agent's competence can be expressed in a wide range of actions (including ones that an agent is normally entitled to perform) as well as in omissions (i.e., decisions *not* to give). I now consider in more detail what it means for a behavior or policy to express an insulting judgment, in the sense relevant to identifying philanthropic paternalism.

A subjective test, classifying behaviors and policies as paternalistic just when the people affected by them *feel* paternalized, would be both over- and underinclusive. Overinclusive, because it is possible for people unreasonably to feel insulted by actions that do not plausibly express insulting judgments. A curator at a nonprofit art gallery might feel that her competence is insulted by a disappointingly small donation from a rich patron; but absent any special claim on the money or other facts about the case, the mere act of making a small donation does not seem paternalistic. Moreover, people differ both in how often they encounter paternalistic treatment and in how sensitive they are to perceived slights to their competence. People who are accustomed to being treated with deference may feel insulted when they are treated "merely" as equal to others in their capacity for autonomous choice and action.

A subjective test would also be underinclusive, because paternalism can occur without the people affected being aware of the relevant behavior or policy at all or of the features that make it paternalistic. Perhaps donors to a local food bank insist that the organization stop supplying foods that are popular but that have low nutritional value; this seems paternalistic even if the food bank's clients mistakenly attribute the changes to market shortages of the foods in question.[35] Even when people are aware of the details of paternalistic policies and behavior, it is possible that they will not feel insulted by forms of treatment that are nevertheless disrespectful. Perhaps the paternalized themselves do not believe that they are the moral or social equals of the paternalizer, and so they do not believe there is anything insulting in judgments about their inferiority as agents. The paternalized's acceptance of paternalistic behavior might be morally important in some ways (e.g., it will affect how third parties ought to respond to paternalism), but it does not necessarily disqualify forms of treatment as objectionably paternalistic provided they exhibit the other relevant characteristics.

In addition, identifying the expression of an insulting judgment is not centrally about inquiring into the subjective motivations of the putative paternalizer. As Nicolas Cornell points out, "Paternalism is, at least sometimes, a feature of behavior that makes that behavior impermissible. But there is good reason to think that the intent with which an action is performed does not affect the permissibility of the action," even if it does affect our evaluations of the agent performing the action.[36] Of course, motivation and expression will often overlap. Negative judgments about people's capacities often *do* motivate paternalistic behavior, and people often (whether intentionally or unintentionally) succeed in expressing the judgments that motivate them. Motive and expression may be especially likely to overlap in philanthropic contexts, since benevolent donors presumably give careful thought to whether they can best help recipients by allowing them more or less scope for choice. But in principle, Cornell is correct to argue that expression and not motivation is what matters: for a behavior or policy to count as paternalistic, it is neither necessary nor sufficient that it be motivated by a subjective belief in another agent's incompetence.[37]

If we do not want the identification of paternalism to turn (or turn only) on the subjective experience of the paternalized or the subjective motivations of the paternalizer, then we need to look for another standard. What does it mean to evaluate when an action or policy expresses a judgment that people are not competent to decide and act well on their own behalf? This must be a matter of asking what reasonable interpretations a policy or behavior can support—in its particular context and given the meanings ascribed to specific behaviors or policies within the relevant community. In practice, this is very similar to the work that motive-based accounts of paternalism need to do, at least as they apply to government.[38] Critics of paternalism are used to inquiring into the justifications available for (or rationales implicit in) programs or policies that may have multiple and even crosscutting motivations.[39] The practice of looking for such rationales and justifications (as opposed to subjective motivations) can be extended to the activities of philanthropists; if doing so is novel, this may be because philanthropy is often not thought to require justification in the same way.

How do we go about identifying paternalistic expressions in the case of philanthropy? As in the case of government action, we look at how policies are shaped and how benefits are structured and conferred, and we ask what aims those choices suggest and what judgments they communicate in the relevant social and political context.[40] What is the purpose of a program for food stamps distributed by a government or of in-kind food aid distributed by a private actor or organization? "To benefit the poor" may be the most natural answer. But this is not specific enough: there are many ways to benefit the poor, the most obvious of which are cash transfers. When we ask about the reasons underlying a philanthropic program or policy, we want to know not only or even primarily the philanthropist's motive for giving in the first place but rather the judgments expressed by the form that giving takes—what observers in the relevant social context would conclude about why the policy has been shaped in the ways that it has. It is not the desire to help poor people that might make the provision of in-kind aid paternalistic but rather the judgement that might be implicit in a philanthropist's choice to distribute in-kind aid rather than cash: that the poor can best be helped by giving them the goods that *he* thinks it would be in their best interests to have; that the poor can best be helped by constraining *their* scope for choice and action.

This standard will not pick out a set of actions and behaviors as (always) paternalistic, since very similar behaviors might be paternalistic or not depending on the context: the rationales plausibly available for an action or policy matter for its classification as paternalistic. Offering in-kind food aid with the implication that you are unable to make healthy choices for yourself is paternalistic while offering the same kind of aid because I need to dump a surplus and am openly unwilling to sacrifice in any other way is not. (Though neither, perhaps, covers me in ethical glory.) What makes paternalism a distinctive and morally interesting category is the kind of judgment that it expresses about the person paternalized and also (as I explain in the following section) the relationship it attempts to put in place (or preserve) between the parties. This will vary with context: in-kind food aid from a poor farmer who only has food to give does not plausibly express the same kind of negative judgment about recipients as do programs of in-kind food aid from large-scale donors or nonprofits.

The fact that motive alone is not what matters also helps to block an objection that might be made here. Often, philanthropists pursue aims that are broader than the good or welfare of the specific people who might be targeted by a program or policy. It therefore seems open to them to claim that the conditions or limitations they put on gifts are motivated not by a negative judgment about people's ability to choose or act well *for their own good* (narrowly construed) but rather by a negative judgment about their ability to promote the *common* good. The expressive account can handle that objection more easily than the intent-based one: it is the expressive content and the effects of the conditions and limitations, rather than their specific objectives, that make them paternalistic. And rightly so: we should not define paternalism only as influence exerted over the paternalized's strictly self-regarding actions (since that may be a very small category). This is in line with Dennis Thompson's suggestion that "paternalism refers not to a distinct class of *actions*, but to a class of *reasons* that we may use to justify or condemn restrictions even on actions that affect other people as well as the person being helped."[41] On this interpretation, showing that a person's actions have other-regarding effects does not end the discussion. Rather, "Paternalistic reasons for actions can usually be distinguished even when the actions themselves cannot be classified as paternalistic because their aims and effects are too complex and extensive."[42] Actors may express paternalistic judgments even when aiming at a broader social good than that of the paternalized.

So far, I have been considering mostly cases in which there are two parties: a donor who might paternalize and a beneficiary (or beneficiaries) who might be targeted by paternalism. But of course, in contemporary philanthropy, there is often an intervening agent—a nonprofit organization that receives donations from philanthropists and whose activities (the philanthropists hope) will create benefits either for specific intended beneficiaries or for a more diffuse public. In such cases, the most visible and direct exercises of philanthropic power are over the recipient organization: it is that organization, rather than beneficiaries, whose activities are most obviously constrained by conditions on philanthropic gifts or by decisions against providing general operating support. It might therefore seem that the risk of philanthropic paternalism toward beneficiaries is mitigated when philanthropists exercise their power through intermediaries. However, the insulting expression that characterizes paternalism can inhere in restrictions on intervening agents, and both donors and recipient organizations can act paternalistically toward the people affected by the organizations' activities.[43]

It should be clear that paternalism can operate through intermediaries, exerting influence over actors whose good or welfare is not the target of the paternalistic policy or behavior. Accept, for the sake of an illustrative example, that Prohibition was a paternalistic policy.[44] If so, the targets of its paternalism were members of the general public. It was not for the good of saloon operators that they were barred from selling alcohol, and the law implied no negative judgment about the ability of saloon owners to choose or act well on their own behalf. Rather, temperance laws limited the behavior of saloon owners for the purpose of changing *other* people's behavior (by limiting the options available to them, even though the consumption of alcohol was not illegal). Similarly, when philanthropists impose conditions on their gifts to recipient organizations, those conditions may sometimes be a way of paternalizing the people whom those organizations serve.

Granted, matters are a little more complicated in the philanthropic case. Prohibition operated (let us assume) against the will of saloon owners, whereas nonprofit organizations that accept gifts with paternalistic conditions attached become (at least) accessories to donors' paternalism: such organizations (unlike saloon owners under Prohibition) share moral responsibility for any paternalistic treatment that their clients encounter. The question of how to divide moral responsibility and blame between donors and recipient organizations in cases of objectionable paternalism is complicated and is not my primary interest here. But it is unlikely that responsibility is zero sum: the negative expression that characterizes paternalism can occur at multiple levels and be compounded (rather than laundered) through intervening agents' actions.[45] The mere fact that a philanthropist imposes conditions on gifts to nonprofit organizations rather than on beneficiaries directly does not mitigate worries about paternalism.

The presence of two potential paternalists (the donor and the operating nonprofit) complicates matters in another way. In some cases, donor paternalism targets people who were *already* being paternalized or targeted for paternalism (i.e., by the employees of the operating nonprofit: doctors and nurses, university professors and administrators, case workers, etc.). Where that is the case, does it mitigate the worry about *donor* paternalism—does it matter much *who* paternalizes the intended beneficiaries of paternalistic behavior or policies? I argue that it can; seeing why requires exploring paternalism's moral weight and relational context in greater detail.

Paternalism's Moral Weight and Relational Context

Paternalism is presumptively wrong both because it is generally disrespectful and because it is subversive of egalitarian social relations.[46] But paternalism's moral weight is not uniform; it can vary depending on the specifics of the paternalistic treatment and (crucially) its relational context. This explains why some cases of philanthropic paternalism are more objectionable than others and why philanthropic paternalism in general raises distinctive moral worries.

There are at least two ways that *particular cases* of philanthropic paternalism can be presumptively more objectionable. The insult that paternalism conveys—and, with it, the presumptive wrongness of paternalistic behaviors and policies—varies according to two distinct factors: (1) the depth and significance of the disrespect expressed for the paternalized's capacity for and entitlement to make autonomous choices; and (2) the degree to which the paternalism expresses the judgment, or reinforces widely held judgments, that some person or class of persons is less able to choose and act well on their own behalf than others are. In comparison, instances of philanthropic paternalism that involve only trivial slights to an agent's competence and that do not single out some people as less competent than others are generally less objectionable.

The first condition concerns the depth, significance, and scope of the insult to an agent's competence; it reflects the standard antipaternalist concern with respect for autonomy. Jonathan Quong argues that "all paternalistic acts towards sane adults" commit the wrong of "treating an adult as if he or she (at least temporarily) lacks the ability to rationally pursue his or her own good. In treating adult persons in this way their moral status is demeaned or diminished."[47] This expression of disrespect will be more or less serious, depending on how seriously someone's ability to choose and act well on her own behalf is impugned. (At the extreme, imagine a donor mandating sexual-orientation "conversion therapy" in exchange for benefits. Having some kinds of choices or behavior constrained, manipulated, or even simply incentivized strikes much more deeply at a person's autonomy than others.)

But the moral weight of paternalism does not depend only on the degree to which it expresses an *absolute* denial of the moral status of the paternalized. Paternalism also involves a *relative* or "comparative" wrong: "paternalistic acts typically involve one party treating another as having an *inferior* status . . . one way in which paternalistic acts are typically wrong is that the paternalizer fails to accord the paternalizee *equal* status."[48] Quong himself does not dwell on the distinction between the two ways in which paternalistic behavior is presumptively wrong because, in his view, they typically go together. But we will underestimate the seriousness of much paternalistic behavior if we focus only on the noncomparative wrong: some cases of paternalism are objectionable *primarily* for their subordinating character—for the ways that the paternalized is treated as *less* competent than the paternalist (or, we might add, than other people whom the paternalist chooses not to target with paternalistic treatment).

The comparative wrong also helps to explain why even behaviors and policies that express *accurate* judgments about a person's cognitive or volitional deficiencies can be objectionable.[49] Many accounts of paternalism emphasize the accuracy of the paternalizer's judgments as a key variable for justifying paternalism.[50] That is, the wrongness of paternalism is thought to scale with how competent of a decision maker the paternalized is: paternalistic treatment that is appropriately matched to an agent's irrationality or weakness of will is often thought to be less objectionable than paternalistic treatment of a fully rational agent (even if the less-than-fully-rational agent is above a minimum threshold of autonomy such that paternalism is still somewhat objectionable). This might seem to license a great deal of paternalism (e.g., that could be defended as welfare promoting and not very seriously disrespectful). As defenders of paternalism often point out, all people have cognitive biases and are prone to weaknesses of will in ways that sometimes frustrate their ability to promote their own good.[51] But what makes some paternalism insulting is not only or even primarily an inaccuracy in the paternalizer's estimation of the capacities or weaknesses of the person paternalized; it is rather the asymmetry in the judgments and treatment some people encounter compared with other people. I can reasonably complain of disrespect when my competence to decide and act on my own behalf is (merely) accurately assessed if other people (including, perhaps, the paternalizer) benefit from forms of respect and deference that treat them as more competent than they are. Here, the objection to paternalism is not only about autonomy but also, and more centrally, about equality.

Philanthropic paternalism is capable of committing both the absolute and the comparative wrong, but it is distinctively prone to the comparative one. This is especially true when philanthropy targets people who (perhaps because of characteristics such as poverty, social class, race, gender, gender identity, disability, or sexual orientation) are particularly likely to have their ability to manage their own lives and pursue their own good called into question.[52] But the identities of donors matter here too. Because philanthropic power is so concentrated among the very rich (a group that is demographically atypical in other ways—more white, more male, and older than the general population), it is *very easy* for it to express and reinforce judgments that people are not equal in their ability rationally to pursue their own good. One implication here is that philanthropic paternalism will be presumptively more suspect the more that the donor-beneficiary relationship tracks background social inequalities.

Considerations of relative status explain why cases of "paternalism from below"—where the putative *paternalizer* enjoys *less* power or status than the other party—often look odd as cases of paternalism at all. This is true even of paradigmatic cases of paternalistic behavior. Consider an anonymized example: A hides B's cigarettes out of concern for B's health and willpower. In most cases, this will describe a paternalistic action on A's part. But this judgment might change depending on how we fill in the details. Suppose that A (the putative paternalizer) is B's six-year-old child. With this specification, a complaint of paternalism by B against A will sound neurotic. More than saying that (genuine) paternalism is more *excusable* when committed by a child, I doubt whether we should register A's action as paternalistic at all—it lacks the moral weight that paternalistic behavior generally has.[53] An insult to B's competence may be present in some sense, but that insult is socially and politically inert. The paternalizer cannot reasonably be interpreted as exploiting or attempting to put in place a subordinating relationship: she lacks the power to do so. Between adults, relationships of power and status are often less one-sided and clear-cut: parties may have different sources of power and status (or one without the other) so that the possibilities for paternalism are sometimes more symmetrical between parties. But it is precisely because wealthy philanthropists generally enjoy both greater power and higher status relative to their beneficiaries that their paternalism is threatening. Philanthropists have fungible forms of influence that are often *not* offset by countervailing vulnerabilities and which they may use to create or reinforce enduring social structures and relationships.

Suppose, for example, that a rich philanthropist attaches paternalistic conditions to his gifts in the area of K–12 education (say, an emphasis on testing, longer school days or years, and the adoption of school uniforms).[54] The moral weight of the paternalism might look quite different depending on the identities of the philanthropist and the intended beneficiaries and the socioeconomic differences between them. The paternalism will look worse, I think, if we specify further that the donor makes these conditioned gifts to a city's public schools but sends his own children to a private school organized on a different model (perhaps one that deemphasizes testing and instead promotes children's creativity and self-expression). Attention to the comparative dimension of paternalist disrespect can help explain why the donor in the latter case might be charged not just with hypocrisy but with a graver kind of paternalism: even if well intentioned, his giving expresses a judgment that more structure and regulation (e.g., longer school days and stricter uniform policies) are appropriate for poor, disadvantaged children—but not for his own. Racial inequalities also play an important role here: scholars such as Janelle Scott and Noliwe Rooks have called attention to the ways that U.S. educational philanthropy by white funders has reflected as well as reinforced prevailing ideas about the different social roles and curricula appropriate for Black as opposed to white students.[55] Even when philanthropy produces important welfare benefits and creates educational opportunities that might not otherwise have existed, relations of asymmetric paternalism raise concerns about invidious distinctions and the lack of reciprocal influence between social groups.

Conversely, a donor's personal history and social ties can also soften the disrespect that philanthropic paternalism generally conveys. Contrast the case described above with that of the I Promise School in Akron, Ohio, a public (noncharter) school opened in 2018 with the support of the LeBron James Family Foundation. (Akron is James's hometown.) The school aims to serve disadvantaged children who are at risk of falling behind in their studies, with initiatives including a longer-than-average school year, services for families (including job services and an on-site food bank), and "activities to prevent the kids from having too much idle time and potentially getting into trouble."[56] We would need more information about the specifics of these initiatives to make a judgment about the degree of paternalism they involve or whether that paternalism is justified, all things considered. But the case illustrates some ways that donors' identity and expressions can matter. In his public statements, James has repeatedly stressed his common history and identification with the school's target students (e.g., his struggles in fourth grade due to circumstances at home and his resulting high rate of absences). In a video announcement, he claims, "I know these kids, basically more than they know themselves. I've walked the same streets. I've rode the same bikes on the streets that they ride on. I went through the same emotions, the good, the bad, the adversity—everything that these kids are going through, the drugs, the violence, the guns, everything that they're going through as kids, I know."[57] The point here is not that paternalism is less objectionable from donors *with accurate information or knowledge* about a target population's needs. It is rather that the expressions of superiority and inferiority that characterize paternalism may be affected by the identities of the parties.[58]

Of course, the cases just considered concern the paternalistic treatment of children. Since young children are not fully autonomous, autonomy-focused accounts of paternalism typically do not treat such cases as objectionable (at least to the extent that paternalism promotes the well-being and the future autonomy of its targets). But the account of paternalism developed here suggests that there can be an equality-based objection even to paternalism that targets people who are not fully autonomous: the comparative dimension of paternalistic disrespect can apply even where there is no autonomy-based objection. Moreover, our normative evaluations of paternalism, even when practiced toward nonautonomous agents, do and should depend on its relational context. In some cases, paternalism may be *fully* justified by its relational context; paternalism within some relationships may not even be presumptively wrong. The case of parents and their children is the most obvious example: few people object to parents trying to make their children good, at least so long as those efforts respect certain bounds (so that violent punishment is ruled out, but boring Sunday school is acceptable). But this is not because there is a standing permission for every adult to paternalize any child. To justify paternalism, we need to appeal not only to features of agents but to the social relationships in which paternalistic behavior is embedded. Some relationships can appropriately be pedagogical; in some arenas, we accept efforts on the part of some agents to improve others. But the conditions that can make paternalism appropriate in some cases are generally absent in the philanthropic one.

Consider again the case in which a donor exerts influence over institutional actors who might be paternalizing their clients anyway. The complaint can be that donor intervention short-circuits a relationship of *justified* paternalism. (Note that the baseline relationship may range from fully justified in its paternalism to containing a measure of objectionable paternalism.) For example, university professors can act paternalistically toward their students, but pedagogical paternalism is often justifiable (e.g., provided that paternalistic treatment is limited in scope, does not involve invidious distinctions between students, and is regulated by appropriate accountability mechanisms). There is generally no objection to professors choosing what their students ought to learn or taking the average student's cognitive and volitional capacities into account when setting assignments. But it does not follow that university donor influence over course content (exercised through conditions on gifts) would likewise be unobjectionable in its paternalism. It matters who is paternalizing you, though this point is often underemphasized. (And authors who do note it often draw the wrong conclusions from it—i.e., that the identity of the paternalist matters for whether he has reliable knowledge about what would benefit the paternalized.) The fact that you would be willing to defer to the judgments of some agent does not prevent you from resenting similar forms of treatment from a different agent (indeed, it may be exactly *why* you resent paternalistic treatment from the latter kind of actor—it displaces or disrupts a valuable relationship).

The importance of relational context, including the paternalized's opportunity to influence her own exposure to paternalistic treatment, helps explain what can be particularly troubling about private and philanthropic paternalism. Although objectionable paternalism can occur even with the paternalized's specific consent (e.g., in the case of offers with paternalistic conditions attached), genuine accountability of the paternalizer to the paternalized would mitigate the worry considerably. The kinds of thick accountability required to mitigate the worry are often absent in cases of government paternalism. But they are almost definitionally absent in philanthropic cases. The relational context of philanthropic paternalism is one of *unaccountable* power.

This is not, of course, to suggest that democratic governments cannot act paternalistically. They can, and do, in ways that may be justified or not, all things considered. In some cases, government and private paternalism might look quite similar. Particular policies can be designed in ways that are more or less paternalistic. A hospital's doctors, for example, might act toward their patients in more or less paternalistic ways (by keeping them more or less informed about their treatment or more or less involved in decision-making about which course to follow). And these characterizations would hold whether the hospital was a public or private one. Or, to return to the case of aid to poor people, policies can be designed in such a way as to allow them more or less freedom in spending their aid-allocated funds. We can arrange cash transfers, choice-limiting options such as food stamps, and in-kind aid along such a spectrum. Once again, the degree of paternalism in policy design seems to be independent of whether the policy is administered publicly or privately: rather, we can say that the regime is being administered such that beneficiaries will have more or less scope for choice (and that choice-limiting options frequently express more negative appraisals of beneficiaries' competence to choose well on their own behalf). New direct-giving programs facilitating simple cash transfers to poor people (of which GiveDirectly is the best known) are an example of philanthropy that recognizes this dimension of the problem and attempts to overcome it. Part of the objective is to design philanthropic programs to allow recipients maximum scope for choice and "empower the poor to set their own priorities."[59] Direct-giving programs are often promoted (and contested) on the grounds of their supposed efficiency, but they are also important for their challenge to the traditional view that donors are most competent to decide— on behalf of recipients and especially on behalf of the poor—how charitable money should be spent. At the level of policy design, private and public programs may face similar choices about whether and how to paternalize their intended beneficiaries.

But there are also important structural differences between public and private actors that matter for our assessments of objectionable paternalism. Defenders of paternalism often assume the portability of their arguments across different kinds of social, economic, and political relationships. Often, the differences between governmental and private paternalism are literally glossed over in parentheses. For example, Abhijit

Banerjee and Esther Duflo (founders of MIT's Poverty Action Lab and recent Nobel laureates) argue for policies that "nudge" (but don't force) people to do what is best for them: "The government (*or a well-meaning NGO*) should make the option that it thinks is the best for most people the default choice, so that people will need to actively move away from it if they want to. So people have the right to choose what they want, but there is a small cost of doing so, and as a result, most people end up choosing the default option."[60] Similarly, Sigal Ben-Porath notes that "through instituting default rules, the state (*or employer, or other regulator*) can affect levels of participation in different programs, thus advancing what seems to be preferable . . . without imposing a change of motivation or preference on individuals, and without infringing upon their freedom."[61] What is missing is adequate consideration of the possibility that the government, "well-meaning NGO," and "other regulator" might enjoy different degrees of reliability or legitimacy in designing such "nudges." Through mechanisms of democratic accountability, people are able to signal their displeasure at the way that governments exercise power and manipulate incentives. They do not have institutionalized ways of responding to similar agenda setting by NGOs. Because it is not subject to democratic accountability (or, often, to market accountability either) philanthropic paternalism lacks important avenues of recourse for the paternalized to contest their treatment, which are available (though imperfectly) in cases of paternalism by government authorities. This lack of accountability is not just instrumentally significant but also reveals something important about the parties' relational standing: hierarchical authority is more troubling when subordinates do not have reliable ways of contesting their treatment. This further underscores the point that the relational context of paternalism, and not only forms of treatment abstracted from context, matter for paternalism's moral weight. I have considered the ways that different *social* contexts and relationships matter, but the *political* structures behind paternalistic relationships are also central. Democracy is a particularly important relational context, and the presence or absence of democratic accountability can affect paternalism's moral weight.

Democracy might matter in other ways too. Although I have been drawing a distinction between the large-scale democratic concerns of the previous chapter and the worries about paternalism in this chapter (which do not necessarily implicate outcomes of common concern), the two sets of egalitarian worry can also overlap. Resentment of paternalism and the insult it involves can sometimes be an appropriate response to philanthropy aimed at outcomes of common concern in a democracy. This is certainly true if Shiffrin is right that paternalism is not necessarily about benefiting the person paternalized so much as it is intervening on her appropriate domain of agency (which might include shared political agency). But even on a narrower definition, one that merely allows for attempts to benefit collectives to count as paternalistic, some attempts at political influence may qualify. The kinds of usurpation of democratic authority discussed in the previous chapter may also convey the kinds of insult discussed in this chapter. Philanthropic acts may express disrespect for the agency of the democratic public as well as the immediate recipients. In the pursuit of worthy goals, philanthropists may seek to reserve the capacities of judgment and action to themselves. When they do, the problem is not just a background inequality in resources or power but the expression of superiority suggested in the exploitation of that inequality: this condescension can itself be a democratic offence.

Conclusion

A focus on paternalism gives us a fuller picture of philanthropy's threat to democratic equality. Beyond undermining political equality and exercising objectionably plutocratic influence over matters of common equal concern, philanthropy can wrong its intended beneficiaries by paternalizing them.

I have argued that paternalism is presumptively wrong, but I have not claimed that it is always wrong, all things considered. The action-guiding force of identifying philanthropic paternalism is not decisive: the moral weight of paternalistic behavior and policies (which can vary according to factors considered in the previous section) must be balanced against other important moral values. So it is not true, for example, that a degree of paternalism automatically makes a philanthropic action or program morally impermissible or (still less) means that third parties (including the state) ought to step in to block or restrict the transaction.

The presumptive wrongness of paternalism gives philanthropists reason to avoid and to minimize paternalism in their giving. This does not mean that they should prefer not to give at all rather than to give in ways that involve elements of paternalism. Philanthropy can promote values that are of great moral importance—for example, by contributing to improvements in human welfare and the welfare of the unjustly disadvantaged;

such important values need to be weighed against the presumptive wrong of paternalism. But the choice between paternalistic giving and not donating at all will rarely be (and should not be assumed to be) binary. Paternalism is a matter of degree and it will usually be possible for donors to reduce considerably the paternalism of their giving, often at no cost at all to the other values they are trying to promote. This is a matter both of project design and of communicative choices: as I argued with reference to the case of in-kind aid, the rationales plausibly available for and imputed to a policy should influence its classification as paternalistic. Donors who think they have sound *non*paternalistic reasons for giving in ways that might *seem* paternalistic can show respect for their beneficiaries by offering them justifications for giving in choice-limiting ways rather than treating the provision of benefits as self-justifying.

Prospective donors are not the only parties with a responsibility to minimize philanthropic paternalism and its effects. Recipient institutions have a responsibility to limit their clients' exposure to donor paternalism by resisting donor attempts at conditionality and control. And the state can likewise take regulatory steps to minimize people's exposure to paternalistic forms of philanthropy—for example, it can attempt to raise the costs of paternalism for philanthropists (using either material or nonmaterial incentives), decline to enforce some philanthropic contracts, or restrict public funding of charities that deploy some kinds of paternalistic offers or conditions (as in the Indiana food bank case). Here, though, beneficiaries' attitudes and (especially) consensual choices can matter a great deal. A *philanthropist's* action may be objectionably paternalistic without third parties (including the state) having any entitlement to block it. In cases of a collective failure to secure justice, it might compound the baseline wrong and itself be paternalistic to prevent beneficiaries from exercising what they take to be their best available option. The point here is not that beneficiaries' consent removes the presumptive objection to paternalism: on the contrary, the philanthropic action remains morally objectionable to the extent that it fails to show respect for its beneficiaries. But respect for beneficiaries and their judgments also constrains how third parties may act.[62]

Again, though, the choice is not a binary one between blocking or acquiescing to philanthropic paternalism. In addition to shaping philanthropists' opportunities for and beneficiaries' exposure to paternalism, third parties can attempt to mitigate and offset its effects. Public criticism is an appropriate response even to some forms of philanthropy that are all-things-considered worth permitting (e.g., when welfare-improving programs contain unnecessary paternalistic elements). In addition to disincentivizing paternalism, such criticism can act as a countervailing force on social relations: to the extent that philanthropists express the judgment that they know better than recipients, it matters a great deal whether states and members of the public act as though they *agree* with that judgment. Philanthropic paternalism is more harmful when greeted with deference than with indignation.

I have focused so far on philanthropy that reinforces relationships of inequality. But there is an alternative image of philanthropy, one more characteristically promulgated by the nonprofit sector (perhaps especially in the United States). According to this image, philanthropy is an expression of solidarity and reciprocity, and it promotes democratic rather than hierarchical relationships. Now, at times this may be no more than rhetoric; to proclaim solidarity is not to stand in a solidaristic relationship. But sometimes the rhetoric is worth taking seriously. In the following chapter, I expand my focus beyond elite philanthropy and consider how (and under what conditions) mass and associational philanthropy can either support or subvert egalitarian social relations.

CHAPTER FIVE

Ordinary Donors and Democratic Philanthropy

In democratic nations associations must take the place of the powerful private individuals who have been eliminated by equality of conditions.—Alexis de Tocqueville, *Democracy in America*

Face it, we all have a bit of the robber baron turned philanthropist in us.—Curtis White, "The Idols of Environmentalism"

In the preceding chapters, I developed two objections to philanthropy: philanthropy can be an exercise of plutocratic power, and it can be objectionably paternalistic. Both objections position philanthropy as potentially undemocratic and inegalitarian. But recently, some observers have suggested that the cure for undemocratic philanthropy is more philanthropy: that we might "democratize" philanthropy and the nonprofit sector by broadening the base of contributors and encouraging (or more generously subsidizing) ordinary citizens' voluntary contributions of their money and their time.

In this chapter, I argue for skepticism about such proposals and the conceptions of democracy on which they implicitly rely. In the first section, I argue that neither *mass philanthropy*, or philanthropic initiatives whose financial base comes from a large number of small donors, nor *associational philanthropy*, or philanthropic initiatives conducted by membership or participatory associations, necessarily models or supports egalitarian social and political relations.[1] Mass philanthropy can be undemocratic or inegalitarian in its aggregate effects, and even internally democratic and egalitarian associations can act undemocratically or paternalistically toward nonmembers (including intended beneficiaries). Democratizing the nonprofit sector requires more than broadening the base of philanthropic contributors or increasing their active participation. In the second section, I consider the conditions under which some forms of mass and associational philanthropy can support egalitarian social relations and promote the democratic goal of ensuring that citizens share authority in an ongoing way over the social and political outcomes that affect them in common.

Philanthropy as Democratic Pluralism and Participation?

Mass Donations

Millionaires and even billionaires can be outspent. In the United States, giving by philanthropic foundations accounts for a growing, but not the largest, share of charitable donations.[2] As I argued in chapter 3, what makes foundation giving (and elite philanthropy in general) exceptional is not only its magnitude in dollar amounts but also the forms of control that it permits donors to exercise. In that chapter, I suggested some remedies aimed at partly addressing the undemocratic aspects of elite giving, but it might be charged that I gave short shrift to the most obvious one: perhaps expanded, reinvigorated, or more generously subsidized forms of mass giving could be a countervailing force. If high-volume, small-dollar-amount donations by ordinary citizens are not vulnerable to the same objections as giving by economic elites, mass giving might seem to be a positive force for democratizing the nonprofit sector.

Hence, proposals to "democratize" the nonprofit sector by broadening and more equitably subsidizing the base of contributors to charitable organizations. Pevnick, for example, argues for eliminating the tax-deduction mechanism for subsidizing charitable contributions and instead "taking public funding for nonprofits and distributing it—in the shape of vouchers—equally across the voting age population (rather than attaching it to donations)."[3] People would then be able to allocate these vouchers to the (qualifying) nonprofits of their choice. Although a reform of the charitable tax deduction might be defended solely on the grounds of tax fairness, Pevnick argues that it would also enhance the democratic character of the nonprofit sector itself: "We should expect the nonprofit sector under such a system to be responsive to a far wider range of needs, interests, and preferences than the existing system"; the reform "would help to create a nonprofit sector far better incentivized to serve the needs of the citizenry as a whole, rather than the small portion of the citizenry with the means to give large gifts."[4] The voucher system "provides increased incentive for art museums and orchestras to seek financial support partially by reaching out to and serving the broader public rather than simply catering to elite supporters. It is in this sense that the voucher system holds out the promise of a democratized nonprofit sector—a sector much more closely tethered to the public's interests. It thus shows the way to a nonprofit sector directed by and for a community of equals."[5]

I share the aspiration for a nonprofit sector that reflects the ideal of "a community of equals." But we should be skeptical of attempts to realize that ideal primarily by broadening the base of charitable contributions (even when such attempts occur through public subsidy rather than mere exhortation). This is for two main reasons.

The first, already touched on in chapter 3, is empirical: although a voucher system would surely cause some changes to patterns in the sources and destinations of charitable donations, it is less clear that it would significantly redistribute power. Absent other changes, ordinary citizens would still struggle to exert the kinds of concentrated and durable influence over nonprofit organizations that economic elites enjoy. When an ordinary person makes (say) a $100 holiday donation to Oxfam (or even, in the hypothetical, sends Oxfam her yearly $200 government voucher), her gifts do not come with strings attached or give her lasting influence over the organization's activities. She probably has less incentive to monitor the organization's activities or to attempt to hold it accountable, and she certainly has less leverage should she try. Successfully pressuring the organization would likely require her to engage in time-consuming forms of coordination with other small donors. While the aggregate effects of a voucher system might be significant in distributional terms, it is not clear how far such a system would erode the more concentrated and entrenched influence of elite donors.

Relatedly, but more importantly, we should question the account of democracy or of a "community of equals" that underlies arguments for democratizing philanthropy through the promotion of mass donations. Whether subsidized by vouchers or not, mass donations might make the nonprofit sector responsive to more people's preferences while leaving some citizens subject to others' undemocratic power. Although individual small donors do not exercise undemocratic power, the aggregation of small donations can create problems that are more closely analogous to democratic concerns around elite philanthropy. While donors to Oxfam and other charities may not exercise significant political power, the *organizations* themselves can exercise unaccountable and undemocratic power.[6] A nonprofit organization, just like a for-profit corporation, is a kind of group agent. Arguably, it undermines democratic equality if such an agent enjoys outsized control over social outcomes of common concern, just as if the agent were a flesh-and-blood person. Whether the organization is funded by mass donations or by a handful of billionaires is not in itself relevant to those concerns.

The possibility of a broad base of donations leading to undemocratic concentrations of influence is not merely hypothetical. The role of religious institutions in providing public goods is particularly important to consider in light of any proposed voucher scheme, since we can predict that huge numbers of Americans would choose to allocate their vouchers to such institutions: churches and religious organizations claim nearly one-third of total charitable giving in the United States and an even higher percentage of giving by individuals, and so are arguably the institutions that stand most to gain from a voucher system.[7] In some forms, this could further erode citizens' shared authority over important social institutions and outcomes.

Consider the dilemma posed by the trend of nonprofit (and especially Catholic) health care providers merging with or replacing public ones. In general, nonprofit privatization has not attracted the same degree of scrutiny as for-profit privatizations of state services (e.g., in the case of prisons). Some of this may be explained by greater confidence in the good intentions of nonprofit providers or the expectation that their incentives are less distorted by the search for profits. And, indeed, Catholic and other nonprofit health care providers may fill gaps in state provision and serve those who are poor, live in rural areas, lack insurance, or are otherwise neglected by public services. On the other hand, Martha Minow has surveyed the costs of relying on such providers, or of diverting public funds in response to their presence:

[A] study of Texas hospitals indicates that public hospitals afforded greater charity health services than nonprofits, including Catholic hospitals. Mergers that reduce the presence of public hospitals can lead to a net reduction in the provision of care for the poor, even when the new entities involve religiously identified organizations. In addition, mergers with specifically Catholic hospitals affects the availability of reproductive services and assisted technology, abortion, counseling for persons who are HIV positive about the use of condoms, vasectomies, and end-of-life choices.[8]

Minow cites a number of reports indicating that abortion, family planning, and sterilization services disappear from formerly public institutions following mergers with Catholic ones. Physicians working at these institutions may not be permitted to provide services that Catholic teaching frowns upon, regardless of the physicians' own religious beliefs.[9] As Minow points out, this can represent a serious restriction of reproductive freedom for people living in communities served exclusively by Catholic hospitals: "Especially in small cities and rural areas, the mergers reduce or even eliminate choice about health care providers and risk imposing Catholic rules on many who would not choose them."[10]

A person who complains of her reduced access to services because of such developments does not complain of her undemocratic domination by a single wealthy citizen. The problem is rather that authority over significant questions of medical access has been outsourced to private actors. Some of these are general problems with the privatization of state services, whether by for-profit or nonprofit actors.[11] Some people might intuitively suppose nonprofit privatization to be the lesser evil of the two. In fact, this is far from clear, at least to the extent that the concern is accountability. In both cases, service delivery becomes shielded from mechanisms of democratic accountability; and, compared with for-profit providers, nonprofits may in some cases be more likely to refuse to provide services that clients want or to supply ones for which there is little demand. In this respect, nonprofit provision risks combining the pitfalls of public and private service delivery. (And this could be true regardless of how internally democratic the nonprofit looks, just as a corporation with an internally egalitarian shareholding structure could be vulnerable to complaints that it is subverting or distorting democratic outcomes.)[12]

Mass philanthropy also fails to overcome concerns about philanthropic paternalism. Even as individuals, relatively small donors can behave paternalistically: it is possible to condescend even from moderate heights, as the case of Victorian- and Progressive-era "friendly visitors" illustrates. Paternalistic power can also be exercised by mass-funded organizations. We are perfectly familiar with paternalism perpetrated by groups or corporate agents (paradigmatically, by the state); a mass organization, funded by small donations, is another kind of group agent whose actions and policies can paternalize its intended beneficiaries (and other affected parties). In some ways, the strains of relying on paternalist aid might be mitigated when aid is dispensed by a mass-funded organization rather than by a single wealthy individual. But even this is not obvious: to the degree that an expression of disrespect can be attributed to many people, it may become more serious. Organizations that rely on soliciting mass donations may also have incentives to rely on paternalistic messaging (e.g., in their advertising and fundraising appeals). Many factors may affect paternalism's moral weight, but there is no reason to treat collective paternalism as less objectionable in principle.

In general terms, the risk is that when we speak loosely of "democratized" forms of mass philanthropy, we continue to imagine models of philanthropy focused on the activity and the empowerment of donors rather than beneficiaries (or others affected). Recent models of "civic crowdfunding" highlight the ways that even comparatively decentralized forms of mass philanthropy (i.e., that do not result in the undemocratic empowerment of a particular individual or institutional actor) can nevertheless reflect and extend subordinating social relations. Civic crowdfunding adapts commercial crowdfunding models (e.g., Kickstarter) to philanthropic purposes. An early and well-known example is DonorsChoose.org, which allows public school teachers to solicit online donations for specific classroom needs. When a project meets its funding goal, DonorsChoose.org ships the materials to the school. The organization's advertising highlights the ways that this model empowers small donors and offers them the elite philanthropist experience: "You can give as little as $1 and get the same level of choice, transparency, and feedback that is traditionally reserved for someone who gives millions."[13] Donors receive information about the projects they fund and thank-you notes from teachers; those who give over $50 are also entitled to receive handwritten thank-you notes from students. Given inadequate public funding and inequalities in educational resources, fundraising models that allow teachers to articulate and meet classroom needs have some instrumental value. On the other hand, it is troubling to see models of educational philanthropy that emphasize the benefits of choice and control for donors and, conversely, of gratitude for recipients. (In its advice to teachers on how to get projects funded, the organization stresses that "a solid thank-you note [from the teacher] is the crucial final step in any project's success" and will also "get your gratitude endorphins flowing";[14] for students, it suggests that writing thank-you notes is "just good manners, the kind that plenty of teachers strive to foster in any classroom.")[15] Contrary to DonorsChoose's organizational messaging, we should question the aptness of the gratitude here and worry about the message conveyed in asking public school students to write thank-you notes to benefactors. When ordinary donors contribute to civic crowdfunding appeals, they may in one way help to offset the public injustice of inadequate and inequitably distributed educational resources. And they generally will not exercise undemocratic control on a scale comparable to elite philanthropists. But their actions can nevertheless communicate disrespectful and subordinating messages—for example, by encouraging students whose schools rely on DonorsChoose funding to think of the educational resources they receive as gifts (for which they should express gratitude) rather than entitlements. Donations that may be valuable in distributive terms can contribute to reinforcing and legitimating unjust inequalities of status and concern.

If a broad financial base alone does not "democratize" philanthropy, what would? In the next section, I consider a second influential answer, which turns not only on the base of financial contributions but also on the modes of participation and engagement that accompany them.

Associations and Civic Externalities

Civic or "social capital" arguments for philanthropy (discussed in chapter 1) celebrate the educative potential of participation in voluntary associations and the positive externalities such participation has for political communities. On such arguments, the democratic promise of philanthropic (and other) associations need not inhere in the substance of their activities or in their internal structures and norms. Rather, associations contribute to democracy by eliciting broad-based forms of citizen engagement, socializing people into practices of cooperation, and contributing to social cohesion and trust.

Civic-benefits theorists generally attribute greater significance to organizational membership and participation than to the mere fact of donating money.[16] Indeed, some, like Mill, explicitly deny that merely donating money, without any practical involvement in its management, will bring significant educative benefits for the giver.[17] The civic case for associational activity will therefore vindicate only a subset of nonprofits and philanthropy; in particular, it will have little to say about the merits of nonmembership organizations. These account for the majority of public-benefit nonprofits: while regular donors may feel strong ties to a 501(c)(3) charity, such organizations generally do not accord their contributors formal membership or voting rights (analogous to those of shareholders in a for-profit corporation) and instead choose a simpler, board-driven governance structure.[18]

Voluntary associations are much more likely to have members. But rates and forms of member participation may still fall below the threshold at which civic benefits can be expected to accrue. Contemporary contributors to the literature on civic engagement recognize that civic justifications are not equally applicable to all forms of associational life. Nancy Burns, Kay Lehman Schlozman, and Sidney Verba note that the advent of mass mailing and telephone solicitation produced "a transformation in the nature of organizational affiliations," with many members limiting their involvement to the payment of dues while leaving management of the money and the organization itself to a professional staff; they suggest that "While this form of affiliation may facilitate the accomplishment of joint purposes, it is probably not very effective in cultivating the civic endowments that are said to accompany active involvement."[19] While the philanthropic sector accounts for a large share of Americans' associational affiliations,[20] rates of active involvement in these organizations appear to be relatively low.[21] If charitable and social service organizations are instruments for involving and empowering their members, they are at best inefficient ones compared with other forms of associational life. Empirical questions aside, there is also something unsatisfying about arguments for associational philanthropy that are too reliant on its democratic externalities. Not only can the relevant externalities be produced as or more efficiently by nonphilanthropic associations and activities, but they also do not seem to capture very well what people value about associational *philanthropy* (as opposed to associational life more generally).

As in the case of the "democracy through mass donations" model discussed above, we need to question the account of democracy lurking behind this conception, one that equates democracy with participation and presence (through either donating time or money). Call these "turnout" conceptions of democracy: democracy as "ordinary people doing things" and as threatened when people do less of those things. While popular participation is an important ingredient of democracy, it would be a mistake to fixate on it to the exclusion of attention to social relations and relations of power. Philanthropy may easily exhibit the density of participation that we sometimes associate with democracy, without incorporating the egalitarian relations that also form a part of the democratic ideal.

For an example of philanthropic activity that satisfies civic and participatory goals but falls short of modeling democratic relationships, consider the case of "giving circles." Angela Eikenberry describes this model, in which members pool resources and make joint decisions about where to give them away, as "something different" from older philanthropic models ("such as foundations, federated giving programs, or check-writing") and as "indicative of new efforts to 'democratize philanthropy.'"[22] Eikenberry points to some democratic effects of giving circles but also recognizes that "what may be democratic for a member of the giving circle as donor and participant does not necessarily translate into democratic outcomes for the larger society."[23] Moreover, we must distinguish both the civic benefits for members and possible positive externalities from relationships that can cogently be described as democratic. It is easy to forget that democracy involves not only groups voting, but groups voting (in provisionally binding ways) on matters of common concern. Claims that a group decision is democratic in character become more difficult to sustain the less that the group making the decision and the group affected by it overlap. Giving circles are not democratic bodies but highly deliberative aristocratic ones. Relationships *within* the giving circle may be characterized by a rich and rewarding reciprocity—but then, so might relationships within an oligarchic elite. The lack of reciprocity between givers and recipients is what limits the democratic potential of the giving circle model.

The *locus classicus* for civic arguments for philanthropy is, of course, Alexis de Tocqueville's *Democracy in America*. Tocqueville observes that "Americans of all ages, all conditions, and all minds are constantly joining together in groups. . . . Americans associate to give fêtes, to found seminaries, to build inns, to erect churches, to distribute books, and to send missionaries to the antipodes. This is how they create hospitals, prisons and schools. If, finally, they wish to publicize a truth or foster a sentiment with the help of a great example, they associate."[24] But invocations of Tocqueville in philanthropic contexts truncate his account of what made American associational activity democratic when they focus on its participatory rather than relational elements. Tocqueville is interested in civic associations not merely as vehicles for citizens' active participation but as sites for negotiating social (and especially class) relationships. For him, the democratic character of American associational life depends on background conditions of social equality and the "reciprocal action" of citizens on each other. These points have not always been emphasized but represent, I argue, a better guide to what is normatively valuable in some forms of mass and associational philanthropy.

Tocqueville's observations on the mania of ordinary Americans for forming associations are best remembered for positioning associations as a desirable substitute for state action: "A government could take the place of some of the larger American associations, and several individual states of the union have already attempted to do so. But what political power could ever hope to equal the countless multitude of small ventures in which American citizens participate every day through their associations?"[25] Even if an expanded government could carry out all the projects undertaken by associations, such a substitution would be ethically, economically, and democratically corrosive: "The morals and intelligence of a democratic people would be no less at risk than its business and industry if governments were everywhere to take the place of associations."[26] No surprise, then, that Tocqueville's archetypal role in American political discourse is as the champion of civil society. His observations are often marshaled in support of private philanthropic activity and as a caution against either declining rates of citizen altruism and voluntarism or the substitution of state for associational action.[27]

However, Tocqueville also describes American associational life as the substitution of one form of private philanthropic action for another. Associational action is an alternative not only to state provision of services but also to the independent action of aristocrats: "Whenever there is a new undertaking, at the head of which you would expect to see in France the government and in England some great lord, in the United States you are sure to find an association."[28] The most familiar celebrations of Tocqueville privilege the contrast with France: in democratic America, spontaneous associational activity replaces statism and micromanagement by government. But Tocqueville also contrasts America's democratic civil society with its hierarchical English counterpart.[29] Associations are the democratic alternative to aristocrats as well as to bureaucrats: "Aristocratic societies always include, along with a multitude of individuals who can do nothing by themselves, a small number of very powerful and very wealthy citizens, each of whom can undertake great ventures on his own."[30] In such societies, "each wealthy and powerful citizen is like the head of a permanent, compulsory association comprising all who are dependent on him and whose cooperation he enjoins in furtherance of his designs."[31] For Tocqueville, the democratic character of American associational life is a feature of its class structure as well as of mass participation: "In democratic nations associations must take the place of the powerful private individuals who have been eliminated by equality of conditions."[32] American associational activity is philanthropy for a world without aristocrats: "aristocracy cannot be reestablished in the world. But ordinary citizens, by associating, can constitute very opulent, very influential, and very powerful entities—in a word, they can play the role of aristocrats."[33]

The problem to which Tocqueville introduces associations as a solution is not in the first instance state overreach, but democratic individualism: the "reflective and tranquil sentiment that disposes each citizen to cut himself off from the mass of his fellow men and withdraw into the circle of family and friends," leaving "the larger society to take care of itself."[34] Now, it is not that egalitarian social relations are Tocqueville's preferred antidote to individualism; on the contrary, individualism "is democratic in origin, and it threatens to develop as conditions equalize," without the organic social ties and willingness to sacrifice for one's dependents and descendants that (according to Tocqueville) characterize aristocratic societies.[35] But aristocratic solutions to individualism are, in Tocqueville's view, inadmissible in democratic countries. Indeed, the mistake that the rich in newly democratizing countries make lies in attempting to relate to other citizens in philanthropic rather than cooperative or solidaristic ways: "They readily consent to do good for the benefit of the people but prefer to keep them scrupulously at a distance. They think this is enough; they are mistaken. They could ruin themselves in this way without kindling any warmth in the hearts of the people around them. What is asked of them is not the sacrifice of their money; it is the sacrifice of their pride."[36] In a democratic society, the vehicle for combating individualism cannot be gratitude: "the very magnitude of benefactions, which highlights the difference of conditions, secretly irritates those who profit from them."[37] Associations are vehicles for "pursuing . . . common desires in common"[38] against a backdrop of recognized mutual need and interdependence: "feelings and ideas are renewed, the heart expands, and the human spirit develops only through the reciprocal action of human beings on one another."[39] This reciprocity, and the genuine mutual need and vulnerability that undergird it, are what separate associational life in Tocqueville's analysis from the giving circle model.

Tocqueville's observations can serve as a spur to think about what kinds of philanthropic activity would better promote social and democratic equality between the people involved. It is no longer plausible to think that American democracy tends strongly toward "equality of conditions" and the occlusion of "powerful private individuals."[40] And, as I argued above, there is no democratic magic in the mere fact of high-volume donations or mass participation: especially against a backdrop of economic, social, and political inequality, there is every risk that associations will indeed take the place of "powerful private individuals"—for ill as well as for good. But we should consider what kinds of philanthropy reflect at least an aspiration toward social equality (if not, as Tocqueville thought, evidence that equality has been achieved).

Ordinary Philanthropy and Democratic Equality

The intuition that mass and associational philanthropy represent a democratic improvement on elite philanthropy can be right, but not in all cases or for some of the most familiar reasons. Democratizing philanthropy, I have argued, is not a matter merely of increasing the donation base or of ensuring that philanthropy provides indirect civic benefits (for participants or the broader democratic culture). Rather, a democratic philanthropy should support relationships of social and political equality.

Now, relational egalitarian values are not the only ones that mass and associational philanthropy might promote. Just like any other kind of philanthropy, mass or associational giving can be instrumentally valuable in producing good outcomes (measured in terms of welfare or other values); just like any other philanthropist, an ordinary donor or volunteer may derive personal satisfaction from giving her time or money. My objective here is to ask how relational egalitarian values bear on evaluations of ordinary donors and volunteers. (I am not, for instance, considering the empirical question of whether, compared with elite philanthropy, mass or associational giving does a better or worse job of producing public goods.) My claim is that what is true of elite giving is also true of ordinary giving: a concern for relationships of political and social equality should condition and sometimes constrain the ways that donors and volunteers go about doing good.

The best case for most philanthropy is to provide some instrumental benefit (broadly conceived), without subverting egalitarian social and political relations. This is no easy feat, and where it does occur—whatever the philanthropic sector or source of donation—it is to the credit of the donors, recipients, and the community whose attitudes and practices shape the giving relationship. The subversion of egalitarian relations is a particular danger of elite philanthropy but can arise even from more ordinary donations. Social equality is multidimensional: gaps can open at different points on the scale of economic advantage and in relation to factors other than wealth. The comparative advantage of mass and associational giving is not that these forms of philanthropy automatically avoid subverting equality but that they may sometimes model and promote (and not just avoid subverting) egalitarian social and political relationships. (This may not be impossible for elite giving to achieve either but, in practice, where background inequalities loom large, the hierarchical dimensions of gift relationships can reassert themselves all the more easily.) Some features of mass and associational philanthropy make it more likely to coexist with egalitarian relations, and some examples of mass and associational philanthropy actually do reflect such relationships. But here we should avoid complacency and the temptation to underestimate the challenges. It is difficult even for mass and associational philanthropy to achieve the kind of respect and reciprocity that I have argued are central to democracy: doing so requires institutional creativity, humility, and social and psychological sensitivity. Cultivating these forms of respect and reciprocity therefore relies not only on policy levers but also on the social norms and practices that shape giving relationships.

There are long traditions in charitable practice that aim to mitigate the risks of gift relationships to beneficiaries' dignity and standing in the community. Anonymous giving is one of the most familiar.[41] It is a recurring trope in charitable practice for many reasons. In part, it represents an end-run around the ethical pitfalls of charity for the giver: anonymity may screen out selfish or self-aggrandizing motivations for giving, and this may be important if the giver's motivations affect the value of a charitable act.[42] But devices of anonymity have also been used to protect the recipients of largesse. Recalling the Passover traditions of his childhood, Elie Wiesel describes one such device of anonymity:

> In some towns, before Passover, Jews would raise funds discreetly: One by one, they would enter a room in the community house. There they would find a dish filled with money. Those who had money left some; those who needed money took some. No one knew how much was given or how much was taken. Thus, the needy were taken care of with dignity.[43]

Wiesel's story of the collection box describes an attempt to model *full* anonymity: the structure of charity is designed to conceal who gives, who takes, and how much. It serves both to reduce the scope for prideful or domineering motives among givers and to preserve the self-respect and equal status of the recipients. Anonymous giving, on this model, prevents people in a community from relating to each other as givers and recipients; it represents an attempt to meet people's needs consistent with respect for beneficiaries and their standing as equals.

Now, there is something a little fantastic or romantic about Wiesel's story; we suspect that real flesh-and-blood townspeople would peek behind the veil of anonymity or at least speculate about the identities of givers and recipients. The success of the arrangement may depend on background inequalities not being too great: in a community consisting of very rich and very poor people, everyone would likely have some suspicion of who played the roles of provider and dependent. (But perhaps such a community would be less likely to hit on the collection box arrangement in the first place.) Another important aspect of Wiesel's case may be an expectation of equality and reciprocity over time. Again, this is easier to achieve between people whose chances of someday needing help are not too heterogeneous.[44]

The aspiration that Wiesel's story expresses might be interpreted in different ways. Perhaps the hidden collection box (or anonymous giving more generally) represents an attempt to *quarantine* background social relationships from philanthropic ones: by concealing the identities of givers and recipients, we hope to prevent philanthropy and gift relationships from changing or subverting whatever social and political relationships are currently in place. But we could also see in the story a more substantive relational aim. Whatever the background relationships, we want forms of giving that meet community needs or desires while expressing and enacting a commitment to social equality. Rather than merely quarantining social relationships from the transformative effects of personalized gift relationships, Wiesel's villagers may be using their (carefully institutionalized) giving practice to change social relationships for the better. On this interpretation, the standing of the poor in Wiesel's village has been improved, not only because they have had their needs met, but also because the social practice expresses the right kind of respect for them as equals.[45]

Practices of mutual respect can characterize nonanonymized philanthropy as well, but the obstacles here may be greater. Nina Eliasoph describes "empowerment projects" as an "increasingly prevalent kind of semi-civic life":[46] these are hybrid, top-down projects, relying on a mix of public and charitable funding, and which engage in "empowerment talk" emphasizing the civic benefits of volunteering for participants. Eliasoph acknowledges that these projects are "morally magnetic": "most Americans, myself included, find them to be simply and almost irresistibly good, for reasons that we assume don't need much further explanation."[47] But her ethnographic work reveals reasons to resist or at least interrogate that moral pull: for all their emphasis on the value of diversity and of forging cross-class or cross-cultural connections, empowerment projects may in fact reveal or reinforce perceptions of inequalities. As Eliasoph frames the ambition of youth-oriented empowerment projects: "Volunteer work was supposed to bring different types of youth together: even though participants were not equals in the rest of their lives, just getting their hands dirty, doing the work, walking the walk, was supposed to set them on equal footing right now, in the moment."[48] In practice, the need both to sustain engagement from privileged volunteers and to appeal to donors often subverted the aim of relating as equals: "Disadvantaged youth overheard organizers' constant fundraising efforts, which often included expertly documenting their neediness. Their dependence was publicly visible. It came with a dollar amount."[49] While disadvantaged youth "spoke of themselves as outcomes and variables" and "understood that they themselves were considered the main problem to solve," nondisadvantaged youth learned to assume "that they were supposed to solve the problems of distant others."[50] That the aspiration to engage in practices of "open civic equality" can go awry does not, of course, show that it must always do so. And it might still be true that many empowerment projects have net benefits. But Eliasoph's study does suggest that efforts to insulate charitable practices from broader social relationships (and vice versa) are fraught with difficulties.

Wiesel's collection box models reciprocity, a value that stands in curious relationship to philanthropy.[51] Donors frequently express motivations of reciprocity in announcing or explaining their giving: the language of "giving back" frames philanthropy as an ongoing exchange of benefits between fortunate individuals and society at large. On the other hand, this reciprocity is often understood to be illusory or merely rhetorical: as Nancy Rosenblum puts it in her assessment of the language of "giving back," "Philanthropy is not reciprocity . . . it has nothing of neighbors' rough equality of concrete give and take."[52] Tocqueville's discussion of America's democratic philanthropy focuses on weakness and interdependence: ordinary Americans "can do almost nothing by themselves, and none of them is capable of obliging his fellow men to assist him. Hence they become helpless if they do not learn to help one another of their own free will."[53] This situation of genuine mutual need is what necessitates the cultivation of associations as "artificial aristocrats." One question, then, is the degree to which practices of mutual respect can create reciprocity even in the context of background inequalities, asymmetric need, and greater role differentiation. Another is whether, when philanthropy seems able to promote relational equality, it is best characterized as philanthropy at all.

The COVID-19 pandemic has witnessed a revival of interest in mutual aid, a practice that—like the settlement house movement—is open to interpretation both as a kind of philanthropy and as antiphilanthropic. Theorists and practitioners of mutual aid frequently distinguish it from other forms of assistance by pointing to its relational contexts and goals. Rebecca Solnit describes it as "aid offered in a spirit of solidarity and reciprocity, often coming from within struggling communities, empowering those aided, and with an eye towards liberation and social change."[54] Mariame Kaba, an organizer and activist, also distinguishes mutual aid from the kinds of "empowerment projects" that Eliasoph describes: "It's not community service—you're not doing service for service's sake. You're trying to address real material needs"; without doing so, one cannot "build the relationships that are needed to push back on the state."[55] In mutual aid traditions, it is not anonymity that protects and promotes the dignity of recipients. Rather, features such as the absence of conditions on aid, responsiveness to the needs and desires of beneficiaries, and the cultivation of respectful and sustained relationships are aimed at making personal, even intimate forms of assistance consistent with egalitarian relations.

Despite the institutional and social challenges, some philanthropy may contribute to (and not just avoid subverting) egalitarian social relations. This was Addams's aim, and it survives in contemporary organizing traditions. And, of course, there are mixed cases, where fumbling expressions of disrespect may be a precursor to more genuinely egalitarian social relationships. Jodi Kantor and Catrin Einhorn describe a complicated case of this kind in their reporting on Canada's volunteer-based system for sponsoring Syrian refugees, which the authors present as "the world's most personal resettlement program."[56] As the authors show, relationships between Canadian volunteers and the people they sponsored were genuinely warm and caring, often characterized by the aspiration to relate as equals—and, at the same time, riddled with power struggles as refugees negotiated the degree and terms of their dependence on their sponsors. There are no policy levers that can guarantee the promotion of egalitarian social relationships, which rest ultimately on the choices made and norms cultivated by participants. Public policy can attempt to reduce asymmetric dependence (e.g., by providing robust public options and mechanisms of accountability). But while these are important elements of a solution, a more complete response requires seeing philanthropy itself as a site of political action within which to contest and reshape social relations.

In addition to shaping social relations, philanthropy may also move us closer to the *political* expression of relational egalitarian commitments—to democracy. To see how, we must revise familiar understandings of philanthropy's contribution to pluralism in the provision of public goods.

The value of pluralism is frequently invoked as a reason for embracing philanthropy in general and for favoring some private role in the provision of public goods. On this rationale, nonprofits and philanthropy can act as counterweights to government orthodoxy by supplementing or offering alternatives to government-supplied goods. There are some obvious problems with this justification as it applies to elite philanthropy. Elite philanthropy may be no *counterweight* at all: it often influences or acts in concert with government rather than supplying independent alternatives, and it may further amplify voices that are already overrepresented in government action. (There is also a more zero-sum character to advocacy philanthropy than the pluralism rationale might suggest: often, philanthropists are not providing *additional* options but rather aiming to *change* the unique option set that government provides.) But mass philanthropy might seem to be less vulnerable to these objections and so to represent the best of both worlds; high volumes of small-dollar-amount donations might supply *both* pluralism and a measure of democracy in the sense that more people's preferences count. (This also might provide more decentralization in the direction of public goods than we could expect with elite philanthropy.)

This is the rationale that we have already seen animating Pevnick's argument about the measures that would democratize philanthropy and nonprofit regulation in the United States. But it is an incomplete and potentially misleading account of what we should take democratic pluralism to mean. We should not call philanthropy democratic simply because large numbers of people contribute their time or money, any more than we would call an electoral outcome democratic simply because voter turnout was high. Democracy is a relational and not a merely participatory ideal. What it demands is that power not be exercised over people except in ways that they have a continuing ability to influence. Philanthropy can violate that principle, but it can also aim to realize it. We can see this most clearly when we consider not the first-best role that philanthropy might play in an idealized liberal democracy but, rather, the role it can play in a society that is less than fully democratic.

Rob Reich provides a modular defense of philanthropy's role in democratic societies, which emphasizes, for ordinary donors, the importance of pluralism in the provision of public goods and, for foundations, the goal of "discovery" or an experimentalist approach to public policy.[57] Reich's pluralism-based defense of philanthropy (which applies especially to mass philanthropy) emphasizes its role in providing minority public goods: the government orthodoxy to which philanthropy is to provide a counterweight is assumed to be *majoritarian* orthodoxy. This is a reasonable assumption to adopt if we are discussing a stylized majoritarian democracy (and the role of philanthropy in such a society), but it risks presenting a misleading picture of philanthropy's role in relation to government in existing democratic societies. Existing democratic governments often reflect *minority* preferences about public policy and public goods. This is especially true in the United States, with its strongly countermajoritarian institutions. Under such conditions, we misinterpret the contribution of some philanthropic funding and associational activity if we cast it as a minority counterweight to majoritarian democratic policymaking. Evidence from public polling suggests that American legislators frequently act against the majority of their constituents' preferences on important issues: for example, in restricting access to abortions more—and access to guns much less—than the public would prefer.[58] Nonprofit organizations like Planned Parenthood and Moms Demand Action (working in the reproductive health and gun-control policy spaces, respectively) have attempted to shift public policy on these issues (and, in Planned Parenthood's case, to privately supply services that would otherwise be unavailable). Philanthropy and associational activity in such cases is not necessarily a counterweight to majoritarian democracy; it can function as a second-best attempt to realize majority preferences to which countermajoritarian electoral institutions are unresponsive. Because Reich's argument is about a first-best (not merely remedial) role for philanthropy in democratic societies, it obscures important second-best roles for philanthropy, where private action is made necessary by public failures of democracy.[59]

Of course, elite philanthropy, too, might be defended on the grounds that it shifts policy in a direction that may more closely align with popular preferences. But some mass philanthropy attempts to bring outcomes more closely in line with majority preferences by increasing ordinary citizens' shared influence over outcomes that affect them in common. Elite philanthropy can support goals that align with mass preferences but remains nondemocratic in the means that it employs: even where it does not subvert democratic relations, it does not model them either. Mass philanthropy can bring us closer to realizing something like the anti-oligarchic principle that outcomes of common concern ought not be subject to minority control—whether the minority in question is political or philanthropic. Billionaire philanthropic activity is not able to model democratic relationships (although it may be able to promote them indirectly and in the long run).[60]

We should not focus only on the highest units of political analysis here or limit our attention to advocacy philanthropy aimed at changing national or state policy. A similarly democratic role for ordinary people's philanthropy can play out in community organizing, which is also oriented to the democratic goal of steering policy and the provision of public goods in ways approved and influenced by the people affected. Andrew Sabl calls community organizing in the Saul Alinsky tradition "the most distinctively Tocquevillean politics."[61] Like the settlement house movement and mutual aid traditions, and despite relying on contributions of time and money, community organizing stretches ordinary understandings of philanthropy—it deemphasizes generalized motives of benevolence or impersonal altruism and attempts to close the distance between citizens and social classes.[62] It invites participants to relate to each other politically rather than philanthropically and promotes a sense of solidarity rather than a sense of benevolent prerogative or *noblesse oblige*. The standard philanthropic goal is to confer a benefit on recipients of goods or services decided in advance by the philanthropist. Community organizers focus instead on the importance of empowering target populations to decide their own goals: "Organizers (and Tocqueville) are determined to inspire independent judgment in those organized, even if this works against the organizers' own visions for society. People must be allowed to define for themselves what their interests entail."[63] The focus is on eliciting citizens' perceptions of their own good (and avoiding situations where leaders stipulate the ends of the community as a whole). In that sense, the ethos of community organizing is self-consciously antipaternalist.

It also recalls Addams's rejection of preconceived philanthropic ideals and her open-ended conception of "lateral" social progress. As Vijay Phulwani puts it, Alinsky's "guiding question" was "how power can be acquired and exercised by as many people as possible, starting from conditions of widespread inequality and popular disempowerment."[64] The organizer is therefore "an agent of the democratization of power,"[65] and this is the central difference between the organizer and the funder. Philanthropic funders may pursue ends or outcomes under which power will be more dispersed; organizers insist on a more immediate democratization of power. We are to relate as equals *now*, not at some future point after which philanthropic objectives have been achieved. Hence, in part, organizers' uneasy relationship to movement funders, whom they have often regarded with suspicion: a need to appeal to funders can stand in serious tension with the goal of empowering ordinary people to define their own goals and gain control over their own lives.[66]

In chapter 4, I noted that philanthropic paternalism is a particular concern when it targets people who are already disadvantaged within existing hierarchies of status and power. Similarly, organizers recognize that the very communities it may seem most important to "speak for" are those where it also may be most important that members speak instead for themselves. There are some good reasons to worry less about the internal democracy of a homeowners' association in a wealthy suburb than of a post–Hurricane Katrina neighborhood association.[67] (Of course, we may have greater reason to worry about the homeowners' association's impact on outsiders.)

In evaluating community-based and community-directed philanthropy, we need to consider both its effects on outsiders and its relationship to overall social distributions of power and advantage. The attractiveness of "community self-help" models of philanthropy depends partly on facts about background social justice or injustice. Where the members of an association stand in relation to background injustices—whether they are unfairly advantaged or disadvantaged by social institutions—can make their efforts at self-help morally objectionable or admirable. The activities of some civic and community associations may amount to efforts to hoard club goods. Reich, for example, has criticized the tax deductibility of donations to local educational foundations, which contribute to inequalities in spending on public schools between districts. The tax deductibility of such donations exacerbates the injustice, but even if the donations were not publicly subsidized, they could contribute to educational inequities in objectionable ways. If local school philanthropy becomes a way for rich communities to compound their advantages, the public value of the project diminishes significantly and may quickly become negative. No similar objection attaches to a disadvantaged community's efforts at local improvements or projects for mutual benefit (though social injustice making such efforts necessary or urgent remains objectionable).

That mass and associational philanthropy can promote egalitarian relations is not in itself an argument for philanthropic over public provision.[68] Even the philanthropic models that emerge as particularly valuable from my account may be limited in their ability to achieve more sweeping egalitarian transformations and will often be second best to public provision (or a substitute for it in situations where the public is failing some citizens). A philanthropic association might model the right kinds of relationships between citizens without being the most appropriate provider of a particular good or service. Mass and associational philanthropy, though it can be more democratic than elite philanthropy, is no substitute for the democracy of public power.

Conclusion

Neither mass nor associational philanthropy is a panacea for relational egalitarian worries about the private funding and provision of public benefits; nonprofit activity funded from a broad base of donations or reliant on the efforts of volunteers can subvert social and political equality. Like elite philanthropy, mass and associational philanthropy risks prioritizing the empowerment of donors over beneficiaries. Avoiding this requires more than a participatory or "turnout" conception of what it means to democratize an institution or practice (i.e., a conception emphasizing the value of more people "getting involved," whether by giving their money or their time). We also need to consider a range of different social and relational egalitarian values—reciprocity, respect, protection of people's dignity, recognition of entitlements—and the kinds of institutions, practices, and norms that might promote or subvert them. Democratizing philanthropy requires attending to the power relationships that philanthropy emerges from and, in turn, helps to shape.

The following chapter pursues the question of how philanthropy can confer important benefits consistent with respect for individuals and communities. It considers what democracy and antipaternalism require when philanthropy travels across national boundaries.

CHAPTER SIX

International Philanthropy

Some of the earliest and most famous stories of charitable acts call into question the significance of shared membership in a social or political community. The Biblical parable of the Good Samaritan is introduced as a response to the question "Who is my neighbor?"[1] The parable teaches that it is the traveling Samaritan—a compassionate stranger—who is "neighbor" to the man in need.[2] In this chapter, I show how the general approach to philanthropy developed in this book—treating philanthropy as a problem of relational equality as well as a matter of welfare or distributive outcomes—applies when philanthropic relationships cross borders.

Global giving comprises some of the most ambitious contemporary philanthropic projects and spurs some of the most important contemporary debates about private philanthropy. Although international philanthropy includes a very wide range of activities,[3] this chapter focuses on private donations (to governmental and intergovernmental agencies, to nonprofits and NGOs, or to individuals) intended to attack the causes and offset the effects of severe poverty. I am defining this category loosely and broadly to include, for example, emergency humanitarian relief, public health initiatives (e.g., to improve sanitation or prevent and treat disease), and educational programs, as well as more straightforward efforts to increase the incomes and savings of poor people. I focus on the issue of global poverty both because I take it to be a hard case for relational views in theory, and because it represents an area where usurpation and paternalism are normalized in practice.

Philanthropy aiming to fight global poverty is a hard case for relational views for two reasons. First, material and welfarist concerns are especially pressing in this area: the goal of preventing and mitigating the harms associated with global poverty is so important that it may seem to crowd out relational concerns. Second, relational egalitarian values may seem to have their strongest purchase between citizens and therefore to be less important in evaluating international philanthropy: in contrast with domestic philanthropy, philanthropists, recipient organizations, and beneficiaries often do not share prior democratic relationships. Nevertheless, I argue that we have strong reasons to attend to the problems of philanthropic paternalism and of undemocratic influence in international philanthropy. We have reasons to avoid objectionably paternalistic relationships that do not depend on shared national membership and that apply in the international context: these are reasons that guide the kinds of relationships we ought to form, whether or not we have an obligation to form a relationship in the first place. Turning to democracy, the concern is not simply that international philanthropy gives foreign donors undue influence over particular outcomes, but that it can displace and subvert existing and nascent democratic relations within the receiving country. I begin by explaining the more direct ways that global giving can create or reinforce objectionable relationships before proceeding to the problem of democratic displacement.

Objective Welfare and Relational Vices

Donors, practitioners, and scholars working from different normative foundations converge in evaluating international giving through distributive lenses. This is partly a product of the greater influence of consequentialist moral perspectives on the theory and practice of global giving: to a greater degree than domestically, debates are dominated by questions about how best to promote objective welfare.

Peter Singer's work continues to set the terms of debate around voluntary giving to fight global poverty.[4] In his 1972 article, "Famine, Affluence, and Morality," Singer argues that individual obligations of assistance exist wherever one is in the position to prevent something bad from happening "without thereby sacrificing anything of comparable moral importance."[5] In Singer's famous example, if I see a small child drowning in a shallow pond and can save her at the trivial cost of muddying my clothes, it would be morally repugnant not to assist. Singer's claim is that the moral principle that explains this (noncontroversial) result in the pond case yields radical conclusions. Once we accept that unnecessary deaths and suffering caused by global poverty are bad, we must ask what actions we could take to prevent those bad things from happening and donate to charitable efforts that meet the case. Moreover, we should *continue* donating as long as there are significant harms that we can prevent without sacrificing anything of comparable moral importance. Singer's argument therefore calls for most people living in rich countries drastically to change their lifestyles. Voluntary giving alone will not eliminate global poverty: Singer is aware of the great significance of public policy (in both donor and lower-income countries) for reducing global poverty and its associated harms. But, even in a democracy, a citizen's influence over her own government is usually vanishingly small; her influence over nondemocratic or distant ones is generally nil. Given this, voluntary giving looks like the most practical way to assist, even for people who might prefer that governments do more in the cause of poverty alleviation or who believe that their own (and others') contributions ought to be coerced. So Singer's practical recommendation is that people give money to international NGOs that focus on reducing poverty or addressing its worst effects. For those convinced by his arguments in favor of a moral obligation to give, Singer's recent works propose a sliding scale of suggested yearly donation amounts, with a person's recommended minimum level of voluntary contributions rising in proportion to her income.[6]

Singer is a utilitarian, but it does not require any strong consequentialist premises to conclude that one should rescue the child in the shallow pond case, and his arguments have exercised nonconsequentialists as well. In considering the case for global giving, nonconsequentialists are more likely to distinguish between duties of justice and humanitarian obligations.[7] While some influential liberal egalitarians claim that obligations of distributive justice are global in scope,[8] others, like John Rawls and Thomas Nagel, deny that the demands of egalitarian distributive justice apply internationally:[9] we must invert the Dickensian dictum that "charity begins at home, and justice begins next door."[10] But few deny that there are *at least* strong humanitarian reasons to direct resources to improving the lot of the global poor. And, where giving proceeds outside political institutions and across borders, liberal egalitarians may be as likely as utilitarians to focus on the welfare improvements that philanthropy can promote. Consider Thomas Pogge's formulation of the moral principle that should guide the conduct of international nongovernmental organizations (INGOs):

> Other things being equal, an INGO should govern its decision making about candidate projects by such rules and procedures as are expected to maximize its long-run cost-effectiveness, defined as the expected aggregate moral value

of the projects it undertakes divided by the expected aggregate cost of these projects. Here, aggregate moral value, or harm protection, is the sum of the moral values of the harm reductions (and increases) these projects bring about for the individual persons they affect.[11]

This principle, with its capacious *ceteris paribus* clause, is striking mainly for the fact that a philosopher who sounds like Kant when discussing institutions reads like Bentham when discussing philanthropy. Both deontological liberals and consequentialists frequently weigh alternative options for global giving against each other based on expected welfare effects— whether or not they would apply different standards to domestic philanthropy or to the design of political institutions.

Singer's public advocacy for philanthropic giving to fight global poverty is a major inspiration for the "effective altruism" movement. According to the definition adopted by the Center for Effective Altruism, "Effective altruism is about using evidence and reason to figure out how to benefit others as much as possible and taking action on that basis."[12] Effective altruism is neither narrowly focused on voluntary giving nor exclusively concerned with antipoverty and public health interventions in poor countries.[13] But the latter have long been important areas of focus for effective altruists, because of their extremely favorable cost-benefit ratio. The effective altruism movement therefore encourages charitable giving to the most demonstrably effective organizations working on these causes and promotes giving pledges as commitment mechanisms.[14] GiveWell is the best known of a new generation of charity-rating organizations that, instead of relying on older and often uninformative metrics such as organizational overhead, rank charities according to their demonstrable cost efficiency in saving or improving lives, as well as their capacity to absorb additional funding. This has translated into a strong preference for money targeted to the global poor, as well as for low-cost health interventions such as the supply of insecticide-treated bed nets (demonstrated to be effective in preventing malaria) and deworming treatments.[15]

While effective altruism carries the aspiration for precise estimations of comparative welfare benefits unusually far, many of its characteristic interests and priorities are shared much more broadly. (Indeed, effective altruism's philosophical proponents and billionaire philanthropists not officially affiliated with the movement have expressed mutual admiration.)[16] For example, effective altruism's emphasis on evidence-backed interventions dovetails with (and has fueled interest in) the use of randomized

control trial (RCT) experiments in development research. Abhijit Banerjee and Esther Duflo, the most notable proponents of RCTs, give a good
statement of a much more widely shared perspective when they argue
that "the endless debates about the rights and wrongs of aid often obscure what really matters: not so much where the money comes from but
where it goes. This is a matter of choosing the right kind of project to
fund—should it be food for the indigent, pensions for the elderly, or clin-
ics for the ailing?—and then figuring out how best to run it."[17] Banerjee
and Duflo want to keep the evaluative focus squarely on the efficacy of
particular interventions and prescind from "big" political questions ("Is
democracy good for the poor? Does foreign aid have a role to play? And
so on").[18] We are to think of the challenge of fighting poverty as "a set of
concrete problems that, once properly identified and understood, can be
solved one at a time."[19]

The effective altruism movement attracts significant philosophical and
political criticism: the most common charges are that it recapitulates the
errors of its (putative) act-utilitarian antecedents (e.g., in making excessive moral demands on individuals or in threatening personal integrity)
and that it neglects the importance of structural or institutional change.[20]
Effective altruists themselves contest both the extent to which effective
altruism posits demanding moral obligations regarding how much to give
and the extent to which it relies on act-consequentialist premises. (William
MacAskill, an influential exponent, describes effective altruism as a "project" that individuals might affiliate themselves with for a range of reasons,
rather than as a moral obligation or set of normative claims.)[21] To the extent possible, I want to avoid the interpretive question of what effective altruism's core normative commitments are (if it has any) and focus instead
on the recommendations that issue from the movement's most important
voices.

Effective altruism offers important illustrations of how the pursuit of
morally valuable welfare objectives can not only coexist with but even exert
pressure toward relational vices like paternalism and failures of reciprocity.[22] Of course, these relational vices are not unique to effective altruism
or to other consequentialist approaches to voluntary giving. They can be
features of virtually any philanthropy, regardless of the specific objectives
that a donor is trying to pursue; and, in fact, we should expect a thorough-
going consequentialism to militate against many (e.g., moralistic) forms
of paternalism. But *if* (and to the extent that) greater measurable welfare
benefits can be produced by giving in undemocratic or paternalizing ways,

a maximizing or efficiency-oriented standard for evaluating gifts generates powerful reasons to engage in those kinds of giving.[23] Effective altruism raises this possibility in an especially stark way. While effective altruists often take a more relaxed position than (at least the early) Singer regarding the stringency (or even the existence) of individual obligations regarding *how much* money to give, they are generally *less* flexible regarding the standards that should be applied in evaluating the efficiency of giving. Some philosophical defenses of effective altruism endorse a "conditionally maximizing" obligation to give—for example, Theron Pummer argues that "in many cases it would be wrong of you to give a sum of money to charities that do less good than others you could have given to instead, even if it would not have been wrong of you not to give to any charity at all."[24] He supports this counterintuitive claim by defending the principle that "it is wrong to perform an act that is much worse than another, if it is no costlier to you to perform the better act."[25] Similarly, MacAskill argues that effective altruism is a "maximizing" doctrine *only* in the sense of "trying to increase the effectiveness of the resources that one has dedicated to doing good" and not in the sense of "increasing the amount of resources that one dedicates to doing good."[26] By this reasoning (depending on one's view of the good to be promoted), the option of giving with a view to minimizing relational vices might even be morally foreclosed: while I might legitimately appeal to the costs to myself in order to justify not giving to charity, any and all money I decide to give must be allocated as efficiently as possible (which might rule out altogether giving in ways that are nonpaternalistic or which otherwise reflect relational egalitarian commitments but that are marginally less welfare promoting).

Whether understood as a moral obligation or simply as a (morally permissible) project, the drive to maximize the impersonal good that donations do fuels ongoing debate within the effective altruism movement about *which* welfare-promoting organizations to support in preference to others. The debate over the merits of direct cash transfers to poor people is illustrative. GiveDirectly is a U.S.–based charity that facilitates unconditional international cash transfers (typically of US$1,000, transferred via mobile phone) to extremely low-income households in the seven African countries where the charity currently works.[27] As I argued in chapter 4, GiveDirectly is an important model of antipaternalistic philanthropy. The leading effective altruist organizations are divided on its merits: GiveWell has recommended GiveDirectly as one of its top-rated charities since 2012, while members of Giving What We Can (including MacAskill) have criticized that recommendation, arguing that alternative ways of donating would do more good.[28] MacAskill characterizes cash transfers as a suboptimal way of doing good in part because of uncertainty about how poor people will spend them: "The obvious first question to ask about GiveDirectly is: What do the recipients of these cash transfers do with the money? If they spend it on education, that sounds pretty good; if they spend it on drugs and alcohol, that's worrying."[29] He notes that the most common reported uses of GiveDirectly funds—the purchase of assets like farm animals and the conversion of thatched roofs to iron ones—"seem to have very high returns"[30] but argues that better opportunities for promoting welfare are available. MacAskill acknowledges that cash transfers provide a useful baseline against which to evaluate the benefits of other interventions and writes that "we should only assume we're in a better position to help the poor than they are to help themselves if we have some particularly compelling reason for thinking so."[31] However, his analysis makes clear that this is a question to be adjudicated on the basis of a standard of objective welfare and not one that grants independent significance to poor people's own judgments about what will promote their good.

Preferring other giving options to cash transfers is not always paternalistic. In some cases, providing cash is not sufficient to make important goods (e.g., medical treatments) accessible: where such goods are not readily available through commercial markets or are subject to economies of scale, they may need to be provided in kind or not at all. This should be distinguished from cases where a good *is* available on commercial markets and would become accessible to the intended beneficiaries if they were provided with cash (and, perhaps, information): in that case, the justification for giving in kind is much more likely to look objectionably paternalistic. The existence of distinct and potentially competing interests and perspectives within households also may supply non- (or less)[32] paternalistic justifications for not giving cash (e.g., because of concerns about benefits being disproportionately consumed by adults rather than children or men rather than women). While there are important empirical questions here, I expect that many of the health interventions that GiveWell and other effective altruist metacharities recommend could be defended on either or both of these bases, suggesting that they might well be compatible with antipaternalistic giving.

Yet effective altruism's committed neutrality (subject to evidence of benefits) about the best ways of doing as much good as possible gives no independent weight to relational virtues and vices. Sometimes, welfare maximization will mean that recipients are paternalistically given less preferred benefits on the grounds of (effective altruists') expectations that these will produce greater welfare returns. Elsewhere, it will mean that some people are denied benefits to which (on some moral views) they might plausibly have claims, on the grounds that resources can generate more good elsewhere. In both cases, what is at stake is the assumption of a donor's entitlement to maximize on the pursuit of her own objective, without regard to other important ways of showing respect for beneficiaries and for the relationships that one finds oneself in. Effective altruism has been accused of having a "political blind spot";[33] I am arguing here that the blind spot is wider, and relational.

When relational considerations appear in effective altruist arguments (if they do at all), it is often in discussions of "personal prerogative"—that is, discussions of when and why a donor is entitled to depart from the goal of good maximization and reserve some time and resources for her own preferred projects. Take an example that MacAskill uses (too narrowly, I think) as a test case for whether feeling a close personal connection to a cause justifies focusing on that cause, even if one could do more good by giving elsewhere. In explaining why he can "feel the pull of this objection," MacAskill gives the example of his decision not to donate to the Fistula Foundation, which funds surgeries and follow-up care at the Hamlin Fistula Hospital in Addis Ababa, Ethiopia:

> It was clearly a highly worthy cause, doing a huge amount of good. Ultimately, however, I concluded that you'd probably have an even bigger impact on people's lives by donating elsewhere. . . .
>
> But there was a catch. When I'd visited Ethiopia several years before, I'd visited this hospital. I'd hugged the women who suffered from this condition, and they'd thanked me for visiting them. It had been an important experience for me: a vivid firsthand demonstration of the severity of problems in the world. This was a cause that I had a personal connection with.
>
> Should I have donated to the Fistula Foundation, knowing I could do more to help people if I donated elsewhere? I do not think so. If I were to give to the Fistula Foundation rather than to the charities I thought were most effective, I would be privileging the needs of some people over others merely because I happened to know them. That would be unfair to those I could have helped more.[34]

MacAskill analogizes the arbitrariness of the "set of personal connections" he made in Addis Ababa to the arbitrariness of one's uncle suffering from one disease rather than another. It would be wrong to direct one's charitable donations to an organization simply because it targeted a disease from which a family member was suffering. Rather, we should strive to make donating decisions based on our expectations of impact. We should not unfairly privilege "the needs of some people over others" simply because we know them or feel a personal connection to a cause.

I choose the Addis Ababa example in part because it *has* produced strong reactions among nonutilitarians. Judith Lichtenburg calls the story "a little chilling" because "to most of us it seems neither reasonable nor desirable to expect people to remain untouched by the particular individuals they know and the particular causes that affect them," and Amia Srinivasan cites it as an example of MacAskill "trying to step outside what is unavoidably the scene of ethical action: one's own point of view."[35] These criticisms locate the problem in the wrong place. MacAskill is consistently applying his own ethical point of view, and there is no reason to suppose that it lacks integrity; if there is a problem in this story, we want to explain it in light of the Ethiopian women's perspectives. What should they think of MacAskill's claim that giving to them would have been unfair to beneficiaries elsewhere, in whose hands resources could be converted into impartial good more efficiently? It seems possible, at least, that they might reasonably complain of exploitation, disrespect, or a failure of reciprocity. MacAskill acknowledges that he benefited from the personal connections he made in Addis Ababa. Perhaps the women he visited hoped to benefit as well. When the expectation of a welfare improvement is above some (nontrivial) level, giving in such a circumstance might be justified as a gesture of reciprocity. No similar rationale applies in the case of the imagined uncle: there is no parallel objection to be made on the uncle's behalf if one gives to causes that one expects to promote welfare more efficiently.

Incorporating some kinds of relational conditions on giving need not mean an unlimited permission to adduce personal grounds for preferring one cause to another; it matters, for instance, whether one is attempting to benefit people at low levels of welfare or trying to right or rebalance an unjust inequality. One can acknowledge strong reason to promote a fungible conception of objective good while also acknowledging competing claims; one can think that MacAskill owed *those women* something. While he may not have had reason to give to the Fistula Foundation rather than other organizations before his visit to Addis Ababa, the visit itself could change that. Arbitrary facts can place us in new relationships, which (though we are under no obligation to form them in the first place) we have reason to try to conduct on terms of equality and reciprocity.[36] To the extent that the women MacAskill met might have good reason to feel exploited—to feel that their suffering has here been used and put on display for purposes of motivating donations elsewhere—that complaint might call for some modest departures from marginal welfare maximization. This does not amount to an all-things-considered judgment either about whether MacAskill should have donated to the Fistula Foundation or about whether the women he met have a moral complaint against him. There are, of course, other (perhaps better) ways of expressing respect and reciprocity than by making a donation, and it is possible that the women in question experienced MacAskill's decision against donating to the Fistula Foundation as fully consistent with respect for them as equals. Whatever one's judgment about the case, what is telling are the terms in which MacAskill thinks about it and his framing of his reasons to donate to the Fistula Foundation as ones of personal preference rather than respect or reciprocity. A concern for avoiding objectionably inegalitarian relationships might generate (at least) moral permissions to give in ways that one cannot be confident will *maximize* expected welfare (or a donor's other objectives in giving), as a way of showing appropriate respect for the people with whom one forms relationships. In such cases, a concern for avoiding relational vices is not best understood as an assertion of personal prerogative but as a rejection of it.

A concern for showing respect and relating on terms of equality with beneficiaries and other affected people should inflect donors' promotion of their objectives in giving—even when the objective is a reasonable and morally important one, such as the promotion of objective welfare. Donors should try to promote welfare while minimizing relational vices like paternalism, disrespect, and failures of reciprocity. Where they do not, they can wrong recipients and other affected people even when they benefit them in distributive terms.[37]

Consequentialists may not be convinced and will be tempted to treat paternalism and other relational vices as unobjectionable to the extent that they produce welfare benefits. In a chapter on public health interventions (e.g., vaccination programs and efforts to control drug availability), Banerjee and Duflo anticipate objections about paternalism with the warning that "it is easy, too easy, to sermonize about the dangers of paternalism and the need to take responsibility for our own lives, from the comfort of our couch in our safe and sanitary home. Aren't we, those who live in the rich world, the constant beneficiaries of a paternalism now so thoroughly embedded into the system that we hardly notice it?"[38] Presumably, they have in mind vaccination requirements and other public health measures (e.g., water fluoridation) that are common features of government policy in rich countries. And, their reasoning goes, if such paternalism is unobjectionable in rich countries, it must be all the more acceptable in places where welfare needs are even greater. Even granting Banerjee and Duflo's characterization of some welfare-promoting public policies as acceptably paternalistic, it would be a mistake to explain the justifiability of such policies solely with reference to their welfare benefits. To the extent that public health policies are applied universally, democratically authorized, and administered by democratically accountable actors, many can avoid both the insulting expression and the forms of subordination that characterize objectionable paternalism. Because the same factors are generally not present in privately administered international aid programs, the latter raise more serious concerns about objectionable paternalism. Even welfarists have reason to worry here, since unaccountable private paternalism may less reliably promote welfare; as Leif Wenar has argued, Singerian perspectives on giving often fail to adequately account for risks of harm from NGO activity.[39] Against the view that paternalism is less objectionable in the case of global philanthropy, because the welfare benefits may be even greater, we should treat it as especially suspect, because relationships of accountability and reciprocity are generally absent.

In evaluating when paternalism is objectionable, other theorists will be tempted to distinguish between duties of justice and humanitarian aid.[40] On familiar interpretations, these two kinds of duties differ in respect to the kind of control that recipients are entitled to exercise over benefits.[41] T. M. Scanlon offers an illustration of this point in the course of a discussion of the differences between subjective and objective criteria of well-being: He writes that the former seem "insensitive to differences between preferences that are of great relevance when those preferences are taken as the basis for moral claims."[42] In the case of duties of mutual aid, "the strength of a stranger's claim on us for aid in the fulfilment of some interest depends upon what that interest is and need not be proportional to the importance he attaches to it. The fact that someone would be willing to forego a decent diet in order to build a monument to his god does not mean that his claim on others for aid in his project has the same strength as a claim for aid in obtaining enough to eat (even assuming that the sacrifices required of others would be the same)."[43] Of course, matters would be different if the stranger had a claim of *justice* on some set of resources: in that case, the obligation to transfer the resources to him would not be contingent on his use of them. It might therefore seem that donors acting on humanitarian duties may permissibly use conditions and other forms of influence to ensure that their humanitarian goals are met (or, failing that, direct the goods to different beneficiaries, who will put them to better use—since, by hypothesis, no claim of justice would be violated in so doing). However, I believe that a sharp distinction between duties of justice and humanitarian duties, with respect to the requirement to turn over control to the recipient, looks far less plausible when we consider the kinds of relationships put in place by donors acting on duties of either kind. To adapt Scanlon's case, if we imagine instead an *ongoing* relation involving yearly or even monthly transfers to some recipient or group of recipients, a donor's insistence on control will look more troubling. Whether or not benefits are owed ex ante, they may be given in ways that create objectionable relationships. This is especially true when the donor's control subverts not only individuals' preferred projects but the possibility of their organizing together politically in the democratic pursuit of shared goals.

International Philanthropy and Democratic Displacement

What many of the perspectives discussed in the preceding section have in common is a focus on getting the content of aid right, regardless of the relationship between the agent delivering aid and the people receiving it. I argued that this can lead to forms of aid that are objectionable (e.g., because they are paternalistic) in ways that parallel relational egalitarian objections to some domestic philanthropy but are often overlooked or treated as less important in international giving. In this section, I argue that we should not ignore the risks of philanthropy subverting democratic relationships, even when philanthropists and their intended beneficiaries do not share democratic citizenship.

Other authors have recognized that international philanthropy risks displacing democratic accountability relationships (though this risk is more often understood to impose obligations on operational NGOs rather than on their donors). Jennifer Rubenstein advances a democratic procedural critique of international NGO advocacy practices. She defends an interpretation of INGOs as "holding and exercising quasi-governmental power," where "governmental power" is understood as "the power to shape the policies and practices of coercive institutions, either directly or by influencing public opinion."[44] Her "minimize displacement principle" holds that "INGOs should minimize the extent to which they displace vulnerable groups and their (more) legitimate representatives and advocates, taking into consideration other ethical constraints."[45] It is perhaps not surprising that democratic and relational concerns have attracted more attention in cases where INGOs are primarily engaged in advocacy rather than in running health or welfare programs. Compared with other NGO activities (e.g., funding or operating health and welfare services), advocacy is (as Rubenstein notes) more often interpreted as an act of "representation."[46] Advocacy is a "speaking for others" problem[47] and invites speculation as to how people might be empowered to speak for themselves. But other philanthropic roles can also involve displacement: compared with advocating on others' behalf, paying for a service is perhaps less easily interpreted as putting in place a political relationship, but it can likewise displace decision-making power and relations of democratic accountability.

A displacement of political authority could occur directly and intentionally; for example, donors could use their financial influence and bargaining power to affect the policymaking of elected representatives and public officials. The use of conditionality by intergovernmental lending institutions, like the World Bank and IMF, has long been studied (and criticized), but less has been written about conditional giving by private philanthropists. Philanthropists, like for-profit companies, often engage in public-private partnerships with governments and public agencies and typically enjoy greater bargaining power in lower-income countries. The motives of profit-seeking partners may raise greater concerns than those of philanthropists, but power imbalances between host country governments and private partners can raise concerns in philanthropic cases as well.

The philanthropic usurpation of democratic authority also need not occur in a direct way (e.g., through attempts to rewrite the policies of host-country governments). Instead, philanthropic programs may bypass or displace domestic political actors and subvert domestic accountability relations in subtler ways. The Bill and Melinda Gates Foundation's work in Africa has attracted criticisms along these lines. Consider the case of Botswana, one of Africa's most stable democracies[48] and also a country afflicted with one of the highest rates of HIV/AIDS prevalence in the world.[49] In 2000, the Gates Foundation and drug company Merck & Co. chose Botswana as the host for the African Comprehensive HIV/AIDS Partnerships (ACHAP), a $100 million pilot program for HIV/AIDS prevention and treatment. Between 2000 and 2005, deaths from AIDS fell significantly (though new infection rates and surveys testing knowledge of HIV/AIDS indicated that prevention efforts were less successful).[50] Over the same time period, child mortality (from all causes) rose and pregnancy-related maternal deaths rose sharply, leading to speculation that, by giving doctors the opportunity to more than double their salaries by working in the HIV/AIDS sector, the Gates initiative had drawn too many of Botswana's best doctors away from primary care.[51]

Other criticisms of ACHAP focused less on welfare outcomes and more on the structure of the program and conduct of the private partners. Festus Mogae, then president of Botswana, had played an important role in attracting attention to the country's HIV/AIDS crisis. Nevertheless, his reaction to the implementation of the Gates-Merck partnership was mixed: "We (the government of Botswana) pride ourselves on our ability to manage donors, the Swiss, Norwegians, and others. We implement, and they monitor progress. But ACHAP was different. They thought they would strengthen our capacity and they would have their own program with us. We didn't understand."[52] He also expressed disappointment at the partners' preference for contracting with NGOs rather than delivering programs through government agencies: "They said they wanted to work with NGOs. ACHAP thought NGOs were better. We think we [the government] are better."[53] Similarly, Botswana's then minister of health commented, "I understood that this kind of relationship should be done in some countries with poor financial management systems and endemic corruption. But this is not the case in Botswana."[54] These complaints reflect not only concerns about the program's results, but the thought that donors were bypassing or usurping the authority of a democratic government.

The displacement of domestic democratic relationships matters in part for instrumental reasons: such relationships are important predictors of people's long-term access to welfare. In a famous study, Amartya Sen explains the incidence of famines with reference not just to the food supply but to relations of democratic accountability. What matters, Sen argues, are publicly recognized *entitlements* to food: even with a food supply that could, under some distribution, feed everyone, people can starve when a lack of transparency or accountability prevents the enforcement of entitlements to food. This is the principal weakness of charity and other "non-entitlement transfers":[55] beneficiaries lack the ability to express demands to an accountable political actor; for this reason, they cannot be confident that their claims will continue to be met in the future. It is the contingent and discretionary character, rather than merely the fallibility, of philanthropic assistance that presents the problem. Even philanthropic assistance that is optimally designed and managed in a particular case delivers something different from what is provided by democratic political institutions (including with regard to expected effects on welfare).

Still more troubling is the possibility that philanthropic transfers can negatively affect the status of entitlement relations, either by eroding existing entitlement relations or by preventing them from developing. In a study that extends and complicates Sen's work, with reference to the activities of humanitarian relief agencies in Africa, Alex de Waal argues that aid is objectionable to the extent that it impedes the development of political contracts for famine prevention. De Waal defines the latter as including "a political commitment by government, recognition of famine as a political scandal by the people, and lines of accountability from government to people that enable this commitment to be enforced."[56] He argues that whatever its material benefits to host populations, "the aid relationship is . . . fundamentally different from a political contract. The benevolent ethos of aid should not obscure the practical and ideological ways in which it erodes the basis of political contracts."[57] De Waal suggests that successful programs by private aid agencies are possible but rare and "depend upon a strong pre-existing political contract" between the government and citizens of the host country. What de Waal writes with specific reference to the case of famine relief could apply equally to cases of, for example, public health emergencies: the risk is that donor activity will create a reversal or displacement of accountability relationships, where requests for assistance addressed to private actors crowd out claims on government. Conscientious donors, as well as their public partners and regulators, should aim not only to deliver health and welfare benefits in the short term, but to do so in ways minimally disruptive of domestic political contracts. If Sen and de Waal are right about the paramount importance of democratic relationships for the long-term promotion of welfare, then even effective altruists and other donors whose focus is exclusively on the promotion of a welfarist conception of the good should pay more attention to the risk of distorting democratic relations.[58]

Displacement is a particular risk when donors work outside government. Donors to public health programs in Africa have often preferred

"vertical programs," or selective interventions delivered outside a country's general health system, to "horizontal programs," where services are
delivered through a country's public health system.[59] In part, the choice
between vertical and horizontal programs represents a trade-off between
expected short-term results and the long-term strength of a country's
health system (and the political contracts supporting it, which may become confused or weakened in the context of multiplying loci of authority).[60] Some donors and NGOs have been attentive to these risks. For
example, Paul Farmer, founder of Partners in Health, is a well-known
advocate of funding basic care and of a holistic approach to health delivery systems.[61] In addition, other NGOs have signed a code of conduct
committing themselves specifically to avoiding "internal brain drain" and
the distorting effects of higher salaries for health care workers in areas of
donor priority.[62] On the other hand, the director of the Global Fund to
Fight AIDS, Tuberculosis and Malaria (a major recipient of Gates Foundation grants relating to public health in Africa) acknowledged in 2007
that vertical programs and salaries targeted to particular sectors "may
have had a distorting effect" but argued that "we're a Global Fund for
AIDS, TB, and malaria. We're not a global fund that funds local health."[63]
That is, the Global Fund reserved the right to focus on the direct effects
of most interest to it (i.e., the reduction in AIDS deaths) while disclaiming responsibility for other possible effects of its initiatives. Similarly,
Dr. Tadataka Yamada, the executive director of the Gates Foundation's
global health program from 2006 to 2011, defended vertical approaches
narrowly targeted to the foundation's areas of focus, partly on the grounds
that the foundation did not want governments to become dependent on
foundation money: "What we can't do is fill the gaps in government budgets. . . . It's not sustainable."[64] Rather, "What we do is we catalyze. . . . We
are not replacement mothers."[65]

These comments gloss over two things. First, the concern here (and in
other criticisms of donors' unintended effects on public health in Africa)
is not just that donors have declined to fill gaps in government budgets; it is
that donors have spent money attracting personnel to their work—money
that government budgets are unable to match and which potentially
threatens government priorities. More than just directing funds to the private sector rather than the public, they have redirected some of the most
promising doctors, researchers, and organizers. Second, channeling funds
through NGOs and other groups rather than through the state apparatus
and retaining independent policy control do not guarantee that countries

will not become dependent on Gates Foundation money. Whether or not the relationship between the foundation and the host state is formalized as a long-term investment, we can expect states to respond to the patterns of donor giving by redirecting funds in light of donor priorities and the gaps that remain. If plugging holes in government budgets is unsustainable, so too may be government budgets drawn up in the expectation of continued donor interest and involvement. Aside from any particular effects of Gates Foundation programming, what is worrying here is the combination of impulses reflected in Yamada's comments—the desire to have significant effects on (some) health indicators in a country while disclaiming any more general or long-term responsibility for public health (especially for health indicators that fall outside the foundation's areas of primary interest). Philanthropists cannot establish democratic relations by fiat, but the relationships that philanthropists do establish nevertheless call for justification. Yamada's comments—and the more general tendency that Rubenstein notes whereby INGOs *deny* that they are engaging in representation[66]—reflect something more than donor restraint; they also suggest a desire by philanthropists to disclaim a political relationship with beneficiaries. Political relationships entail demanding obligations—including an obligation to share authority on equal terms—which philanthropists may be unwilling to assume.

The focus on promoting specific welfare outcomes does not always result in a marginalization of government actors, and the Gates Foundation itself has increasingly emphasized partnerships with domestic political actors. While the foundation's work in Botswana illustrates the risks of displacing government authority, its work in India has attracted what might seem to be the opposite criticism—that it has aligned itself too closely with government partners. In September 2019, the foundation drew criticism for its presentation of a "Global Goalkeeper" award to Indian Prime Minister Narendra Modi, recognizing the achievements of his government's Swachh Bharat Abhiyan (Clean India Mission), which set ambitious targets for improvements in sanitation and for the elimination of open defecation. In a *New York Times* op-ed, Sabah Hamid explained her decision to resign her position with the Gates Foundation (as a communications officer in the foundation's New Delhi office) following the announcement of its award to Modi: "The Gates Foundation has chosen to celebrate a single, questionable initiative of Mr. Modi's government. It has completely disregarded how his politics have filled the lives of marginalized communities in India and the territories it controls with fear and insecurity, let alone that he has transformed India into a majoritarian, Hindu nationalist state."[67] In a statement to the BBC, the foundation defended the award with the same narrow focus on sanitation outcomes that Hamid criticizes: "Before the Swachh Bharat mission, over 500 million people in India did not have access to safe sanitation, and now, the majority do. There is still a long way to go, but the impacts of access to sanitation in India are already being realized. The Swachh Bharat Mission can serve as a model for other countries around the world that urgently need to improve access to sanitation for the world's poorest."[68]

While this controversy was different in substance, it is in one respect traceable to a common complaint: that the Gates Foundation's focus on measurable progress in meeting its own priorities had crowded out attention to its impact on domestic political relationships. The concern is not with philanthropy displacing *government* actors per se.[69] Democratic objections can arise both when philanthropists work outside or around government and when they work too closely with government. The underlying problem is philanthropists paying inadequate attention to their political effects and to the risks of subverting *democratic* relationships in the countries they aim to benefit. This is especially disturbing when donors' decisions about the values to sacrifice in pursuit of expected welfare gains are not transparent or accountable to the people impacted: when efforts to produce sweeping effects on other political communities go hand in hand with disclaimers of even discursive or rhetorical accountability to domestic democratic actors.

We can grant that, in 1999, Bill Gates was not responsible for the state of public health in Botswana. But having chosen to become involved, even with a narrow focus on HIV/AIDS, the Gates Foundation acquires responsibility for other health indicators—for overall spending patterns and the structure of incentives facing health workers and for political as well as welfare outcomes. A policy that improves health outcomes (in some ways or even on balance) can nonetheless justly be criticized as subversive of democracy.

How Relational Views Travel

International philanthropy can create objectionably hierarchical and paternalistic relationships between donors and their intended beneficiaries, and it can subvert or displace valuable relationships between beneficiaries (and other affected parties). Donors have strong reasons to avoid these relational vices. Some of these reasons can themselves be expressed in instrumental and welfarist terms. Because people are often better judges of their own good than even well-intentioned outsiders can be, paternalism risks undermining long-term welfare.[70] Likewise, because democratic accountability relations are important predictors and guarantors of future well-being, philanthropy that displaces, stunts, or undermines democratic relationships is instrumentally objectionable. Egalitarian and democratic relationships also have noninstrumental value. Donors fail to show respect for their beneficiaries when they paternalize them. Respecting people as equals also requires respecting their claims to shared authority over matters of common concern. When donors and recipients or beneficiaries do not share democratic membership, the requirements of respect for political equality may be less clear. A complete account of those requirements would need to specify whether the demands of democracy are global in scope and how this affects the responsibilities of philanthropists in their engagement with intergovernmental and transnational institutions. But some more determinate, largely negative, demands can be specified even absent such an account. There may not be an obligation to stand in relations of political equality internationally; there may not be an obligation to be in political relations at all. But there are contingent relational obligations that arise through engagement: (1) to avoid putting in place exploitive or paternalistic relationships (e.g., between a donor and people in the host country) and (2) to avoid subverting existing or incipient domestic democratic relationships. In terms of the end being pursued, the *donor's* standing relative to beneficiaries is often not the primary concern; the primary concerns are the standing of beneficiaries and other affected parties in relation to each other and the health of domestic accountability relations.

I do not claim that the relational egalitarian demands that I have identified are always decisive. In the easy cases, they give us reasons to reject paternalistic or undemocratic philanthropy when the evidence for its welfare value is weak or absent. In harder cases, donors may face genuine trade-offs between welfarist objectives and democratic or relational egalitarian values. They will often be too quick to prioritize the former and neglect or undervalue the latter. What Onora O'Neill has called the "spurious precision" of some consequentialist approaches to global justice poses a particular risk of enabling relational vices.[71] Marginal welfare gains realized in the short term—or more easily measured in randomized control trials—may be used to justify paternalistic or undemocratic models of giving whose negative effects may be less immediate or more difficult to measure.

Instead, donors should adopt a presumption against giving in paternalistic ways or in ways that threaten to displace domestic democratic relationships. This is a complicated task, to the point where some authors have suggested that giving democratically would require the construction of new global, deliberative institutions within which the global poor could be empowered to decide among themselves how philanthropic funds should be used.[72] However attractive such sweeping institutional proposals might be on their own terms, we also should seek more piecemeal strategies for giving respectfully and democratically in the absence of fully inclusive and robustly democratic deliberative institutions.[73] This can involve direct giving to individuals as well as striving to minimize paternalism in the design of other programs (e.g., by forgoing the use of paternalistic conditions and by communicating any nonpaternalistic justifications for providing some goods in kind). It also can involve cooperating with host-country governments in contexts where there are strong preexisting relationships of democratic accountability; granting as much control as practicable to accountable political actors domestically; and, more generally, recognizing the ways that donor activity threatens to displace or subvert domestic democratic relations. Donors should pursue the important aim of alleviating global poverty and its harms while respecting the choices and the democratic relationships of the people whom they try to benefit—their actual choices, and their existing democratic relationships, as imperfect and incomplete as our own.

Conclusion

In the final section of *The Waste Land*, "What the Thunder Said," T. S. Eliot draws on a story from the Brihadaranyaka Upanishad. The thunder's "DA" is (mis)heard in three different ways by audiences who consequently arrive at different understandings of what the thunder is saying: *datta* ("give"), *dayadhvam* ("sympathise"), and *damyata* ("control").[1] Philanthropy invites at least these three competing interpretations: it can be at once an act of generosity, sympathy, and control; and givers, recipients, and observers will often understand the same transactions in different ways.

This book has developed an interpretation of philanthropy as a vector of influence and control and as a potential threat to relationships of democratic equality. This is not the dominant lens through which we interpret philanthropy today; evaluations are more likely to focus on what is given or on where the giver's sympathies lie. I have tried to show that these narrowly distributive or ethical perspectives give an incomplete and often misleading picture of philanthropy's political significance.

Social and relational perspectives on philanthropy are not new. Anthropologists and sociologists have long recognized the potential of gift giving to enhance the status of some people relative to others. Marcel Mauss claims that contemporary societies retain an archaic moral principle: "The unreciprocated gift still makes the person who has accepted it inferior. . . . Charity is still wounding for him who has accepted it, and the whole tendency of our morality is to strive to do away with the unconscious and injurious patronage of the rich almsgiver."[2] Political theorists including Tocqueville, Mill, and Addams have recognized philanthropy's potential tension with egalitarian social relationships and with democracy. And stretching as far back as ancient Greece and Rome, anxieties about philanthropy have been closely tied to the question of what kinds of social and political relationships are desirable; even those who would strongly reject the general moral or political value of *egalitarian* relationships treat some sources of status or forms of influence as morally inappropriate or politically threatening.

A central aim of this book has been to revive this tradition of political and relational thinking about philanthropy, one capable of speaking both to contemporary philanthropic practice and to political theory. This could not be accomplished simply by presupposing and applying a freestanding relational egalitarian perspective (examples of which exist in contemporary political theory, although they have had surprisingly little to say about philanthropy). Instead, I have tried to show how philanthropy can illuminate the grounds, scope, and content of relational ideals rather than just furnishing a new context for their application. Thinking politically about philanthropy brings into focus democratic concerns of which philanthropy itself is not the only or even the most important instance.

Aristocratic Virtues and Democratic Justifications

If Seneca's complaint, that "we neither know how to bestow nor how to receive a benefit," holds true in the case of philanthropy, this is at least in part because we have been thinking of the transactions involved solely in terms of benefits. We are used to thinking of philanthropy as a practice that rearranges distributive shares or that summons previously nonexistent public goods into being. But philanthropy can also transform the relationships of people to each other, to political institutions, and to public goods and services. It can shape relationships of deference, authority, and control. This matters for the form that a democratic justification of philanthropy must take; it also tells us something about the appropriate form of democratic justification generally.

Existing democratic societies fail their members in a range of ways, and it is tempting to understand both the causes and solutions in distributive terms. Seeing the extent to which people are underserved by democratically elected politicians, we may be drawn to conceptions of democracy that stress the quality of substantive interest representation. Viewed through this lens, some philanthropy will look comparatively acceptable as a substitute for government action; some donors may seem likelier than politicians to have the public's interests at heart or to have the right answers to intractable political problems.

Like any observer, I have faults to find with many philanthropic funders and programs. But this book's arguments are not premised on the claim that philanthropic action tends to produce substantively worse outcomes than would have occurred in its absence (i.e., leaving in place the status quo, whether of government action or inaction). To the contrary: I grant (and not just for the sake of argument but in reasonable confidence that it is true) that some donors have a better grasp of the measures that would best promote people's substantive interests than the elected officials whom they are seeking to influence or bypass. Some of the failings of electoral institutions are well known. Officials may be prone to capture by powerful interests. But even more robustly democratic and egalitarian electoral institutions might have biases that hamper good policymaking: they might, for example, be prone to presentism or short-termism, since both politicians and the electorate may discount future benefits and risks, and elected officials are incentivized to take actions whose good results will be quickly felt.[3] The COVID-19 pandemic revealed startling shortfalls in governments' capacity and political will to respond effectively; meanwhile, philanthropists like Bill Gates, who had long expressed concerns about global pandemic preparedness, moved quickly to commit to funding new vaccines and treatments. In such a context, it is no wonder that philanthropic activity is welcomed and widely perceived as legitimate.

However, I have argued against neglecting philanthropy's relational effects even when we welcome its (other) substantive outcomes. Institutions that are plainly undemocratic in their relational structure and effects might well promote some goods that democratic institutions do not. Consider again the concern about democratic presentism and ask what other kinds of social or political relations might be justified by appealing to long-term public goods. Tocqueville, for example, worries that some goods he associates with aristocratic societies will be lost in democratic ones. Where "families maintain the same station for centuries" in the same place, time horizons lengthen: a man "willingly takes upon himself duties to both ancestors and progeny, and will frequently sacrifice his personal pleasures for others who either no longer exist or have yet to be born."[4] The aristocratic man "can already see his great-grandsons" in his mind's eye, "and he loves them."[5] Aristocratic institutions also "create close bonds between each man and a number of his fellow citizens," keeping people "closely tied to something outside themselves," in contrast with democratic societies in which "the bond of human affection slackens."[6]

This enumeration of aristocracy's virtues has significant overlap with contemporary defenses of philanthropy. As unaccountable, perpetual institutions, philanthropic foundations are insulated from electoral pressures and can afford long time horizons: they face no electoral disincentive to act in what they take to be the long-term public interest and may be uniquely positioned to place risky bets on untested strategies for the provision of public goods. Philanthropic activity is also celebrated for its positive contributions to social trust and cohesion. Tocqueville himself casts philanthropic and other associations as artificial aristocrats to replace the endangered human prototypes. But benefits-focused defenses of philanthropy risk eliding the distributive and the relational questions in ways that Tocqueville does not. To offer a *democratic* vindication of an institution or practice, it is not enough to point to (some) good outcomes. Justifying forms of power and influence requires evaluating not only the outcomes they produce but the kinds of social and political relationships they put in place. As Tocqueville recognizes, aristocratic trusteeship over the public good is democratically unacceptable. Democratic societies need different ways of promoting reciprocity and long-term attention to the public good—ones that do not require reliance on the competence and goodwill of hereditary or economic elites.

Contemporary philanthropy has not yet solved this problem. While it produces many benefits, it also produces forms of social and political relationships that stand in deep tension with democratic equality. The aristocratic forms of solidarity that Tocqueville describes risk replicating themselves within democratic societies unless countervailing relational forces emerge. This was what organizers like Addams and Alinsky aimed for: forms of solidarity that were not rooted in altruism (however intuitively welcome altruism must seem) and that would shift (not eliminate) the burdens of deferring to someone else's judgments of the good.

As I have argued throughout, political theories of philanthropy therefore need to pay close first-order attention to philanthropic relationships. The point is not to ignore or deny the benefits that philanthropy can produce but to recognize that these are, at best, an incomplete justification of the role of philanthropy in a democracy. Efforts to democratize philanthropy—and, indeed, other social institutions and practices—must aim at relational and not only distributive targets. A democracy that has the wrong relationship to (even) its benevolent elites is failing itself in important ways.

Philanthropy and Midlevel Democratic Theorizing

Philanthropy sits in a blind spot for many contemporary political theories. Familiar notions of justice and democracy, oriented to the normative evaluation of public political institutions or to appreciations of voluntarism and participation, will not flag for us when and why philanthropy can be democrat-ically objectionable. Even political theories that engage philanthropy as an issue often make the case for its political character in narrow terms—for ex-ample, by focusing on the inequitable distribution of "public money" through tax subsidies that favor the wealthy. Criticisms of regressive tax policies have merit, but philanthropy is not a political issue only to the extent that the money spent has a public provenance. It is political because of its public effects and its ability to shape relationships between people in society. Those are the features that make giving—and, indeed, accepting—philanthropic gifts political acts, appropriately subject to political theorizing and political criticism.

Philanthropy is a case where political theorists have made mistakes—and, notably, mistakes that earlier generations of theorists did *not* make—about the kinds of institutions, transactions, and relationships that have democratic political significance. It therefore helps us recognize lacunae in what we register as political or not and in our judgments about what counts as an appropriate object for political theory and why. In particular, the case of philanthropy shows the importance of midlevel theory and intermediate institutions and practices; we cannot rely exclusively on high-level politi-cal institutions to resolve downstream democratic deficits. Even relational egalitarian political theories often focus either on the abstract citizen-citizen relation (mediated through formally public institutions) or, on the other hand, on personal and even intimate relationships between friends, partners, and family members. But much lies in between.

In what Danielle Allen has called "the dreamscape of democracy," politi-cal communities "are supposed to rest on consent and open access to happi-ness for their citizens": "No one ever leaves the public arena at odds with the communal choice; no one must accept political loss or suffer the imposition of laws to which she has not consented."[7] Allen argues that dreams of democ-racy as a "static end state that achieves the common good by assuring the same benefits or the same level of benefits to everyone" ignore the realities of democracy as a political practice and render invisible the sacrifices of those citizens who benefit less and nevertheless accede to democratic decisions.[8] A similar problem haunts both some political theories that discuss philan-thropy and many that ignore it. In the dreamscape of democracy, managing the problem of citizen beneficence might be as unnecessary as managing the problem of sacrifice: major social institutions could be counted on reliably to discharge duties of justice for the political community as a whole and to secure the required kinds of equal standing for all. But this is a dream that abstracts dangerously from social facts about where and how status is made and unmade. Philanthropy can neither be a matter of individual conscience alone nor folded into a public conception of justice; it is a site for negotiating social and political relationships between people, not just a delivery vehicle for personal moral commitments or public goods.

If a narrow view of what counts as an object for democratic theory causes us to miss important problems, it also may cause us to miss sources of democratic hope. An expanded attention to social institutions and practices should also include greater attention to norms and attitudes as sites of democratic change.

We miss the point of a political theory of philanthropy if we interpret its principal task as the provision of moral guidance to billionaires. In philanthropy as elsewhere, it is usually a mistake to interpret democratizing movements as the products of individual moral choices or moral learning. Even individually salient actions are shaped by politics in important ways. They are shaped by the incentives created by political institutions: by the tax code, by legal structures for governing philanthropy, and by public policy that encourages it and gives it wide scope. Beyond that, they are shaped by norms concerning what count as acceptable exercises of power and the appropriate responses to those exercises that occur outside formal structures of democratic accountability. Consider MacKenzie Scott's decision in 2020 to focus her philanthropic donations on unconditional direct-support grants to racial justice organizations. We make a mistake if we register only Scott's individual moral agency: her decision results in significant part from years of social movement activism and criticism that gave greater salience to the importance of people speaking for themselves and to the capacities and needs of Black-led organizations. Scott's *was* a personal moral decision. But it is also continuous with politics, shaped by and likely, in turn, to help shape political change.

Thinking politically about philanthropy helps us understand the ways that it can shape and transform social and political relationships; the forms of deference that often obscure philanthropy's political significance; and the relational values that givers, recipients, and observers should promote in their management of philanthropy and attitudes toward it. Understanding the normative values that philanthropy and philanthropic relations can promote or subvert also helps orient us to our social and political circumstances more broadly.[9]

Private Virtues, Relational Vices

Like other recent work in political theory and political science, I have emphasized nonelectoral institutions and even formally private domains as sites of democratic or antidemocratic action.[10] Authors including Joe Soss, Vesla Weaver, and Elizabeth Anderson have called attention to the ways that, by neglecting nonelectoral institutions, we miss forms of authoritarian government that exist within formally democratic societies.[11] The kind of democratic threat that philanthropy poses is not best understood as an authoritarian one. Instead, I have argued, we can understand philanthropy's threat to democracy and democratic relations in terms of a set of linked relational vices—usurpation, subordination, failures of reciprocity, and paternalism.

Considering philanthropic usurpations of democratic authority helps clarify the grounds and the scope of objections to elite influence. Elite philanthropy standardly confers benefits in forms determined and controlled by the donors. As I argued in chapter 3, it is philanthropy's potential to increase elite control over matters of common concern that constitutes its threat to democratic equality; but this central feature goes largely unrecognized or unaddressed by familiar perspectives on philanthropy. Considered as a private matter of personal ethics, to confer benefits according to one's own best judgment seems permissible or even virtuous. We commonly think it praiseworthy to sacrifice personal consumption in the service of a greater good—hence familiar criticisms of philanthropy that focus on donors' self-interested motivations rather than considering whether altruistic elite influence is inherently less *democratically* objectionable. Many democratic theorists, oriented to distributive or participatory conceptions of democracy, likewise fail to register philanthropy as a potential democratic threat. The objection only comes into focus when we consider the ways in which elite philanthropy can subvert democratic citizens' shared authority over matters of common concern.

This conception of democracy carries over into our understanding of potential democratic solutions. It argues against a too-narrow focus on first-best or highly generalized institutional solutions. We should avoid relying solely on imperfectly democratic public institutions to do the democratic work of bringing outcomes of common concern under the control of the people affected by them. Instead, first-best institutional solutions should be supplemented with more piecemeal attempts to democratize influence. Studying philanthropic relationships helps us bring relational egalitarian values into the real world and demonstrates how they can be advanced one relationship at a time.

Democratic citizens should enjoy presumptively equal status with respect to deciding matters of common concern. They should not have their shared authority over public life usurped, even by benevolent elites. But relating as equals requires respect for areas of exclusive as well as shared authority. Egalitarian relations are threatened if some people are recognized or treated as less competent than others to manage their own lives on their own behalf. Egalitarian relations therefore require protection and norms against private paternalism.

Through the forgoing analysis of philanthropy, paternalism emerges as a core concern not only for liberals but also for democrats. The concern for relating as equals is the link between democracy as a demand for shared influence over public or common outcomes and the value of antipaternalism in (even) private relationships. Familiar liberal arguments against paternalism obscure this link by abstracting from the social and political relationships in which paternalism is embedded. Paternalism is not objectionable just to the extent that it involves interference (however benevolent) with individual liberty or autonomy. It is objectionable when and because it is subordinating; and this objection can hold even when an action (e.g., a conditional gift that the giver was under no obligation to make) is not best understood as an act of interference. We may miss the political import of philanthropy when we treat consent as sanitizing relationships. That is a sociologically blinkered view of how relationships work. Consent at a particular moment can raise the costs of exercising autonomy later. Consensual actions and transactions can put in place objectionably subordinating relationships, and we therefore have reason to endorse public norms and institutions that offer protection against such relationships. Just as some have argued for barring some market transactions (e.g., organ selling) out of concern for people's ongoing ability to relate as equals, we have reason to resist subordinating gift relations.

Philanthropy helps us to recognize underappreciated interdependencies within democratic values and ideals—for example, between the familiar idea that public power should be directed by the shared authority of the people subject to it, and the idea that some forms of private interference in people's lives are disrespectful because they are paternalistic. Usurpations of public authority, some attempts to influence other social institutions and movements, and paternalistic influence over individuals all threaten to impose hierarchies of judgment and status and to subvert valuable relations of social and political equality. Egalitarian relations require protection against such threats to equal status.

Paternalism is not the only relational vice, nor is it always the most important one. People can be subordinated in other, often more harmful ways. But recognizing the special objections that attach to exercising power over someone for (putatively) her own good helps us understand core cases of philanthropic disrespect. It also helps us to understand what might otherwise seem a mysterious theme in analyses of philanthropy (discussed in chapters 2 and 5): the idea that admitting one's self-interested motivations can be a respect-preserving move and that claiming to act from (at least enlightened) self-interest can be more compatible with egalitarian relations than are familiar variants of altruism.

The temptations to rely on philanthropy and to defer to philanthropists can be strong. They are only reinforced by widespread disillusionment with political processes and with the prospects for the more democratic exercise of public power: entrenched minoritarian institutions and partisan polarization make it all the more tempting to look instead to philanthropists for the production of important public goods. Sometimes the benefits philanthropists provide are real. But this tendency is democratically pernicious to the extent that it encourages either a further retreat from attempts to secure equality politically or a failure to recognize what is political in philanthropy.

There is, in the end, an unbridgeable gap between what philanthropy does and what democracy ought to do. The arguments in this book aim to shrink that gap: to show how philanthropy can better avoid subverting important democratic values and so to help point the way toward a more democratic philanthropy. But we should not be satisfied with that or with a merely more philanthropic democracy. We have had the gifts and the sympathy. Relating as equals requires more.

Acknowledgments

At all stages of this project, I have been lucky to benefit from the advice and support of friends, colleagues, and teachers who gave generously of their time and expertise. I am deeply conscious of all that this project owes to them; I am also grateful for relationships that have enriched my life more broadly.

As a graduate student at Harvard University, I benefited from outstanding advice and support from the members of my dissertation committee: Nancy Rosenblum, Dennis Thompson, and Eric Beerbohm. All three were unfailingly generous with their time and guidance. I am especially grateful to Nancy for her mentorship, her constant encouragement, and her example. I am also grateful for the comments, questions, and suggestions I received from Adriana Alfaro, James Brandt, Jonathan Bruno, Joshua Cherniss, Tarun Chhabra, Prithvi Datta, Michael Frazer, Johann Frick, Archon Fung, Adriane Gelpi, Jonathan Gould, Sean Gray, Emily Gustafson, John Harpham, Sean Ingham, Frances Kamm, Tae-Yeoun Keum, Carly Knight, Dave Langlois, Adam Lebovitz, Lindsay Mayka, Alfred Moore, Yascha Mounk, Joe Muller, Eric Nelson, Tomer Perry, Sabeel Rahman, Michael Rosen, Will Selinger, Shauna Shames, Mira Siegelberg, Lucas Stanczyk, Andrea Tivig, Don Tontiplaphol, Richard Tuck, Cheryl Welch, Eleana Whyte, Vanessa Williamson, and Bernardo Zacka. My studies at Harvard were generously funded by a doctoral fellowship from the Social Sciences and Humanities Research Council of Canada, a graduate fellowship from the Edmond J. Safra Center for Ethics, a Democracy Doctoral fellowship from the Ash Center for Democratic Governance and Innovation, and by graduate and dissertation completion fellowships from Harvard University. I am grateful to each of these institutions for their support.

I had the opportunity to further develop my thinking about philanthropy during a postdoctoral fellowship at Stanford University at the
Stanford Center on Philanthropy and Civil Society (PACS). All political
theorists and political scientists with interests in philanthropy have benefited from Rob Reich's field-building work: I have been especially lucky
to count him as a mentor and friend. At PACS, I also benefited from comments and support from Lucy Bernholz, Paul Brest, Kim Meredith, and
Woody Powell. I am grateful to PACS for giving me not only a wonderful
postdoctoral year but also a sustained sense of community with other fellows and visitors past and present.

My time at Stanford was also enriched by the opportunity to participate in the postdoctoral fellows' workshop of the McCoy Family Center
for Ethics in Society. I am grateful to Debra Satz, Anne Newman, Joan
Berry, Brian Berkey, Megan Blomfield, Eamonn Callan, Lisa Herzog,
Alex Levitov, Brad McHose, Alan Ryan, Brent Sockness, and Patrick
Taylor-Smith for their warm welcome and their generous comments on
draft chapters. Toward the end of my time at Stanford, I benefited enor-
mously from a manuscript workshop that Rob organized for me; I am
especially grateful to Ryan Pevnick for traveling to join us for the day and
to all in the Stanford community who participated and offered comments
that greatly improved subsequent versions of the book.

After Stanford, I was lucky to take up a position as a Harper Fellow in
the Society of Fellows at the University of Chicago. I am grateful to the
Society of Fellows, the Social Sciences Division in the College, and the
Political Science Department, all of which supported my work and created a wonderful intellectual community. I presented work drawn from
this manuscript on several occasions at Chicago and am grateful to those
who took the time to engage with it and offer comments, especially Gor-
don Arlen, Mark Berger, Austin Carson, Chiara Cordelli, Daragh Grant,
Justin Grimmer, Robert Gulotty, Jared Holley, Jeff Jackson, Sarah John-
son, Ben Laurence, Birte Löschenkohl, John McCormick, Sankar Muthu,
Lauren Perez, Natasha Piano, Jennifer Pitts, Emma Planinc, Bob Reamer,
and Jim Wilson.

Earlier versions of these arguments were presented at meetings of the
American Political Science Association, the Canadian Political Science
Association, the Association for Political Theory, the Edmond J. Safra
Center graduate seminar, the Ash Center Democracy Seminar, and in
other workshops at Harvard, Stanford, and Chicago. I am grateful to the
organizers, discussants, and audiences on each occasion and especially to

Alexander Moon, Nadia Urbinati, Andrew Sabl, Amanda Greene, Ted Lechterman, and Hilary Greaves for helpful comments on individual draft chapters or on strands of the argument that germinated elsewhere in different forms.

I finished this book from my new position as an assistant professor in the Department of Political Science at the Ohio State University. I am grateful to my colleagues in the department and to friends in Columbus for making me feel so at home so quickly, especially Eric MacGilvray, Benjamin McKean, Michael Neblo, Inés Valdez, Dana Howard, Brad Holland, Greg Caldeira, Erin Lin, Vlad Kogan, Jennifer Mitzen, Jan Pierskalla, Alex Thomspon, Amanda Robinson, Sarah Watson, Alex Wendt, and Tom Wood. I would also like to thank Donghye Kim, Emily Ann Israelson, Dominic Pfister, and Jacob Semus, all of whom provided exemplary teaching assistance in the last two years and without whom finishing this book would have been much more difficult.

An earlier version of chapter 3 was published as "Plutocratic Philanthropy" in the *Journal of Politics*, in January 2018. I am grateful to Lisa Ellis for her editorial guidance and to the press for permission to use that material again here.

I owe particular thanks to the generous readers who, in the later stages of this project, provided detailed comments on the full manuscript: Matthew Landauer, Sean Ingham, Eric MacGilvray, Rob Reich, and two referees from the University of Chicago Press. I am grateful to all of these readers for the improvements they helped me to make to the book; the remaining mistakes are of course mine alone.

I am grateful to Chuck Myers at the University of Chicago Press for believing in this project and for his wonderful editorial guidance. Thanks also to Jenni Fry, Alicia Sparrow, and Holly Smith for shepherding the book through editing and production, to Suzanne Rapcavage for copyediting the manuscript and to Jim Curtis for compiling the index.

I have relied throughout this project on the support my family. Here, I especially wish to thank my mother, Eileen Saunders; my sister, Katie, and my brothers, Patrick and Owen; Ron, Owen, and Richard Saunders; Fred Wilmot-Smith and Jane Reisman; and Hollis, Melissa, and Rachel Landauer. Michael Landauer's kindness was a gift and his memory is a blessing.

Nobody has contributed more intellectual help or moral support to this project than Matthew Landauer—the first, last, and most generous reader of all that is written here. I owe him more than I can say.

This book is dedicated with love to my mother and to the memory of my father, Ross Hastings. He did not see the final product, but along the way he cut out newspaper clippings to send me, read early versions of these ideas or discussed them over glasses of wine, contributed his sociological imagination, and knew that he made it possible.

Notes

Introduction

1. Seneca, *On Benefits*, 1.1.

2. Mandeville, *The Fable of the Bees*.

3. For example, as I argue in chapter 3, consumption spending (whatever we think of it morally) may not be a uniquely politically problematic use of private wealth.

4. At least in the usual sense of "payment"; this definition is meant to exclude ordinary for-profit market transactions, not donations that are incentivized or rewarded with tote bags, opera tickets, or naming rights (even if those inducements motivate the donation). I also do not count donations to political candidates or campaigns as philanthropy, although in practice the line between political and philanthropic donations is blurred (see chapter 3).

5. When a philanthropic donation supports a harmful or trivial public purpose, this definition makes it a case of destructive or trivial philanthropy, not of *non*philanthropy.

6. See Steinberg and Powell's introduction to *The Nonprofit Sector*, 2–3.

7. Ibid., 1–3. It should be stressed here that "nonprofit" status is not synonymous with reliance on philanthropy. Philanthropy and nonprofits raise many parallel issues (for example, around privatization and private influence in welfare services), but philanthropy can be directed toward individuals and organizations that are not formally designated as nonprofits, and nonprofits may rely for their budgets on fees for service or on government grants rather than on philanthropic contributions.

8. Americans gave an estimated $449.64 billion to charity in 2019. In the first two decades of the twenty-first century, charitable giving in the United States has increased or stayed flat (in inflation-adjusted dollars) every year, with the exception of 2008 and 2009 during the Great Recession (*Giving USA 2020*, 42).

9. Randy Kennedy, Monica Davey, and Steven Yaccino, "Foundations Aim to Save Pensions in Detroit Crisis," *New York Times*, January 14, 2014, A1.

10. Suzanne Perry, "Proposed Detroit Grants Test Limits of Philanthropic Aid to Cities," *Chronicle of Philanthropy*, January 14, 2014, online edition, http://phi lanthropy.com/article/Foundation-Efforts-to-Help/144003/.

11. Quoted in Perry, "Proposed Detroit Grants."

12. Newark Mayor Cory Booker played an important role in attracting the Zuckerberg donation, and in response to the donation, New Jersey Governor Chris Christie agreed to cede back to the city some control of the Newark school system (which had been declared a failure and taken over by the state in 1995). See Richard Pérez-Peña, "Facebook Founder to Donate $100 Million to Help Remake Newark's Schools," *New York Times*, September 23, 2010, A27; and Russakoff, *The Prize*.

13. Barbara Crossette, "After Long Fight, U.N. Agrees to Cut Dues Paid by U.S." *New York Times*, December 23, 2000, A1. As Crossette notes, Turner's money had to be channeled through the state department, since the UN may not accept money directly from individuals to pay for a country's dues.

14. See, e.g., Reich, *Just Giving* and "Toward a Political Theory of Philanthropy"; Pevnick, "Democratizing the Nonprofit Sector"; and the essays in *Philanthropy in Democratic Societies*, edited by Reich, Cordelli, and Bernholz.

15. Reich's political theory of philanthropy in *Just Giving* focuses on just such institutional questions. For Reich's argument about the need for political theories of philanthropy, see *Just Giving*, 12–17.

16. The terms *nonideal theory* and *realist theory* are not equivalent; they denote different intellectual traditions. However, some similar criticisms of idealized theories of philanthropy are possible from the vantage point of each.

17. Rawls, *Theory of Justice*, 9.

18. For further exposition of Rawls's distinction between ideal (or "strict compliance") and nonideal (or "partial compliance") theory—and his explanation for the priority of the former—see also his *Theory of Justice*, 245–46, and Rawls, *Justice as Fairness*, 13 and 65–66. For useful discussion of the distinction, see Stemplowska, "What's Ideal About Ideal Theory?"; and Valentini, "On the Apparent Paradox of Ideal Theory" and "Ideal vs. Non-ideal Theory." For defenses of the priority of ideal theory, see G. A. Cohen, *Rescuing Justice and Equality*; Estlund, *Democratic Authority*, 258–75, and *Utopophobia*; and Simmons, "Ideal and Nonideal Theory." For a history of "justice theory," see Forrester, *In the Shadow of Justice*.

19. Critics of ideal theory contest this claim. See Wiens, "Against Ideal Guidance," for the argument that political ideals are not just unnecessary or insufficient but utterly uninformative" for "specifying the directive principles we should aim to satisfy in our world" (434).

20. See, e.g., and in different ways, Shklar, "The Liberalism of Fear" and *The Faces of Injustice*; C. Mills, "Ideal Theory as Ideology"; and Sen, *The Idea of Justice*.

21. See, e.g., Williams, *In the Beginning Was the Deed*; Geuss, *Philosophy and Real Politics*; Galston, "Realism in Political Theory"; Sabl, "History and Reality" and *Hume's Politics*; D. Miller, *Justice for Earthlings*; Rossi and Sleat, "Realism in Normative Political Theory"; and Levy, "There's No Such Thing as Ideal Theory." Not all of these authors self-identify as realists, though they subscribe to a similar set of concerns.

22. Jubb, "The Real Value of Equality," 679.

23. For argument about the inescapability of political inequality in liberal democracies, see Green, *The Shadow of Unfairness*.

24. See Walzer, "Socialism and the Gift Relationship," for the argument that significant scope for philanthropy would remain even under dramatically more generous welfare states.

25. See, e.g., R. Dworkin, "What Is Equality?," parts 1 and 2, *Philosophy & Public Affairs* 10 (1981), and reprinted in *Sovereign Virtue*; Arneson, "Equality and Equal Opportunity for Welfare"; and G. A. Cohen, "On the Currency of Egalitarian Justice."

26. Cohen, "Currency of Egalitarian Justice," 906. Cohen and other distributive egalitarians acknowledge that this concern for distributive justice must be balanced against other values; nevertheless, the value of equality itself is understood as demanding the equal distribution of *something*.

27. Anderson, "What Is the Point of Equality?" 313.

28. Ibid. In addition to Anderson, see Scheffler, "What Is Egalitarianism?" and "Choice, Circumstance, and the Value of Equality"; M. O'Neill, "What Should Egalitarians Believe?"; D. Miller, "Equality and Justice"; Norman, "The Social Basis of Equality"; Hinton, "Must Egalitarians Choose between Fairness and Respect?"; Schemmel, "Distributive and Relational Equality"; Kolodny, "Rule Over None II"; Scanlon, *Why Does Inequality Matter?*; Wilson, *Democratic Equality*; and the essays in *Social Equality*, edited by Fourie, Schuppert, and Wallimann-Helmer.

29. Distributive conceptions of equality often incorporate some claims about just (e.g., democratic) relationships, and relational conceptions often suggest a general idea of a just distribution (e.g., as instrumentally important for people's ability to relate as equals). And, in the real world, it will often be possible to advance significantly both distributional fairness and respectful social relations. On relational egalitarian reasons for valuing distributive equality, see Scanlon, *Why Does Inequality Matter?*; M. O'Neill, "What Should Egalitarians Believe?"; Schemmel, "Why Relational Egalitarians Should Care about Distributions"; and Elford, "Relational Equality and Distribution."

30. As Jonathan Wolff puts it, egalitarianism starts from a "collection of values" that may not be reducible to a fundamental distributive principle. Wolff, "Fairness, Respect and the Egalitarian *Ethos* Revisited," 342.

31. Anderson, "What Is the Point of Equality?" 288.

32. M. O'Neill, "What Should Egalitarians Believe?" 129–31.

33. See Pettit, *Republicanism* and *On the People's Terms*.

34. Like distributive egalitarians, neorepublicans "reject the idea of forcing the less well off to have to rely . . . on voluntary forms of philanthropy" (Pettit, *On the People's Terms*, 113), although they may arrive at this conclusion by different routes. While distributive egalitarians often ground their arguments on people's claims to fair equality of opportunity and to a fair share of the benefits of social cooperation, republicans object to a situation in which "[t]he needy will depend on the goodwill of voluntary benefactors" for security against interference, "which already comes dangerously close to being dependent on their goodwill in a dominating way" (ibid.). It is to prevent or eliminate "relations of such dependency" that Pettit argues for public forms of social insurance. This analysis of an objectionable philanthropic relation is helpful for understanding the wrong of inadequate public assistance, but it has less to say about when and why different forms of philanthropic assistance might be more or less objectionable.

35. See, e.g., Markell, "The Insufficiency of Non-Domination," arguing that "usurpation" is a problem distinct from domination: while domination involves subjection to arbitrary power, usurpation involves subjection to "stifling" or "stultifying" forms of (even nonarbitrary) power that displace one's agency or involvement. See also Kolodny, "Being under the Power of Others," arguing that familiar republican objections to domination are best understood as objections to "being under the power of a superior" rather than being exposed to arbitrary interference per se; on this reading, the concern about domination is itself grounded in a more general concern "to stand in relations of social equality, or nonsubordination, with others" (94).

36. Chapter 6 considers the somewhat more complicated issues that arise in evaluating philanthropic relationships between members of different societies.

37. Wilson makes a similar point about the value of negative conceptions in his catalogue of the vices of inequality (and, in particular, of oligarchy): as he puts it, "certain vices might be easier to identify than their complementary goods." Wilson, *Democratic Equality*, 41.

38. On the plurality of reasons for valuing equality and/or for finding inequality objectionable, see M. O'Neill, "What Should Egalitarians Believe?"; Scanlon, *Why Does Inequality Matter?*; Tawney, *Equality*; and Young, *Justice and the Politics of Difference*, chap. 2.

39. See, e.g., Douglass, *My Bondage and My Freedom*, 171–72; Mill, *The Subjection of Women*; and Kolodny, "Rule Over None II" and "Being under the Power of Others." This is a recurring theme in the republican, Afro-modern, and feminist traditions of political thought.

40. On democracy's role in promoting and/or constituting relations of social equality or mutual respect, see especially Christiano, *The Constitution of Equality*; Anderson, "Democracy: Instrumental vs. Non-Instrumental Value"; Kolodny, "Rule Over None II"; Viehoff, "Democratic Equality and Political Authority";

and Wilson, *Democratic Equality*. These arguments have significant overlap with neorepublican defenses of democracy as guarding against both public and private relations of domination; see Pettit, *On the People's Terms*. Rousseau and Tocqueville are frequently cited as ancestors to democratic theories that link democracy to a broader conception of people interacting as social equals rather than superiors or inferiors.

Chapter One

1. Katie Warren, "Here Are All the People and Companies Who Have Collectively Pledged Nearly $730 Million So Far to Help Rebuild Notre-Dame After the Disastrous Fire," Business Insider, April 16, 2019, https://www.businessinsider.com/people-who-pledged-money-to-rebuild-notre-dame-fire-paris-2019-4.

2. Paul Sullivan, "Notre-Dame Donation Backlash Raises Debate: What's Worthy of Philanthropy?" *New York Times*, April 26, 2019, http://www.nytimes.com/2019/04/26/your-money/notre-dame-donation-backlash-philanthropy.html.

3. As has the question of what counts as charity or philanthropy. I continue to use the terms loosely and interchangeably to describe voluntary contributions of private resources for broadly public purposes. This definition does not require any particular (e.g., altruistic) motive on the part of the giver.

4. This point is not specific to social or relational egalitarian accounts of democracy: my more general aim in this chapter is to show how the political regulation and social reception of philanthropy is undertheorized and often internally inconsistent and therefore how virtually any liberal democratic political theory could benefit from thinking more clearly about philanthropy.

5. Machiavelli, *Discourses on Livy*, 3.28.1. Reich cites the same passage as a historical example of willingness to constrain philanthropy and of the fear that "public influence obtained through private wealth might be injurious to the state for, by example, threatening the authority of the ruling class." See Reich, "Toward a Political Theory," 177.

6. Machiavelli, *Discourses*, 3.28.1.

7. Ibid.

8. Livy, *Early History of Rome*, 4.13.

9. The quotation is from the then-sitting president, William Taft. For a more detailed retelling of the Rockefeller controversy, see Reich, *Just Giving*, 17 and 137–40.

10. Will of James Smithson, cited in Harmon, "The Transformation of American Philanthropy," 22.

11. Cited in Harmon, "The Transformation of American Philanthropy," 28–29. Notably, the objection was not that these senators did not want to establish an institution of the kind proposed; Preston's view was that the United States had better use its own funds to establish such an institution.

12. Giridharadas, *Winners Take All*.

13. On Gates, see, e.g., Jane Wakefield, "How Bill Gates Became the Voodoo Doll of Covid Conspiracies," BBC News, June 5, 2020, https://www.bbc.com/news /technology-52833706; and Monica Evstatieva, "Anatomy of a COVID-19 Conspiracy Theory," NPR, July 10, 2020, https://www.npr.org/2020/07/10/889037310 /anatomy-of-a-covid-19-conspiracy-theory. On Soros, see, e.g., James Wilson, "'Dripping with Poison of Antisemitism': The Demonization of George Soros," *Guardian*, October 15, 2018, online edition, https://www.theguardian.com/us-news/2018 /oct/24/george-soros-antisemitism-bomb-attacks; and David Klepper and Lori Hinnant, "George Soros Conspiracy Theories Surge as Protests Sweep US," AP News, June 21, 2020, https://apnews.com/article/f01f3c405985f4e3477e4e4ac27986e5.

14. Structuring economic incentives also contributes more directly to philanthropists' ability to get other people to do what they want (without those people either being coerced or regarding themselves as morally bound to comply with the philanthropist's wishes).

15. See, e.g., John Arnold, "Attacks and Vitriol Will Not Deter Me from Supporting Fixes to Public Policy," *Chronicle of Philanthropy*, March 31, 2014, https:// www.philanthropy.com/article/AttacksVitriol-Will-Not/153337; and Phil Buchanan, "Philanthropy's Blighted Reputation Threatens Global Giving," *Financial Times*, April 15, 2019, https://www.ft.com/content/1980e4b4-57bc-11e9-8b71-f5b0066105fe. Arnold is a billionaire philanthropist and the cochair of Arnold Ventures LLC (formerly the Laura and John Arnold Foundation); Buchanan is the president of the Center for Effective Philanthropy.

16. Paul Sullivan, "Precious Eyes: Guide Dog Training a High-Cost Charity with a Big Payback," *New York Times*, November 8, 2013, F1.

17. See, e.g., Peter Singer, "The Why and How of Effective Altruism," TED video, March 2013. Transcript available at http://www.ted.com/talks/peter_singer _the_why_and_how_of_effective_altruism/transcript.

18. Two critics (both nonprofit sector consultants) writing in the *Stanford Social Innovation Review* were affronted enough to declare, "We believe a more accurate phase for this concept is 'defective altruism' and will therefore use that term for the remainder of this article." Ken Berger and Robert M. Penna, "The Elitist Philanthropy of So-Called Effective Altruism," *Stanford Social Innovation Review*, November 23, 2013, https://ssir.org/articles/entry/the_elitist_philanthropy _of_so_called_effective_altruism.

19. In contrast, and as I explain in more detail in chapter 6, for effective altruists the value of a philanthropic donation is an *essentially* comparative question.

20. To be sure, there are distinctions between the tax treatment of 501(c)(3) public charities and of 501(c)(4) social welfare organizations (which, compared with 501(c)(3)s, are subject to fewer limitations on political activity and lobbying but are not eligible to receive tax-deductible contributions). Within the 501(c)(3) category, further distinctions are also made between public charities and private

foundations, and churches and religious organizations are exempt from some reporting requirements that apply to other organizations. But these distinctions are
based on formal criteria, not on substantive judgments about the value of different
organizations' aims or about their efficacy in pursuing those aims.

21. For 2019, the tax subsidy for charitable contributions totaled $51.6 billion, a
figure that does not include the value of tax exemptions on charities' earnings or of
estate tax deductions (see Gravelle, Marples, and Sherlock, "Tax Issues Relating
to Charitable Contributions and Organizations"). Claiming the tax deduction for
charitable contributions requires that one itemize one's taxes: the deduction is not
ordinarily available to taxpayers taking the standard deduction. For this reason,
the subsidy for charitable donations is directed disproportionately to wealthier
taxpayers—the more so since 2017, when new federal tax legislation significantly
raised the standard deduction and led to fewer nonwealthy people itemizing their
taxes and claiming deductions for charitable contributions. I discuss egalitarian
criticisms of the existing tax-deduction mechanism in more detail in chapter 3.

22. Treas. Reg. §1.501(c)(3)-1(d)(2) (T.D. 6391) (1959). Like many modern enu-
merations of charitable purposes, this list is influenced by the Elizabethan Statute
of Charitable Uses (1601).

23. Fremont-Smith, *Governing Nonprofit Organizations*, 245.

24. While regulations vary, a broad understanding of "charitable purpose" is
common among countries that offer charitable tax exemptions; this feature of philanthropic regulation is less anomalous than the scale of philanthropy and philanthropic subsidies in the United States. See Harding, *Charity Law and the Liberal
State*, 7–30.

25. Reich, Dorn, and Sutton, "Anything Goes," 4.

26. Fremont-Smith, *Governing Nonprofit Organizations*, 2.

27. Amarante, "Unregulated Charity."

28. See Brody and Owens, "Exile to Main Street." At issue was IRS scrutiny of
groups applying for status as 501(c)(4) social welfare organizations—a classification meant to exclude groups whose primary activity is political. Aiming to identify questionable applications, "the agency opened itself up to charges of political
bias by inappropriately using 'Be On the Lookout' (BOLO) lists that included,
among other screens, organizations with certain terms in their names (including
'Tea Party,' '9/12,' and 'Patriot,'—and, it later transpired, 'Progressive,' 'Occupy,'
'Acorn,' and 'Israel')," although "screening rarely translated into denial" (865–66).

29. Goodwin, "Ask Not What Your Charity Can Do for You," 101–2.

30. *Evans v. Abney*, 396 U.S. 435 (1970). The case is discussed in Friedman,
Dead Hands, 158; and Madoff, *Immortality and the Law*, 98–99.

31. Friedman, *Dead Hands*, 150.

32. Abby Goodnough, "A Wounded Museum Feels a Jolt of Progress," *New York
Times*, March 13, 2009, https://www.nytimes.com/2009/03/15/arts/design/15good
.html.

33. Isabella Stewart Gardner, Will and Codicil of Isabella Stewart Gardner (Probate Court of Suffolk County MA: July 23, 1924), 3.

34. Ibid., 5.

35. Cara Buckley, "Cosseted Life and Secret End of a Millionaire Maltese," *New York Times*, June 9, 2011, https://www.nytimes.com/2011/06/10/nyregion/leona-helmsleys-millionaire-dog-trouble-is-dead.html. According to Buckley, Trouble's actual living expenses amounted to about $190,000 per year, more than half of which was spent on her security team. See also Madoff, *Immortality and the Law*, 114.

36. This is, of course, an imaginary case. As a matter of fact, the Helmsley Charitable Trust (which received significantly more of Helmsley's fortune than Trouble did), *was* created for "purposes related to the provision of care for dogs," as well as for "such other charitable activities as the Trustee shall determine." The latter provision was sufficiently open-ended as to allow the trustees wide latitude in determining which causes and organizations to fund. See Jeffrey Toobin, "Rich Bitch: The Legal Battle over Trust Funds for Pets," *New Yorker*, September 2008, 41.

37. Of course, one possibility is that we should regard judicial nullification of bequests as wrong in both charitable and noncharitable cases: the libertarian solution to the discrepancy in the legal treatment of charitable and noncharitable bequests would be to seek consistency through enhanced deference to testators' noncharitable dispositions of property, rather than the inverse. At this stage, my point is simply to note the discrepancy, not to make an argument about the direction in which we should resolve it.

38. Reich, "Toward a Political Theory," 177, and *Just Giving*, 24–64.

39. Shawna Mizelle, "New York AG Says Black Lives Matter Foundation 'Not Affiliated with the Movement' and Orders It to Stop Collecting Donations," CNN, July 6, 2020, https://www.cnn.com/2020/07/06/politics/new-york-attorney-general-blm/index.html.

40. I do not in this section engage significantly with libertarian arguments that mandate deference to philanthropy as a subset of deference to property rights more generally. While libertarian arguments do provide reasons against government regulation of philanthropy, they can equally supply reasons against government subsidization of philanthropy, and they do not in theory (though may in practice) treat philanthropy as a specially worthy or protected use of money. In this section, I want to focus on reasons not just for protecting property rights in general but for treating donations as a *better* use of property than alternatives (e.g., consumption spending or investment), in ways that might justify the forms of deference canvassed in the previous section.

41. See, e.g., Du Bois, "Negro Education," arguing that "the Negro who comes with his hat in his hand and flatters and cajoles the philanthropist—that Negro gets money. . . . The Negro who shows the slightest independence of thought or character is apt to be read out of all possible influence not only by the white South but by the philanthropic North" (178).

42. See, e.g., Du Bois, *Black Reconstruction in America*, 637–69.

43. Du Bois, "Postscript," 58. Although Rosenwald was more active in funding Du Bois's rival Booker T. Washington, he also contributed to Du Bois's work, including his editorship of *The Crisis*. See Diner, *Julius Rosenwald*, 191 and 199.

44. Du Bois, "Postscript," 58. However, for a more mixed assessment, see Rooks, *Cutting School*. While acknowledging that "Rosenwald schools did more to further the cause of Black education than did any other educational entity of the time" (70), Rooks also notes that the Rosenwald Fund mandated a narrow focus on vocational education and required heavy fundraising and investment by Black communities before matching funds were made available (68–69). As I will argue in chapter 4, such conditions may be objectionably paternalistic even when they occur in the context of philanthropic donations that deliver important benefits.

45. Information available at https://www.holeinthewallgang.org.

46. See Hansmann, "Economic Theories of Nonprofit Organization."

47. Weisbrod, *The Nonprofit Economy*, 25.

48. Ibid., 25–31. Weisbrod borrows the language of "mini governments" from Clark's "Does the Nonprofit Form Fit the Hospital Industry?," where Clark notes that nonprofit "minigovernments" can be interpreted either as voluntary and "democratic" or as elitist in character (1438).

49. However, economic accounts also express versions of the worry that philanthropic provision will "let the state off the hook" for providing some services, or result in an excessive transfer of welfare burdens to the voluntary sector. Against the view that permitting voluntary provision alongside government provision will always lead to Pareto improvements, Weiss notes that it could lead to the exploitation of "high demanders" of public goods by low demanders, who might vote for lower levels of public goods provision in anticipation of free riding on the voluntary contributions of high demanders. Weiss, "Donations: Can They Reduce a Donor's Welfare?"

50. See Hirschman, *Exit, Voice, and Loyalty*. For the argument that poor people's exposure to domination would be reduced by replacing public welfare with publicly subsidized charitable aid (provided that sufficient competition among nonprofit providers could be assured), see Taylor, "Donation without Domination."

51. At least in theory (and setting aside any opportunity costs arising from tax subsidies). This is not an argument available to those who support philanthropy as a *complete* substitute for state provision. On such an arrangement, there might still be net gains in the choice available to clients, but there would also be significant losses.

52. For example, Frumkin suggests that the absence of coercion is a normative point in favor of philanthropy: "nonprofits occupy a moral high ground of sorts when compared to public-sector organizations that have the ability to compel action and coerce those who resist" (Frumkin, *On Being Nonprofit*, 18). Not everyone will share this intuition: in many cases, we might think that the moral high

ground is occupied by organizations that distribute burdens more equally among contributors. (This point is often made in debates about the relative merits of volunteer armies and drafts.)

53. Notably in the case of the movement for school choice and charter schools; see Scott, "The Politics of Venture Philanthropy."

54. See Reich, *Just Giving*, chap. 4. Reich (*Just Giving*, 219n26) traces the use of the phrase "risk capital" to describe the activities of philanthropic foundations to Arnold J. Zurcher's article "Foundations: How They Operate as Society's Risk Capital," *Challenge* 4 (1955), 16–19.

55. See, e.g., Fleishman, *The Foundation*; Acs, *Why Philanthropy Matters*; and Reich, "What Are Foundations For?" and *Just Giving*.

56. Reich, "What Are Foundations For?" 12.

57. The Rockefeller and Ford Foundations invested heavily in the Green Revolution in the 1950s and 1960s. The Gates Foundation is a leading funder of global public health initiatives, including prevention and treatment programs for HIV/AIDS, tuberculosis, and malaria, as well as major vaccination and immunization programs (including childhood immunization programs and, more recently, efforts to ensure widespread access to COVID-19 vaccines and treatments).

58. On "auditioning," see Beerbohm, "The Free Provider Problem." Of course, some examples of philanthropic innovation will look like better candidates for eventual public adoption than others. In some cases, citizens may reject the solutions identified by philanthropic innovators. In others, they may judge that philanthropy is succeeding in meeting a need without government action.

59. In principle, I accept something like this argument about when some forms of deference to philanthropy might be justified, all things considered; however, in later chapters I raise doubts about how much of our existing deference to philanthropy can be justified by the efficient extraction of public benefits.

60. As noted above, this is only true of taxpayers who itemize their taxes; people taking the standard deduction are not able to claim additional deductions for charitable contributions.

61. See, e.g., Andrews, "Personal Deductions in an Ideal Income Tax"; and Bittker, "Charitable Contributions."

62. Reich, "Toward a Political Theory," 179–80.

63. Philip Rucker and Rosalind S. Helderman, "Romney: I've Paid at Least 13 Percent Tax Rate in Each of Past 10 Years," *Washington Post*, August 16, 2012, http://www.washingtonpost.com/politics/romney-ive-paid-at-least-13-percent-in-taxes-for-past-10-years/2012/08/16/bf4b5944-e7be-11e1-8487-64e4b2a79ba8_story_1.html.

64. Bill Gates, "Why Inequality Matters," *The Gates Notes* (blog), October 13, 2014, http://www.gatesnotes.com/Books/Why-Inequality-Matters-Capital-in-21st-Century-Review#.

65. Ibid.

66. Ibid.

67. Singer, "What Should a Billionaire Give?"

68. One of Buffett's children, reflecting on his experience in the philanthropic sector since 2006, has written critically about contemporary philanthropy and "'conscience laundering'—feeling better about accumulating more than any one person could possibly need to live on by sprinkling a little around as an act of charity." Peter Buffett, "The Charitable-Industrial Complex," *New York Times*, July 26, 2013, https://www.nytimes.com/2013/07/27/opinion/the-charitable-industrial-complex.html.

69. The anecdote appears in Aubrey, *Brief Lives*, 446. For a more recent "warm glow" account of giving, see Andreoni, "Impure Altruism and Donations to Public Goods." "Warm glow" models can also incorporate the expectation that donors crave less exalted returns like status and prestige: see Harbaugh, "What Do Donations Buy?"

70. Attempting to distinguish between genuinely foregone consumption and cases where the giver receives some benefit would also point to a very different kind of tax deduction, one that excluded the most "consumption-like" philanthropy and included benefits for other nonconsumption spending. Reich gives the examples of donations to for-profit corporations (in which one does not hold stock) and donations to foreign countries and charities, which are not currently deductible under U.S. law but which seem equally to represent foregone consumption opportunities of which the tax system should take account. See Reich, "Toward a Political Theory," 180–81.

71. For philanthropy aimed at policy advocacy and policy change, the analogy to political spending might be very close; chapter 3 presents a deflationary picture of the differences between elite political spending and elite philanthropy.

72. Rosenblum, in *Membership and Morals*, argues that even illiberal, inegalitarian, and antisocial civil society groups have psychological and moral benefits for members (and can act as "safety valves" that also benefit society at large).

73. Putnam, "Bowling Alone," 67.

74. Tocqueville, *Democracy in America*, vol. 2, 595–99. I discuss these arguments of Tocqueville, and associational arguments for philanthropy more generally, in chapter 5.

75. Mill, *On Liberty*, 305.

76. Putnam, *Bowling Alone*, especially chap. 7–8.

77. I should emphasize again that this catalogue is not meant to be exhaustive; in particular, I have focused on third-person reasons for valuing philanthropy, not on all the reasons that donors themselves might have for viewing their philanthropy as important (e.g., a desire to preserve and pass on a family legacy of philanthropic leadership). While such reasons may certainly be important in motivational terms, they do not refer to projects that a liberal state should exert special effort in promoting (unless they can be shown to have other positive externalities).

78. See, e.g., Madoff, "When is Philanthropy?"; Cullman and Madoff, "The Undermining of American Charity"; and Andreoni, "The Benefits and Costs of Donor-Advised Funds."

79. To maintain their tax exemption, private foundations in the United States are required to pay out (in grants and qualifying administrative expenses) a minimum of five percent of the average market value of their net investment assets each year.

80. Some large-scale philanthropists have voluntarily mandated spend-downs for the foundations that they created or helped to fund. Rosenwald's example has already been mentioned; more recent examples of limited-life foundations include the John M. Olin Foundation (a conservative foundation whose founder was concerned with preventing ideological drift over time, and which completed its spend-down in 2005), Atlantic Philanthropies (which ceased operations in September 2020), and the Bill and Melinda Gates Foundation (the structure of which is currently in flux following Bill and Melinda Gates' divorce in 2021).

81. On charitable choice, see Minow, *Partners, Not Rivals*; Kennedy and Bielefeld, "Government Shekels Without Government Shackles?"; and Gilman, "Charitable Choice and the Accountability Challenge." On the role of nonprofits in the American welfare state more generally, see Smith and Lipsky, *Nonprofits for Hire*. For an extended argument against the legitimacy of privatization, see Cordelli, *The Privatized State*.

82. Though the distinction between time and money might also break down in places.

Chapter Two

1. Relational egalitarians generally recognize that a *public* policy's impact on equality cannot be reduced to or straightforwardly inferred from its distributional effects (e.g., Anderson, "What Is the Point of Equality?"). I argue both that this point generalizes to philanthropy and that philanthropy is an independently significant site of "action" for relational equality: the virtues and vices and good or bad effects of philanthropic relationships are not simply derivative of the virtues and vices and good or bad effects of social institutions.

2. Utilitarian and other consequentialist theories have paid more attention to voluntary giving as a mechanism for bringing about good outcomes, especially in the case of giving for global poverty relief. I discuss these perspectives in more detail in chapter 6 (where I consider philanthropic giving that crosses borders, and where givers and beneficiaries do not share membership in a democratic community). Welfare consequentialist perspectives on giving are considerably less interested in ideal theory or in the specification of institution-specific principles of justice, and they are correspondingly more likely to register philanthropy as a

practice of normative interest. However, as I argue in chapter 6, consequentialist and nonconsequentialist views generally overlap in advancing distributive rather than relational standards for evaluating voluntary giving.

3. For Rawls's own explanation for the primacy of the basic structure as subject of justice, see Rawls, "The Basic Structure as Subject," in *Political Liberalism*, 257–88. For other defenses of social institutions as the primary bearers of duties of justice, see Nagel, *Equality and Partiality*; Pogge, "On the Site of Distributive Justice"; and Julius, "Basic Structure and the Value of Equality." Liam Murphy and G. A. Cohen are two of the most important exceptions to the generalizations that I make above: both argue that the same principles of justice that apply to social institutions also impose personal duties of justice on individuals (beyond the duty simply to support and comply with just institutions). See Murphy, "Institutions and the Demands of Justice"; and Cohen, "Incentives, Inequality, and Community," "Where the Action Is," and *Rescuing Justice and Equality*.

4. As I use the term, to call an act of voluntary giving *philanthropy* is compatible with its having been owed to the recipient as a matter of justice or special obligation; the term reflects the giver's space of legal, rather than moral, discretion. Nevertheless, to call something a charitable or philanthropic gift certainly *connotes* moral discretion, in ways we might find misleading or objectionable.

5. For some, state funding is primarily a means to guarantee the just distribution of important goods, leaving open a possible role for private funders. Others argue that obligations of distributive justice are agent-relative and belong to citizens collectively so that there is an important moral remainder in cases where private funders discharge (what should be) public obligations of distributive justice. See Beerbohm, "The Free Provider Problem."

6. See Rawls, *Political Liberalism*; R. Dworkin, "Liberalism" (in *A Matter of Principle*) and *Sovereign Virtue*; Larmore, *Patterns of Moral Complexity*; and Barry, *Justice as Impartiality*.

7. R. Dworkin, "Liberalism," in *A Matter of Principle*, 191–92.

8. Ibid.

9. Brighouse, "Neutrality, Publicity, and State Funding of the Arts." R. Dworkin himself argues that state support for the arts can be justified if it is content neutral and looks "to the diversity and innovative quality of the culture as a whole rather than to (what public officials take to be) excellence in particular occasions of that culture" (*A Matter of Principle*, 233). Anderson defends state subsidy of the arts by appealing to the importance of providing citizens with equal opportunity to access artistic culture; see *Value in Ethics and Economics*, 149.

10. This version of the argument might implicate not only *direct* state funding of the arts but even their indirect subsidy (e.g., in the form of charitable tax deductions). Liberal neutralist arguments about the appropriate division of labor between government and philanthropic spending should be distinguished from arguments about the merits of government subsidy of philanthropy; some ways of

grounding the institutional division of labor may rule out subsidies for (at least some) charitable donations, while others might see an arms-length, content-neutral subsidy as consistent with the demands of neutrality.

11. Arguments along these lines include Pevnick, "Philanthropy and Democratic Ideals," and Beerbohm, "The Free-Provider Problem." Pevnick argues that tax deductions, credits, or other mechanisms of public subsidy for philanthropy could allow the state "to provide support for a society's cultural structure while outsourcing judgments about the relative quality or value of different pursuits" to individual citizens, thus avoiding concerns about perfectionism (235–38).

12. Recall that, in Rawls's formulation, ideal theory investigates "the nature and aims of a perfectly just society" (*Theory of Justice*, 9) under (1) the assumption of full compliance by citizens with principles of justice and just institutions and (2) the assumption of favorable background conditions. Nonideal theory relaxes both assumptions and aims to articulate principles for responding to injustice and reforming less-than-just institutions. See introduction, note 18, for works that explicate and defend the priority of ideal theory. See also introduction, notes 19–21, for authors who question the priority and, in some cases, even the cogency of ideal theory. I do not here take a general position on the value of ideal theory, but I do make the case for detaching nonideal theories of *philanthropy* from claims about the role that philanthropy would play in a perfectly just society.

13. For example, suppose it were true that—assuming social institutions and the distribution of primary goods are just—there is an antiperfectionist objection to government spending on the opera and no antiperfectionist objection to philanthropic spending on the opera. It is unclear whether that conclusion is sufficient to favor philanthropic spending on the opera (or to rule out public spending on the arts) under conditions of unjust inequalities.

14. Discussed in chapter 1.

15. A variant of the second position would focus voluntary giving on political objectives: we should donate not so as to approximate just institutions but rather so as to help bring them about. But this recommendation would leave significant scope for philanthropy, both because philanthropy can be a way of pursuing political objectives (see chapter 3) and because presumably there will be times when a donor can achieve better distributive outcomes directly than she could through attempts at electoral influence or institutional reform. See Murphy, "Institutions and the Demands of Justice," 281–82.

16. Arguments along these lines include Murphy, "Institutions and the Demands of Justice," and Cordelli, "Reparative Justice and the Moral Limits of Discretionary Philanthropy." Cordelli argues that, in circumstances of unjust inequality, philanthropists should understand themselves to be spending money to which they are not morally entitled and which is not really "theirs." They should therefore exercise no moral discretion regarding where to give but donate entirely with a view to mimicking or promoting just institutions. More controversially, she argues that

political institutions are justified in incentivizing philanthropists to comply with these duties of reparative justice (e.g., by extending tax incentives for donations to justice-promoting causes but not to other kinds of donation). This suggestion presents problems in nonideal theory, since presumably it often will be the case that the relevant political institutions are partially *responsible* for unjust inequalities. They are therefore not best placed to incentivize compliance with a (correct) conception of justice. (And, even if they were, they could probably promote that conception in more sweeping and efficient ways than by adjusting the tax treatment of philanthropy.) A further complication is how to divide attention between addressing domestic and global injustices and inequalities.

17. To some degree, consequentialist theories suffer from the opposite problem: they supply exacting moral standards for evaluating voluntary giving but are often criticized for treating the institutional backdrop as fixed.

18. The contemporary literature on social or relational equality has paid considerable first-order attention to such relationships (see introduction, note 28). However, this contemporary literature has had surprisingly little to say about charity or philanthropy—perhaps because it is taken as obvious that dependence on voluntary charity has no place in a relational egalitarian ideal.

19. Veyne, *Le pain et le cirque*.

20. Tocqueville, *Democracy in America*, vol. 2, 2.4. For discussion of this passage and the claim that, for Tocqueville, this preference for philanthropic rather than political engagement is "perhaps the hallmark of an upper-class outlook," see Sabl, "Community Organizing as Tocquevillean Politics," 3. Analyzing white supremacy rather than class relations, Du Bois makes a point strikingly similar in structure to Tocqueville's: He claims that "in matters of simple almsgiving, where there can be no question of social contact" the white South is "generous to a fault. The black beggar is never turned away without a good deal more than a crust, and a call for help for the unfortunate meets a quick response. . . . And yet this does not touch the kernel of the problem. Human advancement is not a mere question of almsgiving, but rather of sympathy and cooperation among classes who would scorn charity" (*The Souls of Black Folk*, 146).

21. Huyssen, *Progressive Inequality*, 9. In addition to dynamics of prescription and cooperation, Huyssen discusses class conflict as the third important kind of class interaction.

22. Ibid.

23. Tocqueville, *Memoir on Pauperism*, 31.

24. Ibid. Tocqueville also claims that private charity is less degrading than public assistance to the recipient's self-respect: a poor man "turning to individual charity, recognizes, it is true, his condition of inferiority in relation to the rest of his fellow men; but he recognizes it secretly and temporarily"; public aid, on the other hand, "publicizes inferiority and legalizes it" (*Memoir on Pauperism*, 30). This argument has some interesting overlap with contemporary egalitarian concerns

about the problem of "shameful revelation" (see, e.g., Wolff, "Fairness, Respect, and the Egalitarian Ethos").

25. Spencer, "The Proper Sphere of Government," 105.

26. See, e.g., Walzer, *Spheres of Justice*; Anderson, "The Ethical Limitations of the Market" and *Value in Ethics and Economics*; Radin, *Contested Commodities*; Sandel, *What Money Can't Buy*; and Satz, *Why Some Things Should Not Be for Sale*. Most of these authors focus on how commodification transforms the meanings of goods and social practices; Satz places the most emphasis on commodification's effects on relationships and on people's ability to interact as equals.

27. Titmuss, *The Gift Relationship*.

28. Note that this is a position about how blood should be *collected* (i.e., from donations rather than paid contributions); it is consistent with the view that public agencies should control the *distribution* of the blood supply. For an account that complicates Titmuss's picture and that stresses the importance of organizations and organizational choices in mediating the effects of marketization, see Healy, *Last Best Gifts*.

29. See, e.g., Satz, *Why Some Things Should Not Be for Sale*, 80; Sandel, *What Money Can't Buy*, 122–26. Though herself a critic of marketization, Radin has questioned the view that "market-inalienabilities are necessary to encourage altruism" and the assumption that "permitting any commodification engenders a domino effect," whereby a good becomes commodified for everyone such that the possibilities of altruism and reciprocity are foreclosed (Radin, *Contested Commodities*, 96–99).

30. As Walzer puts it, "there is a virtue in private giving, and [Titmuss] would rightly doubt that this virtue can be duplicated by public taking, even when the taking is mandated by a democratic decision" (Walzer, *Spheres of Justice*, 93).

31. Walzer, *Spheres of Justice*, 94. Egalitarians will be quick to recognize the limitations of these arguments in conditions of significant background inequality, and Walzer himself argues (with "community chest"–type cases in mind) that it is a backdrop of equality that "redeems charity." Worries about dependency and subordination can most easily be overcome in contexts (analogous to the blood case) where both the capacity to contribute and the chance of needing help are relatively widely or evenly distributed. (See Walzer, 93–94.) Different arguments would be necessary to redeem elite philanthropy or other kinds of giving against the backdrop of serious inequalities.

32. Arrow, "Gifts and Exchanges," 359.

33. Ibid.

34. Ibid.

35. Ibid.

36. Singer, "Altruism and Commerce"; Sandel, *What Money Can't Buy*, 126–27.

37. Smith, *Wealth of Nations*, 1.2. Smith continues, making the contrast with (and limitations of) charity explicit: "Nobody but a beggar chooses to depend

chiefly upon the benevolence of his fellow-citizens. Even a beggar does not depend upon it entirely. The charity of well-disposed people, indeed, supplies him with the whole fund of his subsistence. But though this principle ultimately provides him with all the necessaries of life which he has occasion for, it neither does nor can provide him with them as he has occasion for them. The greater part of his occasional wants are supplied in the same manner as those of other people, by treaty, by barter, and by purchase. With the money which one man gives him he purchases food. The old clothes which another bestows upon him he exchanges for other old clothes which suit him better, or for lodging, or for food, or for money, with which he can buy either food, clothes, or lodging, as he has occasion."

38. Satz, *Why Some Things Should Not Be for Sale*, 25. See also Anderson, *Private Government*, 1–5.

39. As well as on the externalities of transactions. We also should not assume that permissible forms of political regulation will overlap with our moral evaluations of the people seeking to make voluntary contributions. For example, we might admire young people who are willing to volunteer for unpaid internships at public agencies, while also seeking to restrict the use of unpaid internships out of concern for equality of opportunity (e.g., to access interesting and opportunity-generating work, for people who cannot afford to work for free).

40. Adam Cureton explores this case in more detail in "Offensive Beneficence."

41. Brennan and Jaworski stress the contingency of social meanings in "Markets without Symbolic Limits," (where they argue against "semiotic objections" to commodification, rather than to gifts or offers of help).

42. This is partly because, until relatively recently in human history, only the most radical thinkers have imagined the abolition of poverty or supposed that the needs of the poor could be met without charity. On the historical pervasiveness of belief in the inevitability of poverty, see, e.g., Katz, *The Undeserving Poor*. Thomas Paine's *Agrarian Justice* (1797) is an early and important exception: perhaps the first case of a canonical thinker imagining the eradication of severe poverty through a tax on landed property and unconditional transfers to all citizens (including a one-time payment of £15 for each new adult reaching the age of twenty-one, as well as annual payments of £10 to all adults over the age of fifty). Paine insists that "it is justice, and not charity, that is the principle of the plan" (332) and that transfers should be made to rich and poor alike "to prevent invidious distinctions" (327). His proposal thus combines an argument about distributive justice (i.e., that people deserve compensation for the appropriation of land from the common "natural inheritance") with attentiveness to the relational effects of candidate solutions.

43. Mill, *Principles of Political Economy*, 962.

44. Mill, *Subjection of Women*, 330. I discuss Mill's critique of women's charity and its relationship to his feminism in more detail in Saunders-Hastings, "No Better to Give Than to Receive."

45. Mill, *Subjection*, 330.

46. Knight, *Citizen*, 148. Knight notes that Addams likely read the American edition of *The Subjection of Women*, published in New York by Henry Holt and Sons in 1885 and that her personal library also included an edition of *On Liberty* (452n52).

47. Addams quotes this line (which appears in *Subjection*, 338) in her speech "Outgrowths of Toynbee Hall," which she revised and published as "The Subjective Necessity for Social Settlements." The Mill passage appears in both.

48. Mill, *Subjection*, 330 and 338–39. The former passage is quoted above; in the latter, Mill argues that "to practise [charity] usefully, or even without doing mischief, requires the education, the manifold preparation, the knowledge and the thinking powers, of a skilful administrator. There are few of the administrative functions of government for which a person would not be fit, who is fit to bestow charity usefully. In this as in other cases . . . the duties permitted to women cannot be performed properly, without their being trained for duties which, to the great loss of society, are not permitted to them."

49. Addams, "The Objective Value of a Social Settlement," 55.

50. Ibid.

51. Again, see especially Mill, *Subjection*, 330 and 338–39. Considering Addams's repeated quotation of a line from the latter paragraph, it is interesting to consider whether Mill's critique of traditional "feminine" charity helped shape Addams's aspirations for the settlement movement.

52. Mill, *Subjection*, 330.

53. Addams, "A Modern Lear." Although the essay was not published until 1912, Addams wrote it in 1894 (shortly after the Pullman strike) and read it to audiences in Chicago and Boston.

54. Lindsey, "Paternalism and the Pullman Strike," 273. Lindsey uses the word *philanthropic* to describe motives of disinterested beneficence, rather than in the neutral sense of donations of private money for broadly public purposes. In her essay, Addams is more willing to grant that Pullman's motives were "philanthropic" in the sense that he sincerely believed that he was benefiting his workers. The latter point is of course open to doubt—but Addams's point is that even motives of sincere benevolence do not license paternalistic social relations.

55. Addams, "A Modern Lear," 133.

56. Ibid., 135.

57. Ibid., 135.

58. Ibid., 136.

59. Ibid., 135.

60. Ibid., 136.

61. Ibid., 137.

62. Chapter 4, "Philanthropic Paternalism," develops in more detail the argument that philanthropic relationships can be objectionably subordinating even

when recipients give meaningful consent to the terms that philanthropists offer, and even in (the standard) circumstances where philanthropists *add* to recipients' choice sets rather than removing previously available options.

63. Mill, *Principles of Political Economy*, 759.

64. Ibid., 761.

65. Ibid., 761.

66. I have been unable to find evidence that Addams ever read *Principles of Political Economy*, although Mill's critique of philanthropy as essentially a patriarchal mode of relating to recipients is present in *The Subjection of Women* as well. While they may have arrived at this emphasis independently, the convergence between the two thinkers on this point remains striking.

67. Mill and Addams are not puritanical in their calls for relational equality. (Addams was attracted by but eventually rejected Tolstoy's ascetic vision of ethical life.) Their call for egalitarian relations is compatible with at least some attitudes and beliefs (e.g., Mill's distinction between higher and lower pleasures or Addams's interest in bringing "high culture" to the settlement community) that could look elitist or patronizing. Both Mill and Addams acknowledge that wealthy people have had access to a greater range of opportunities and experiences, and it therefore stands to reason that they have something to teach their fellow citizens. Zakaras stresses that, for Mill, egalitarian "open practices" can accommodate and may even require *provisional* inequalities, in the context of an aspiration toward full equality (*Individuality and Mass Democracy*, 140). And, as is well known, Mill did not apply his commitments to equal liberty and to egalitarian social relations in the case of colonial subjects; unlike Addams, he explicitly accepts paternalistic social and political relations in some contexts.

68. Addams, "Objective Value," 56. Neither Mill nor Addams treats voting as the singular focus of social and political responsibility. In part, this may be because both were centrally interested in the lack of voting rights and, at the same time, the social and civic agency of women.

69. Addams, "The Subjective Necessity for Social Settlements," 2. In the same passage, she elaborates, "It is not difficult to see that although America is pledged to the democratic ideal, the view of democracy has been partial, and that its best achievement thus far has been pushed along the line of the franchise. Democracy has made little attempt to assert itself in social affairs. We have refused to move beyond the position of its eighteenth-century leaders, who believed that political equality alone would secure all good to all men" (1–2). Later, she describes the settlement workers' "desire to interpret democracy in social terms" (21–22).

70. Addams, "Subjective Necessity," 22.

71. Himmelfarb, *Poverty and Compassion*, 6.

72. Addams, "Subjective Necessity," 22–23.

73. Ibid.

74. Addams, "A Modern Lear," 137.

75. See Reich, *Just Giving*, chap. 2.

76. Though Mill's and Addams's arguments also suggest that hierarchical relations often will produce outcomes that are worse for having been less inclusive of multiple perspectives. Contemporary arguments about the epistemic properties of democracy make a parallel claim; see, e.g., Anderson, "The Epistemology of Democracy"; and Landemore, *Democratic Reason*, 82–85 and 97–105.

Chapter Three

1. See Bartels, *Unequal Democracy*; Gilens, *Affluence and Influence*; and Gilens and Page, "Testing Theories of American Politics." For other important contributions to the recent literature on inequality at the top and on how wealth translates into unequal political voice, see Hacker and Pierson, *Winner-Take-All Politics*; Winters, *Oligarchy*; Schlozman, Verba, and Brady, *The Unheavenly Chorus*; Page and Gilens, *Democracy in America*; and Page, Seawright, and Lacombe, *Billionaires and Stealth Politics*.

2. Page, Bartels, and Seawright, "Democracy and the Policy Preferences of Wealthy Americans," 67.

3. On the increasing concentration of wealth at the top, see Piketty, *Capital in the Twenty-First Century*; and Piketty and Saez, "Income Inequality in the United States."

4. See, e.g., McCormick, *Machiavellian Democracy*; and Green, *Shadow of Unfairness*. Green denies that liberal democracies (with the inequalities that private property and the private family unavoidably introduce) are capable of fully realizing the ideal of political equality. In this chapter, I do not take a position on whether or not the ideal of political equality is *fully* realizable in a regime that permits economic inequalities; rather, I focus on how democracies might take the ideal of political equality more seriously and advance it in ways compatible with other values.

5. Bartels, *Unequal Democracy*, 252; Lessig, *Republic, Lost*, 312–13. Emphasis added in both cases.

6. Page, Bartels, and Seawright, "Democracy and the Policy Preferences of Wealthy Americans," 52. Emphasis added.

7. Singer, "What Should a Billionaire Give?"

8. Murphy, "Institutions and the Demands of Justice," 282.

9. Ibid., 281.

10. Ibid.

11. Miller and Zinsmeister, *Agenda Setting*, 72.

12. Ibid., 71–73.

13. See, e.g., Mayer, *Dark Money*; Skocpol and Hertel-Fernandez, "The Koch Network and Republican Party Extremism"; Hertel-Fernandez, *State Capture*; and Page, Seawright, and Lacombe, *Billionaires and Stealth Politics*.

14. See Hertel-Fernandez, *State Capture*, for an extended discussion of ALEC's activities and influence.

15. "About ALEC," American Legislative Exchange Council (ALEC), https://www.alec.org/about/.

16. Traditional institutional boundaries are also blurring within the Effective Altruism movement, which is more often accused of being *excessively* morally demanding than of enabling selfish donors. The Open Philanthropy Project (funded by Cari Tuna and Dustin Moscowitz and initially incubated at GiveWell) spun off as an independent group of affiliated organizations, including a 501(c)(3), a 501(c)(4) social welfare organization capable of engaging in some political activity, and an LLC capable of investing in for-profit corporations.

17. Mark Zuckerberg, "I want to thank you all for your heartwarming congratulations on Max's birth and on starting the Chan Zuckerberg Initiative," Facebook, December 3, 2015. https://www.facebook.com/zuck/posts/10102507695055801.

18. Issacharoff and Karlan, "The Hydraulics of Campaign Finance Reform."

19. Ibid., 1709.

20. Rockefeller, *Random Reminiscences of Men and Events*, 140–41. Quoted in Fleishman, *The Foundation*, 99–100.

21. Goodwin, "Ask Not What Your Charity Can Do for You," 97fn98.

22. "Key Facts on U.S. Nonprofits and Foundations," Candid.org, April 2020, https://www.issuelab.org/resources/36381/36381.pdf. Based on IRS filings, Candid counts a total of 119,791 foundations. By far the largest share (107,889) are independent grant-making foundations established by individual donors and families; of the remainder, 7,947 are operating foundations (which run their own programs, sometimes in addition to making grants), 2,888 are corporate foundations, and 1,067 are community foundations.

23. Or, for 2019, an estimated $75.69 billion of the estimated $449.64 billion in total philanthropic giving (*Giving USA 2020*, 22).

24. Ibid. Giving by individuals accounts for an estimated 69 percent of total giving (or, for 2019, nearly $310 billion); bequests account for roughly 10 percent of total giving and giving by corporations another 5 percent.

25. Macdonald, *The Ford Foundation*, 3.

26. See, e.g., Miller and Zinsmeister, *Agenda Setting*, 10–16; Reese, *Backlash Against Welfare Mothers*, 154–57; and Ridzi, *Selling Welfare Reform*, 51–54.

27. See, e.g., Michael Anft, "How One Megadonor Gives to Further His Cause," *Chronicle of Philanthropy*, May 18, 2014, https://www.philanthropy.com/article/how-one-megadonor-gives-to-further-his-cause/.

28. See, e.g., Odendahl, *Charity Begins at Home*; and Ostrower, *Why the Wealthy Give*.

29. See, e.g., Odendahl, *Charity Begins at Home*; Roelofs, *Foundations and Public Policy*; and Giridharadas, *Winners Take All*. Marx and Engels anticipate some of these arguments when they note that "a part of the bourgeoisie is desirous of redressing

social grievances, in order to secure the continued existence of bourgeois society" and that this group includes "philanthropists, humanitarians, improvers of the condition of the working class, [and] organisers of charity" (*Communist Manifesto*, 496).

30. See, e.g., Incite! (eds.), *The Revolution Will Not Be Funded*; Kohl-Arenas, *The Self-Help Myth*; and Francis, "The Price of Civil Rights." For some similar arguments but a more mixed overall verdict, see also Ferguson, *Top Down*.

31. See, e.g., Reich, "A Failure of Philanthropy" and *Just Giving*, 65–105. The latter describes practices of public school fundraising that (in conjunction with tax subsidies for philanthropy) are actually *upwardly* redistributive.

32. It is for this reason that I do not emphasize the case of the Kochs, despite its political importance and fact that far more wealthy donors in the United States support conservative and Republican causes than liberal ones. (See Page, Seawright, and Lacombe, *Billionaires and Stealth Politics*.) The Kochs represent a case where intuitions about elite self-interest, and a rejection of the substance of elite policy agendas, are especially likely to be driving the responses of liberal readers. It is therefore not the best case to consider for insight into the more general democratic concerns that philanthropy raises.

33. See Cordelli, "The Institutional Division of Labor and the Egalitarian Obligations of Nonprofits," "How Privatization Threatens the Private," and *The Privatized State*.

34. Reich, "What Are Foundations For?" and *Just Giving*, 152–67.

35. "Presumptively" because I leave open the possibility that some very rich people could legitimately be authorized to decide matters of common concern (e.g., through competitive elections), subject to appropriate mechanisms of democratic accountability.

36. See, e.g., Anderson, "Democracy: Instrumental vs. Non-Instrumental Value"; Kolodny, "Rule Over None II"; Viehoff, "Democratic Equality and Political Authority"; and Wilson, *Democratic Equality*.

37. Wilson, *Democratic Equality*, 48–72.

38. Thompson, *Ethics in Congress*; Lessig, *Republic, Lost*; and Pevnick, "Does the Egalitarian Rationale for Campaign Finance Reform Succeed?"

39. Again, absent special authorization.

40. See, e.g., Scott, "The Politics of Venture Philanthropy"; Ravitch, *The Death and Life of the Great American School System*; Barkan, "Got Dough?"; Reckhow, *Follow the Money*; and Tompkins-Stange, *Policy Patrons*.

41. Ravitch, *Death and Life*, 200.

42. Thompson, *Ethics in Congress*, 7.

43. Lessig, "Institutional Corruption Defined," 553.

44. See Barkan, "Got Dough?"; Reckhow, *Follow the Money*; Tompkins-Stange, *Policy Patrons*; and Greene, "Buckets into the Sea."

45. Barkan, "Got Dough?" The example is from the Gates Foundation's state-level grant making in 2009.

46. See Reckhow, *Follow the Money*; and Tompkins-Stange, *Policy Patrons*.

47. Of course, there may be other deficiencies in democracy to take account of, such that we could judge an outcome to be inadequately democratic with or without the philanthropic intervention. For example, school board elections often have low voter turnout and are not demographically representative of the populations served by public schools. My central claim here is that elite philanthropy is an undemocratic form of control over (some) public outcomes, not that it is always the only or even the worst one. I address this point in more detail below.

48. On the importance of recognizing the democratic requirement that citizens enjoy equal authority over features of their common life over time, see Wilson, *Democratic Equality*. Privatization and the outsourcing of influence to donors are distinctive threats to equality over time, in ways that a focus on episodic interactions (i.e., the moment when a gift is accepted by democratically authorized actors) might obscure.

49. See, e.g., Dave Levinthal, "Koch Foundation Proposal to College: Teach Our Curriculum, Get Millions," Center for Public Integrity, September 12, 2014, https://www.publicintegrity.org/2014/09/12/15495/kock-foundation-proposal -college-teach-our-curriculum-get-millions.

50. See Anderson, "Epistemology of Democracy"; and Dewey, *The Public and Its Problems*. As Dewey and Anderson both emphasize, the question of what counts as a public problem is to be settled neither by philosophical fiat nor (only) by a simple majoritarian procedure, but through processes of inclusive deliberation. One worry about donor restrictions is that they limit in advance the possibilities for democratic deliberation and debate.

51. This might be the case, for example, for some institutions of high culture: elite control over art galleries only raises democratic concerns in aggregate to the extent that such institutions have public purposes or effects that go beyond reflecting and serving elite tastes.

52. Lessig, *Republic, Lost*, 312–13.

53. Cf. Walzer, *Spheres of Justice*, 100–101.

54. Pevnick, "Philanthropy and Democratic Ideals," 236.

55. Kolodny, "Rule Over None II," 20.

56. Ibid.

57. Kogan, Lavertu, and Peskowitz, "The Democratic Deficit in U.S. Education Governance." The authors find that voters who participate in local school board elections are not demographically representative of the people served by public schools: voters are, in general, whiter, wealthier, and less likely to have children in public schools. Of course, the same is true for many donors, and so one might still claim a comparative democratic advantage for school boards. Against this, one might claim that philanthropic motives and objectives make donors' interests better aligned with those of schoolchildren than are the interests of ordinary adult voters.

58. See Reich, "Toward a Political Theory," 182–83 and 190–91; and Pevnick, "Democratizing the Nonprofit Sector." However, among the COVID-19 relief provisions passed by the U.S. Congress was a temporary expansion of the charitable tax deduction, allowing individual taxpayers taking the standard deduction to deduct up to $300 in charitable giving for the 2020 and 2021 tax years.

59. Pevnick, "Democratizing the Nonprofit Sector," 261.

60. Ibid., 270–71.

61. Ibid., 279.

62. In the United States, for example, the 2017 tax cuts doubled the standard deduction, leading to fewer people claiming the charitable tax deduction, to a smaller proportion of total giving being subsidized, and to an even sharper skew of the subsidy toward donations by the very rich. But the more significant effect of the tax cuts was to leave many rich people with much more money to spend or donate than under the previous scheme of income taxation. Suppose that we preserved the 2017 income tax rates but converted the charitable tax deduction into a voucher system. On one interpretation, the rich would no longer illegitimately be favored in the allocation of public money. But tax policy *as a whole* could be accused of favoring them unfairly and (thereby) shoring up their philanthropic influence—just less directly and explicitly than the deduction mechanism now does. Charges that the tax system favors the rich need to be adjudicated on the grounds of substantive justice; the problem cannot be solved only through the neutral procedural mechanism of redistributing an artificially isolated pool of "public money." We cannot isolate the question of what a fair tax system *with respect to philanthropy* would look like from broader questions of justice in taxation. For a more general argument against narrow evaluations of the justice of particular tax provisions (i.e., without reference to broader questions of distributive justice), see Murphy and Nagel, *The Myth of Ownership*.

63. Pevnick, "Democratizing the Nonprofit Sector," 273.

64. Veyne, *Le pain et le cirque*.

65. Zuiderhoek, *Politics of Munificence*, 10–11.

66. Ibid., 150. Of course, the fact that euergetism may have reflected a commitment to (a version of) political equality should not lead us to assimilate it to a comprehensive relational egalitarian ideal.

67. Atkinson, "Reforming Cy Pres Reform."

68. Ibid., 1143. Recognizing the dim prospects for sweeping legal reforms along the lines he endorses, Atkinson has more recently suggested "piecemeal, practical" strategies that might be deployed by charitable fiduciaries in order to achieve the same goal of "freer, more fungible charitable assets and increased charitable autonomy" (Atkinson, "The Low Road to Cy Pres Reform," 101–2).

69. Founded in the late 1990s, Resource Generation describes itself as "a multiracial membership community of young people (18–35) with wealth and/or class privilege committed to the equitable distribution of wealth, land, and power" (https://resourcegeneration.org/). The organization encourages young people with access to inherited wealth to donate with a view to reducing inequality and, in particular,

to transferring control of funds to beneficiaries and their communities (e.g., by donating to organizations led by activists and community organizers, rather than wealthy boards, and by refraining from asserting control over grantees through familiar techniques such as donor conditions and required impact reporting on grants). See Zoë Beery, "The Rich Kids Who Want to Tear Down Capitalism," November 27, 2020, https://www.nytimes.com/2020/11/27/style/trust-fund-activism-resouce-generation.html; Malia Wollan, "How to Give Away Your Trust Fund," *New York Times*, November 21, 2019, https://www.nytimes.com/2019/11/21/maga zine/resource-generation.html; and Anna Altman, "The Millenials Who Want to Get Rid of Their Class Privilege," *Washington* Post, March 2, 2020, https://www.washingtonpost.com/magazine/2020/03/02/their-families-built-fortunes-these-millennials-are-trying-figure-out-how-undo-their-class-privilege/?arc404=true.

70. For example, in the Athenian system of compulsory liturgies (or the private funding of festivals, military equipment, and other public benefits by wealthy citizens); see Reich, *Just Giving*, 29–35.

71. See Hume, *History of England*, vol. 4, 383–85; and Smith, *Wealth of Nations*, vol. 1, 3.4.10–17. On this thread in Hume, see Sabl, *Hume's Politics*, 66–74 and 221–23.

Chapter Four

1. See, e.g., Suzanne Perry, "The Problem with Paternalistic Donors," *Chronicle of Philanthropy*, May 22, 2007, https://www.philanthropy.com/article/The-Problem-with-Paternalistic/191677; and Ian Wilhelm, "A Paternalistic View of Philanthropy?" *Chronicle of Philanthropy*, May 5, 2008, https://www.philanthropy.com/article/A-Paternalistic-View-of/192421.

2. Dickens, *Bleak House*, 106.

3. Ibid., 446.

4. See, e.g., Yunus, *Banker to the Poor*, 249; George Soros, quoted in Lewis, "The Speculator"; and Ira Magaziner, a Clinton Foundation executive and spokesperson, quoted in Rauch, "This Is Not Charity."

5. I am most indebted to the following for my understanding of paternalism: Shiffrin, "Paternalism, Unconscionability Doctrine, and Accommodation" (offering a definition focused on the paternalist's attempt to substitute her judgment or agency for that of the person paternalized); Quong's "judgmental definition" of paternalism (*Liberalism Without Perfection*, 80); and, especially, Cornell, "A Third Theory of Paternalism." Cornell's account is closest to my own because he focuses on the external meaning of paternalistic actions rather than on the motive of the paternalist (which is Shiffrin and Quong's focus). See Cornell, "A Third Theory of Paternalism," 1308fn43. I use the formulation "on her own behalf" rather than the more common "for her own good" in order to preserve the possibility of classifying as paternalistic behaviors and policies whose aims seem to be broader than

their target's *own* welfare, happiness, or values. Like Shiffrin and Cornell, I believe that actions whose primary motive is to benefit someone other than the person paternalized can count as paternalistic (provided that they express the requisite negative judgment about the competence of the paternalized to decide or act in matters properly under her control). My definition could be amended specifically to include interventions that aim to benefit someone other than the agent herself (i.e., by eliminating the second condition's "on her own behalf" clause or substituting it with a condition like "in her legitimate sphere of agency," as Shiffrin does). I avoid doing so here in order to argue from a more widely accepted understanding of what paternalism involves. The "on her own behalf" formulation can be interpreted both narrowly (as equivalent to the popular "for her own good" formulation) or broadly (in line with Shiffrin's definition). My argument that philanthropy can be paternalistic relies only on the narrower interpretation but is compatible with either (although the choice of interpretations will affect the class of cases that count as examples of paternalism).

6. See, e.g., G. Dworkin, "Paternalism"; Arneson, "Mill versus Paternalism"; de Marneffe, "Avoiding Paternalism"; and Richardson, "Only in the Ballpark of Paternalism." On the other hand, for arguments that coercion or liberty limitation is not a necessary feature of paternalism, see Gert and Culver, "Paternalistic Behavior"; Shiffrin, "Paternalism"; Quong, *Liberalism Without Perfection*; Cornell, "Third Theory of Paternalism"; and Tsai, "Rational Persuasion as Paternalism." A middle case is Sunstein and Thaler's "libertarian paternalism," which accepts the possibility of noncoercive paternalism but denies that such paternalism is generally objectionable in the ways that coercive paternalism is (Thaler and Sunstein, *Nudge*).

7. See, e.g., Shiffrin, "Paternalism"; and Quong, *Liberalism Without Perfection*. For persuasive argument *against* the view that motive is the important aspect of paternalistic behavior, see Cornell, "Third Theory of Paternalism."

8. Shiffrin, for example, claims that paternalism "manifests an attitude of disrespect" and that "paternalist doctrines and policies convey a special, generally impermissible, insult to autonomous agents" (Shiffrin, "Paternalism," 220 and 207). Quong claims that paternalism is wrong "because of the way it denies someone's moral status as a free and equal citizen" (*Liberalism Without Perfection*, 74). Quong's specific argument is framed in Rawlsian terms: He argues that liberalism is committed to a conception of citizens as free and equal; paternalistic actions are inconsistent with such a conception because "paternalism involves one person or group denying that another person or group has the necessary capacity, in a given context, to exercise the second of the two moral powers: the capacity to plan, revise, and rationally pursue their own conception of the good. To treat someone paternalistically is thus (at least temporarily) to treat that person as if he or she lacks the second moral power. This means there is always a strong moral reason not to treat a sane adult paternalistically, and this is why paternalism is *prima facie* wrong" (101). Shiffrin and Quong attribute the insult or manifestation of

disrespect to the *motive* of the paternalist; I agree with Cornell that the "external meaning of the behavior," rather than the subjective motivation of the paternalist, is what accounts for the insult and for paternalism's presumptive wrongness. (See especially Cornell, "Third Theory," 1308, n43.) Cornell places the insulting expressive content of paternalistic behavior front and center, arguing that "Paternalistic actions imply that the actor knows better than the subject with regard to a matter within the subject's sphere of control, and paternalistic actions are impermissible insofar as this expression is offensive. That is, paternalism is impermissible to the extent that it expresses something insulting" (Cornell, "Third Theory," 1314–15).

9. Hill, "Homes of the London Poor," 12.

10. Ibid., 12.

11. Zelizer, *Social Meaning of Money*, 131.

12. For example, Milton Friedman rejects public housing programs with the argument that they "can be justified, if at all, only on grounds of paternalism; that the families being helped 'need' housing more than they 'need' other things but would themselves either not agree or would spend the money unwisely. The liberal will be inclined to reject this argument for responsible adults" (Friedman, *Capitalism and Freedom*, 178). Friedman makes a similar argument against Social Security programs (or the "compulsory purchase of annuities"), and defends a negative income tax partly on the grounds that it avoids the paternalism of other social welfare programs. More recently, Matt Zwolinski criticizes the welfare state in its current form as "heavily paternalistic": "benefits are often given in-kind rather than in cash precisely because the state doesn't trust welfare recipients to make what it regards as wise choices about how to spend their money (Zwolinski, "The Pragmatic Libertarian Case for a Basic Income Guarantee").

13. Himmelfarb, *Poverty and Compassion*, 7.

14. See, e.g., Katz, *In the Shadow of the Poorhouse*, 79 and 165; Zelizer, *Social Meaning of Money*, 119–42; and Huyssen, *Progressive Inequality*, 64–66 and 76–80.

15. Richmond, "Friendly Visiting Among the Poor," 47.

16. Carnegie, "The Gospel of Wealth," 16.

17. Ibid., 17. The latter judgment follows in part from Carnegie's view that "those worthy of assistance, except in rare cases, seldom require assistance. The really valuable men of the race never do, except in case of accident or sudden change."

18. Ibid.

19. See, e.g., Fleishman, *The Foundation*, 99–102 and 118.

20. See, e.g., Letts, Ryan, and Grossman, "Virtuous Capital: What Foundations Can Learn from Venture Capitalists"; and Bishop and Green, *Philanthrocapitalism: How the Rich Can Save the World*.

21. Zunz, *Philanthropy in America*, 19.

22. Buteau et al., "New Attitudes, Old Practices," 10. The report also notes that program officers report "the existing relationship the foundation has with a

grantee" as the most important factor in decisions about whether to provide multiyear GOS, and that this factor "can disadvantage organizations led by people of color," which are less likely to enjoy established relationships with funders (11).

23. Mill, *On Liberty*, 223. The concept of an "exercise of power" is potentially much broader than that of coercion or liberty infringement, but the qualifier "against his will" implies a narrower definition of prohibited acts.

24. G. Dworkin, "Paternalism," 65.

25. Feinberg, "Legal Paternalism." See note 6 above for other authors who accept coercion or liberty restriction as a necessary feature of paternalistic behavior.

26. Feinberg, "Legal Paternalism," 123.

27. Ibid.

28. Tim Evans, "Indiana Food Bank Reaches Compromise on Prayer," *USA Today*, March 29, 2012, http://usatoday30.usatoday.com/news/nation/story/2012 -03-29/indiana-food-bank-prayers/53868650/1. The eventual compromise, which restored the food bank's eligibility for federal assistance, had volunteers wait to suggest prayer until after food was distributed, with a view to "removing any hint of a religious requirement to get the free government food, preserving the constitutional separation of church and state." Of course, the constitutional issue is distinct from the moral one: even if no public funds were involved, one might worry that requesting prayer before distributing food aid is exploitive. And, assuming that many food recipients foresee repeated visits to the food bank, it is not clear that moving the request for prayer until after (each) distribution solves the problem.

29. See the influential account in Nozick, "Coercion."

30. For a discussion of an analogous nonphilanthropic case, of unfair and therefore exploitative offers in circumstances of unequal bargaining power, see Wertheimer, *Exploitation*.

31. Importantly, it also need not rely on full agreement about what goods are owed to whom, by whom, as a matter of justice.

32. The possibility of noncoercive paternalism has been defended by "libertarian paternalists" who argue that public and private policymakers can use "nudges" and "choice architecture" to promote welfare without coercing or actually removing options from the people so influenced. For libertarian paternalists, coercion is what makes the standard examples of paternalistic interventions *objectionable*, not what makes them *paternalistic*. Like many authors, Thaler and Sunstein assume that the chief moral pitfall of (traditional, nonlibertarian) paternalism is the element of coercion; correspondingly, they assume that removing the element of coercion sanitizes their own ("libertarian," "nudging") form of paternalism. By contrast, I argue that paternalism can exist without coercion or option restriction *and that it remains presumptively wrong* in such cases. See Thaler and Sunstein, *Nudge*, 10–11.

33. One of the most sustained investigations of incentives as a form of power is Grant, *Strings Attached*. Grant recognizes that "Incentives always present people

with choices, but they can be an affront to their autonomy at the same time" (12). Grant's argument that incentives can operate as a form of power and as an affront to autonomy is, not coincidentally, accompanied by a definition of paternalism that does not focus on coercion: "Paternalism can be described as treating another person as if he is incapable of recognizing for himself what his purposes ought to be or of rationally pursuing them" (57).

34. Here I differ somewhat from Cornell: I do not think that the element of insult on its own suffices to ground our objections to paternalism (*pace* his claim that "paternalism is wrong because it constitutes an insult, and that is all that needs to be said" ["Third Theory," 1297]). Not all insulting appraisals of a person's competence are paternalistic; recognizing this, Cornell later specifies that paternalism also requires "at least the superficial appearance of providing aid" (1316). But why does (at least the superficial appearance of) providing aid change the character and moral weight of an insulting expression? In my view, it must be because our concern with paternalism is a concern not just with insults but with insulting *ways of exercising power* (and, as I argue in the next section, with subordinating relationships).

35. To the degree that both the food bank's clients and (importantly) other observers are unaware of the rationale, some of the negative relational effects of paternalism might be mitigated: the audience(s) matter for how subversive we should expect an insult to be of people's equal status. But people can be treated disrespectfully even without themselves recognizing it.

36. Cornell, "Third Theory," 1309.

37. Actions can express a negative judgment without that judgment being a part of the actor's motivation. Perhaps someone donates in-kind goods simply out of unthinking habit or in deference to common practice; nevertheless, depending on contextual factors and the alternatives available to her, this behavior can still be objectionably paternalistic. On the other hand, actors may be *motivated* by the kinds of negative judgments that characterize paternalism without their *behavior* expressing the relevant kind of disrespect. Perhaps someone makes an unconditional philanthropic gift, privately motivated by the thought that the recipients are too stupid or immature to accept a gift with restrictions or too incompetent to meet any conditions that the donor would consider attaching. Even if the donor's motivation is contemptuous, it would be odd to classify her *behavior* as paternalistic.

38. Quong, for example, defines paternalism as any act attempting "to improve the welfare, good, happiness, needs, interests, or values" of another agent with respect to a particular decision or situation the agent faces, "motivated by a *negative judgement*" about that agent's ability "to make the right decision or manage the particular situation in a way that will effectively advance [her] welfare, good, happiness, needs, interests, or values" (*Liberalism Without Perfection*, 80). Officially, this is a definition that turns on the intentions of the paternalist, but, recognizing that "it may seem inaccurate to speak of a government's or state's *motivation* for

passing specific pieces of legislation," Quong stipulates that "the term motivation can be used to refer to a government's or state's *rationale* or *justification* for each piece of legislation" (80n21). This shrinks the distance between motivation and expression considerably: rationale and justification are features that need to be assessed with reference to characteristics of the legislation itself, its context, and its effects, and not only the subjective intentions of government actors.

39. This is in line with Waldron's argument that Mill's harm principle as it applies to government is best understood as "a test of legislative intent," and that assessing legislative intent requires us to consider facts about the framing, design, and impact of a law's provisions, not just its stated purpose. See Waldron, "Mill on Liberty and on the Contagious Diseases Acts," 33–34.

40. Waldron, "Mill on Liberty and on the Contagious Diseases Acts," sketches parallel questions that we might ask to elucidate the intent of coercive government legislation, and my account here draws on his.

41. Thompson, *Political Ethics and Public Office*, 153.

42. Ibid.

43. Of course, donor conditionality can also constrain the options of people working at recipient organizations. Since this is one form that paternalism may take, it raises the interesting possibility that nonprofit staff may be paternalized when their actions are constrained by conditional gifts to their institutions (e.g., social service agencies, hospitals, universities). I do not pursue this possibility here. Vindicating it would require appealing to a controversially broad characterization of paternalism, since the staff and experts putatively paternalized here are generally the instruments rather than the objects of donors' benevolence. But the argument that donor behavior toward recipient organizations can be paternalistic is clearly available to Shiffrin, who claims that "Behavior may be paternalist if the motive behind it is simply that the (putative) paternalist knows better than the agent, or may better implement, what the agent has authority for doing herself. An action may be paternalist . . . if it involves a person's aiming to take over or control what is properly within the agent's own legitimate domain of judgment or action." ("Paternalism," 216). This means that "paternalism may occur when a person's concern is to ensure that a project or aim is acquitted properly, if she pursues this concern by substituting her perceived superior judgment or agency for that of the agent who has legitimate control over the project" (217). This aspect of Shiffrin's characterization of paternalism is not widely accepted, since it seems to many authors to have counterintuitively expansive implications for what counts as paternalism. Shiffrin's view strikes me as right in at least some contexts (e.g., it seems right to say that one can sometimes act in objectionably paternalistic ways toward a parent by interfering with her parenting). But the usurpation of judgment and authority can also take forms other than paternalism, and this may be a better way of understanding donor influence over recipient organizations and their employees. Still, since a usurpation of judgment or action is often

an important feature of paternalistic behaviors and policies, it is worth noting as potentially morally significant in this context. Elsewhere, Shiffrin herself raises concerns about foundation grants compromising "recipients' independence and governance procedures," without characterizing the problem as one of paternalism ("The Power and Influence of Grantors").

44. That is, set aside any nonpaternalistic justifications for Prohibition.

45. For a more general argument that "moral responsibility and blame need not be conceived as fixed sums" to be divided between participating actors, see Beerbohm, *In Our Name*, 14. Among Beerbohm's immediate targets is Kamm's argument that moral responsibility is "fully transferable" (so that, for example, a principal can be fully liable for an agent's wrongdoing, with the result that the agent can "permissibly act impermissibly"). See Kamm, *Intricate Ethics*, 311.

46. Again, this does not amount to a claim that paternalism is always wrong, all things considered; a concern for paternalism must be balanced against other values. We will be in a better position to do this once we have a clearer sense of how and why paternalism's (generally) negative moral weight can vary.

47. Quong, *Liberalism Without Perfection*, 101.

48. Ibid. Shiffrin and Cornell both make versions of this point as well. Unlike the "noncomparative" wrong described in the previous paragraph, Quong does not think that this comparative wrong characterizes all paternalistic acts toward sane adults.

49. Cf. Conly, who seems to make accuracy the criterion: "treating people in accordance with their actual abilities is not insulting or disrespectful. Recognition of our actual status is all respect can call for" (*Against Autonomy*, 42).

50. See Conly, *Against Autonomy*, 42. Of course, Conly claims that (even coercive) paternalism is very often morally appropriate. For an argument that paternalistic laws and policies are pro tanto wrong (when directed at competent agents) but that the paternalized's level of competence (above some minimum threshold) matters for the degree of pro tanto wrong, see McKay, "Basic Income, Cash Transfers, and Welfare State Paternalism," 439–40.

51. See, e.g., Thaler and Sunstein, *Nudge*; Conly, *Against Autonomy*; and Banerjee and Duflo, *Poor Economics*. Contrary to Quong, I think there are cases here where the comparative wrong of paternalism can exist without the noncomparative one; there may be no denial of moral status in recognizing some absolute (and widely shared) limitations on our competence, so that concerns about paternalism sometimes arise *only* from behaviors and policies that express comparative judgments.

52. While paternalism and the comparative wrong that it involves need not be group based, I take it that this is a common and practically important exacerbating condition.

53. I briefly discuss the same case in Saunders-Hastings, "Benevolent Giving and the Problem of Paternalism," 119. There, the case appears in the context of an argument about when and why evidence-based, welfare-oriented models of

philanthropy (as promoted by the effective altruism movement) can be objectionably paternalistic.

54. As discussed in the previous chapter, these are all ideas that are or have been popular among philanthropists involved in U.S. primary and secondary education (and among education reformers more broadly).

55. See Rooks, *Cutting School* (especially ch. 2); and Scott, "Venture Philanthropy and Charter Schools." Both note that the Rosenwald schools—despite improving in important ways on the status quo of public non-investment in education for Black children—also "began a pattern whereby groups that were not themselves poor or of color proposed educational curricula and forms offered only to Blacks and the poor" (Rooks, *Cutting School*, 50).

56. James Dator, "LeBron James Opened a Public School in Akron for At-Risk Kids," SB Nation, July 30, 2018, https://www.sbnation.com/nba/2018/7/30/17 629560/lebron-james-i-promise-school-akron.

57. LeBron James (@KingJames), speaking in a video uploaded to Uninterrupted (@uninterrupted) Twitter account, Twitter, July 29, 2018, 3:00 p.m., https:// twitter.com/uninterrupted/status/1023644408397193216?s=20.

58. This is not to say that the donor's identity or personal history, and plausible expressions of solidarity flowing from either, are the only relevant factors; it still matters, for instance, what kind of school James sends his own children to.

59. See GiveDirectly, "Values," accessed March 18, 2014, http://www.givedirectly .org/values.php.

60. Banerjee and Duflo, *Poor Economics*, 66. Emphasis added.

61. Ben-Porath, *Tough Choices*, 11. Emphasis added.

62. I do not mean to suggest that these are the only constraints: respect for property rights or a commitment to toleration may likewise limit the ways that third parties can permissibly respond to objectionable paternalism.

Chapter Five

1. Both of these, but especially mass philanthropy, can be either one-off cases (e.g., donations to post-9/11 relief organizations, the ALS "ice bucket challenge") or ongoing ventures (e.g., Oxfam)—as can elite philanthropy (e.g., Mark Zuckerberg's donation to Newark schools versus the Broad Foundation). In some of what follows, I use the terms *mass* and *associational philanthropy* interchangeably (since many cases of high-volume, small-dollar-amount philanthropy count as both). But what I take to be distinctive about mass philanthropy is simply the large number of donors, whereas what is distinctive about associational philanthropy is the organizational structure (even if relatively small numbers of people are involved).

2. For 2019, foundation giving accounted for $75.69 billion (17 percent) of a total $449.64 billion in charitable giving by individuals, corporations, foundations,

and bequests; the largest share ($309.66 billion, or 69 percent) continues to come from individuals (*Giving USA 2020*, 31). (Of course, not all individual giving is from small donors: some is by the very rich.)

3. Pevnick, "Democratizing the Nonprofit Sector," 279.

4. Ibid., 279.

5. Ibid., 280.

6. For an argument about the normative standards that should guide (and be used to evaluate) the exercise of power by international humanitarian NGOs, and Oxfam in particular, see Rubenstein, "The Misuse of Power, Not Bad Representation" and *Between Samaritans and States*, chapter 5.

7. Over the five-year period between 2015 and 2019, giving to religious organizations accounted for 30.5 percent of total charitable giving (from all sources). For comparison, the education sector is the second-largest beneficiary of charitable contributions, receiving about 14 percent of total donations (*Giving USA 2020*, 66).

8. Minow, *Partners, Not Rivals*, 13.

9. Ibid.

10. Ibid., 14. These problems are exacerbated by "charitable choice" legislation in the United States, which permits government to contract with religious organizations for the provision of welfare and health services, and to fund religious providers on the same basis as secular ones. This means that government may sometimes fund (say) a Catholic health care provider *instead* of secular ones.

11. For a more general argument about privatization's threat to legitimacy, see Cordelli, *The Privatized State*.

12. See Cordelli, "Democratizing Organized Religion," for an argument for a pro tanto right to democracy *within* religious institutions; for the converse argument against requiring congruence with democratic norms from churches or other civil society groups, see Rosenblum, *Membership and Morals* and Levy, *Rationalism, Pluralism, and Freedom*. I am not taking a position on whether there is a prima facie case for (or pro tanto right to) congruence with democratic norms within civil society (including religious) organizations and institutions: my concern here is with the forms of power that such groups can exercise over people who have not chosen to affiliate with them or to fund them.

13. "DonorsChoose Mission Statement," DonorsChoose, accessed May 8, 2015, http://www.donorschoose.org/about. This language appears to have been removed from the DonorsChoose website but remains in its online video advertising. See DonorsChoose, "How It Works—DonorsChoose.org," DonorsChoose, posted on July 8, 2015, YouTube video, 1:16:00, https://www.youtube.com/watch?v=ESZHrzp0dR0.

14. Emilia Murphy, "Get Your Project Funded: The 4 Essential Steps," DonorsChoose, May 1, 2018, https://www.donorschoose.org/blog/get-your-classroom-project-funded/.

15. Julia Prieto, "How We Leverage Gratitude to Drive a Business Model," DonorsChoose, November 24, 2015, https://www.donorschoose.org/blog/power-of

-student-thank-you-notes/. Prieto, then director of Donor Appreciation at the organization, adds the following story to her discussion of the merits of the thank-you practice: "We recently received an inquiry from a teacher whose classroom was exempt from creating thank-yous. This happens in rare cases when no $50 donors opt in. This teacher wasn't having that. She wrote in to us demanding that her students create thank-yous for *someone*. In her adamant words, 'It's only right!' We'd like to thank her for saying what we were all thinking." As of this writing, DonorsChoose's student thank-you note program is paused due to the COVID-19 pandemic but is expected to resume sometime after July 2021 ("Guidelines for Student Thank-You Notes," DonorsChoose, accessed March 15, 2021, https://help .donorschoose.org/hc/en-us/articles/201936706).

16. Scholars of civil society who disagree on many other important points agree about this. See, e.g., Putnam, *Bowling Alone*; and Skocpol, "Advocates without Members" and *Diminished Democracy*.

17. See, e.g., Mill, *Subjection*, 330 (he writes that the mistakes associated with short-sighted benevolence are less likely to be made by women who "have actually the practical management of schemes of beneficence. . . . But women who only give their money, and are not brought face to face with the effects it produces, how can they be expected to foresee them?"). For a more detailed discussion of this passage and of Mill's views on women's philanthropy in general, see chapter 2 and Saunders-Hastings, "No Better to Give Than to Receive."

18. See, e.g., Brakman Reiser, "Dismembering Civil Society," 830; and Brody, "Agents without Principals," 486.

19. Burns, Schlozman, and Verba find that, for both men and women, "charitable or social service" organizations represent by far the most common organizational affiliation (with 45 percent of women and 43 percent of men affiliated with at least one). Burns, Schlozman, and Verba, *Private Roots of Public Action*, 76.

20. Ibid., 78.

21. Ibid. Among those affiliated, only 15 percent of women and 12 percent of men had attended a meeting within twelve months of being surveyed. For comparison, the percentages of both men and women affiliated who had attended meetings were above 50 percent (and sometimes far above 50 percent) for the following categories of associations: "'religious,' 'business, professional,' 'literary, art, study,' 'hobby, sports, leisure,' and 'neighborhood, homeowners.'"

22. Eikenberry, *Giving Circles*, ix.

23. Ibid., x.

24. Tocqueville, *Democracy in America*, vol. 1, 393.

25. Ibid., 597.

26. Ibid., 598.

27. On the former, see especially Putnam, *Bowling Alone*, chap. 7. On the latter, see, e.g., Barber, "Searching for Civil Society"; Schambra, "By the People"; and Michael Barone, "The Road Back to Tocqueville: At Last, 19th Century

Values Stage a Revival," *Washington Post*, January 7, 1996. Skocpol criticizes the "zero-sum way of thinking that pits 'state' against 'society'—or the national state against local voluntarism," and argues that it is partly the product of Tocqueville's failure to recognize the American state's role in fostering civil society. See Skocpol, "The Tocqueville Problem," 459–63.

28. Tocqueville, *Democracy in America*, vol. 2, 595.

29. This is not to say that Tocqueville rejects the English version; as discussed in chapter 2, in his *Memoir on Pauperism*, he describes the advantages of private over public poor relief in England, in part by appealing to its superior effects on social relations.

30. Tocqueville, *Democracy in America*, vol. 2, 596.

31. Ibid.

32. Ibid., 598.

33. Ibid., 824.

34. Ibid., 585.

35. Ibid., 585–86 and 824.

36. Ibid., 593.

37. Ibid., 592.

38. Ibid., 596.

39. Ibid., 598. In *Making Democracy Work*, Putnam is attentive to this dimension of Tocqueville's analysis. Sabl emphasizes similar features of Tocqueville's account of American associations in his argument that community organizing is the most distinctively Tocquevillean form of political action. See Sabl, "Community Organizing as Tocquevillean Politics." I discuss the contrasts between philanthropy and community organizing in the following section.

40. See, e.g., Piketty and Saez, "Income Inequality in the United States"; and Piketty, *Capital in the Twenty-First Century*.

41. The best-known valorizations of selfless and anonymous giving are religious. In the Sermon on the Mount, Jesus warns his listeners to "take heed that ye do not your alms before men, to be seen of them: otherwise ye have no reward of your Father which is in heaven. Therefore when thou doest thine alms, do not sound a trumpet before thee, as the hypocrites do. . . . But when thou doest alms, let not thy left hand know what thy right hand doeth: that thine alms may be in secret: and thy Father which seeth in secret himself shall reward thee openly" (Matthew 6:1–4, KJV). In his ranking of the degrees of charity, Maimonides also stresses the superiority of anonymous giving and especially of giving where *neither* the benefactor nor the recipient know each other's identity. See Moses Maimonides, *Mishneh Torah*, 7.10:7–10.

42. In his discussion of beneficence, Kant notes that some people might give from inclination rather than from duty and that such giving lacks moral worth. See Kant, *Groundwork for the Metaphysics of Morals*, 4:398–99. Anonymous giving would not solve Kant's problem—givers' motives would still be inscrutable and

suspect—but would at least mitigate the contaminating influence of "the inclina-tion to honor." Utilitarian theories, in contrast, are generally indifferent to the content of the giver's motivations: if public praise of the rich is efficient in shaking off large donations, so much the better.

43. Wiesel, *A Passover Haggadah*, 24.

44. Some of the same features—double anonymity, genuinely reciprocal chances of mutual need, and broadly distributed capacity to help—appear in practices of blood donation, another gift relationship that avoids significant threats to social equality. See chapter 2 for discussion of social theories of blood donation, which often regard blood as a good appropriately supplied philanthropically.

45. This is contingent on other contextual factors; our overall judgments of the practice should depend on the feasible alternatives (e.g., it would be more difficult to see the collection box arrangement as expressing respect if it survived mainly because the rich preferred it to taxation and the public provision of goods to which the poor were entitled).

46. Eliasoph, *Making Volunteers*, xi.

47. Ibid., x.

48. Ibid., 17.

49. Ibid., 17.

50. Ibid., 11.

51. This is a major way in which Wiesel's story differs from some contemporary arrangements that might otherwise be thought of as, in effect, big collection boxes. Donors to a local food bank or the United Way may not give anonymously, but most receive minimal public recognition and remain unknown to recipients. But recipients cannot make anonymous withdrawals, and there is not the same attempt to frame the transaction as a reciprocal exchange between citizens: the receiving institution plays a mediating role and makes the decisions about how and to whom to disburse benefits.

52. Rosenblum, *Good Neighbors*, 213.

53. Tocqueville, *Democracy in America*, vol. 2, 596.

54. Rebecca Solnit, "'The Way We Get through This Is Together': The Rise of Mutual Aid under Coronavirus," *Guardian*, May 14, 2020, https://www.theguard ian.com/world/2020/may/14/mutual-aid-coronavirus-pandemic-rebecca-solnit.

55. Quoted in Jia Tolentino, "What Mutual Aid Can Do during a Pandemic," *New Yorker*, May 18, 2020.

56. Jodi Kantor and Catrin Einhorn, "Canadians Adopted Refugee Families for a Year. Then Came 'Month 13,'" *New York Times*, March 25, 2017, https://www.ny times.com/2017/03/25/world/canada/syrian-refugees.html.

57. Reich, *Just Giving*, 197.

58. Most Americans (79 percent) support abortion in at least some circum-stances, according to a 2020 Gallup poll; this level of support has been stable over the past decade (see "Abortion," Gallup News, accessed December 19, 2020, https://

news.gallup.com/poll/1576/abortion.aspx). State-by-state analysis of the 2016 Coop-erative Congressional Election Statistics by Data for Progress estimated that sup-port for banning abortion does not reach 25 percent in any state in the country (https://twitter.com/DataProgress/status/1128481533273178112). Despite this, in 2019, Alabama passed a near-total ban on abortion, and states including Louisiana, Geor-gia, Kentucky, Mississippi, Missouri, and Ohio passed laws banning abortion after the first six to eight weeks of pregnancy; none of these laws included exceptions for cases of rape and incest. See Leah C. Stokes, "Alabama State Legislators Are Wrong about Their Voters' Opinions on Abortion," *Monkey Cage* (blog), *Washington Post*, May 28, 2019, https://www.washingtonpost.com/politics/2019/05/28/alabama-state -legislators-are-wrong-about-their-voters-opinions-abortion/; Eric Levenson, "Abor-tion Laws in the US: Here Are the States Pushing to Restrict Access," CNN, May 30, 2019, https://www.cnn.com/2019/05/16/politics/states-abortion-laws/index.html. Sim-ilarly, some gun control measures, such as universal background checks, enjoy ro-bust (and bipartisan) public support, consistently polling above 80 percent, but laws closing the existing loopholes for private gun sales have faltered both feder-ally and in many states. See, e.g., Lydia Saad, "Americans Widely Support Tighter Regulations on Gun Sales," Gallup News, October 17, 2017, https://news.gallup .com/poll/220637/americans-widely-support-tighter-regulations-gun-sales.aspx.

59. This is not to say that there would be no place for the philanthropic provi-sion of minority-supported public goods under genuinely democratic or majori-tarian institutions: pluralism would remain an important value, and philanthropy could be a useful way to fund public goods that democratic governments or majori-ties do not wish to fund.

60. Consider the rapid pace at which MacKenzie Scott began donating her for-tune, after her divorce from Jeff Bezos; over four months in 2020, she moved over $4 billion to charities and social movement organizations (including to many Black-led organizations with a focus on racial justice issues). See Sophie Alexander and Ben Steverman, "MacKenzie Scott Gives Away $4.2 Billion in Four Months," Bloom-berg News, December 15, 2020, https://www.bloomberg.com/news/articles/2020-12-15 /mackenzie-scott-gives-away-4-2-billion-within-four-months. Scott's giving is remark-able not only for its scale but for its focus on upfront, unrestricted donations that charities and social movement organizations can use immediately and as seems best to them. In this respect, it stands a better chance of supporting democratic relation-ships than many other prominent examples of elite philanthropy.

61. Sabl, "Community Organizing as Tocquevillean Politics," 2.

62. On Alinsky as an "unwitting protégé" of Addams, see Maurice Hamington, "Community Organizing: Addams and Alinsky." Hamington suggests that we can account for the overlap in part by the fact that "Addams and Hull House helped shape the sociology department at the university of Chicago, which in turn influ-enced Alinsky's approach to community organizing" (265).

63. Sabl, "Community Organizing," 5.

64. Phulwani, "The Poor Man's Machiavelli," 863–64.

65. Ibid., 864.

66. For example, when Ella Baker and George Schuyler founded the Young Negroes' Cooperative League (YNCL) in 1930, they refused to accept donations from charitable foundations (Ransby, *Ella Baker and the Black Freedom Movement*, 82–84). Baker consistently held that effective organizing required building relationships within particular communities and empowering community members in decision-making processes rather than power resting with outside actors—even activists (ibid., 270). On this theme, see also Incite!, *The Revolution Will Not Be Funded*; and Kohl-Arenas, *The Self-Help Myth*.

67. For an account of community organizing in post–Katrina New Orleans, including organizers' efforts to build ties of mutual accountability and solidarity across cleavages and to correct (rather than replicate) democratic deficits in public institutions, see Stout, *Blessed Are the Organized*.

68. Compare Fung's argument that "participatory democracy has always been, at its core, a way to realize the ideal of self-government," and that this is a reason for rather than against making participatory processes public rather than leaving them solely within the realm of civil society: "When participation is limited to the voluntary sphere of associations, as it has been for resistance and civic-engagement scholars, the reach of citizen participation is arbitrarily truncated to exclude those sites of public decision making that deeply affect ordinary individuals." See Fung, "Associations and Democracy," 533.

Chapter Six

1. Luke 10:29 (KJV).

2. Luke 10:33–37 (KJV).

3. I will retain the understanding of philanthropy that I have been using throughout: private gifts of time and money, whether the gifts are to individuals (e.g., "direct-giving programs" and, for the sake of argument, online microlending programs such as Kiva, though the status of the latter as "gifts" is ambiguous); to nonprofits and NGOs (e.g., Northern NGOs conducting operations in the South, Southern NGOs funded by Northern money, and "federated" INGOs with national chapters, such as Oxfam, Amnesty International, and *Médecins sans frontières*); or to governments and intergovernmental institutions (e.g., gifts to a country's public health agency, or Ted Turner's gifts to the UN).

4. See especially Singer, "Famine, Affluence, and Morality," *The Life You Can Save*, and *The Most Good You Can Do*. Singer's 1972 article spawned a vast literature on the ethics of voluntary giving, inspired both by Singer's conclusions and his argumentative strategy (relying on hypothetical interpersonal cases). See especially Unger, *Living High and Letting Die*.

5. Or, in a much weaker framing of the principle, "without thereby sacrificing anything morally significant" (Singer, "Famine, Affluence, and Morality," 231). Singer himself endorses the stronger version. Brian Barry suggests that the weaker version is "useless," since even small increments of pain or inconvenience (e.g., from getting one's clothes muddy) may have *some* moral significance—to a Benthamite utilitarian, for example ("Humanity and Justice in Global Perspective," 224–25).

6. See, e.g., Singer, "What Should a Billionaire Give?" and *The Life You Can Save*. These recent arguments ought probably to be interpreted as Singer writing "esoterically" and attempting to avoid the potentially counterproductive consequences of "overdemandingness" (the most common objection to his arguments). He has not recanted his original argument that one *ought* to give until further giving would render one worse off than the people one is trying to help.

7. See Barry, "Humanity and Justice."

8. There are further divisions among liberal egalitarians concerning the reasons that duties of global distributive justice exist. Some tie these reasons to claims that a "basic structure" exists internationally (e.g., Beitz, *Political Theory and International Relations*) or that coercive global arrangements harm the global poor and violate negative duties that rich countries and their citizens have (e.g., Pogge, *World Poverty and Human Rights*). Others hold that obligations of distributive justice exist between human beings, without regard to institutional relationships (e.g., Tan, *Justice without Borders*; and Caney, *Justice beyond Borders*).

9. Rawls holds that the demands of egalitarian distributive justice arise only between people who share a (domestic) institutional "basic structure" and who jointly participate in a system of (domestic) social cooperation (Rawls, *Law of Peoples*, especially 113–20). Nagel argues that it is a mistake to speak of demands of justice at all at the international level. Justice is an "associative obligation": it arises from "a special involvement of agency" and "engagement of the will . . . in the dual role each member [of society] plays both as one of the society's subjects and as one of those in whose name its authority is exercised" (Nagel, "The Problem of Global Justice," 128). Nagel argues that this special engagement of agency and will, and the claim to exercise authority in another's name, requires sovereignty as an enabling condition. Some of Nagel's critics share an associative view of justice but argue that the kind of relationships required for obligations of justice to arise can occur across state borders—for example, through relationships of international trade, lending, and investment and the international institutions that regulate them (e.g., Cohen and Sabel, "Extra Rempublicam Nulla Justitia?"; and Julius, "Nagel's Atlas").

10. The line is spoken by Montague Tigg in *Martin Chuzzlewit* (ch. 27).

11. Pogge, "How International Nongovernmental Organizations Should Act," 58–59.

12. "What Is Effective Altruism," Center for Effective Altruism, https://www.centreforeffectivealtruism.org/. For other important definitional statements by

proponents of effective altruism, see Singer, *The Most Good You Can Do*; and MacAskill, *Doing Good Better* and "The Definition of Effective Altruism."

13. For example, policy activism around animal welfare and risks to the long-term future (e.g., from climate change and threats relating to artificial intelligence) are also long-standing areas of interest for effective altruists. One effective altruist organization, 80,000 Hours, aims to help people choose careers with a view to doing the most good possible with one's time (which sometimes, but by no means always, leads to recommendations to seek highly paid careers in order to enable larger charitable contributions).

14. Singer's own The Life You Can Save initiative has already been mentioned. Another well-known effective altruist organization is Giving What We Can (www .givingwhatwecan.org), founded in 2009 by Oxford University ethicist Toby Ord. The latter organization's pledge is somewhat more demanding for lower- and middle-income donors: it promotes a pledge of at least 10 percent of one's income to fight global poverty. On Singer's sliding scale, this tithe is recommended as the minimum donation only for people with annual incomes of $500,000 or more. Both pledges should be distinguished from the Gates-Buffett–led Giving Pledge (www .givingpledge.org), which entails a commitment to dedicate the majority of one's wealth to philanthropy but requires neither that the money be given on an annual basis (or even in one's own lifetime) nor that it be directed to organizations that are demonstrably efficient at promoting welfare or other impartial values. It is therefore significantly less demanding (apart from requiring that signatories be billionaires).

15. More information, and charity rankings, available at www.givewell.org. GiveWell estimates that, in 2018, it moved some $161 million in donations to its recommended charities, including nearly $80 million in grants from (or funded by) Good Ventures (a close partner of GiveWell, and the giving vehicle of Cari Tuna and her husband, Facebook and Asana co-founder Dustin Moscowitz); $18.6 million from other donors giving $1 million or more; and $42.4 million in grants from smaller donors. The remainder (about $20 million) represents GiveWell's "best guess" of additional donations made due to its recommendations (but not made through GiveWell and not reported to GiveWell or to the recommended charity as having been made due to GiveWell's recommendation). The vast majority of these donations went toward health programs in poor countries: over half (52.7 percent) went to two organizations operating antimalaria programs, while another 24.8 percent went to deworming programs. The largest share of nonhealth donations (11.1 percent) went to GiveDirectly, an organization that makes direct cash transfers to poor households. GiveWell, "GiveWell Metrics Report—2018 Annual Review," accessed September 20, 2020, https://files.givewell.org/files/metrics /GiveWell_Metrics_Report_2018.pdf.

16. MacAskill's book features a blurb from Bill Gates, praising the author as a "data nerd after my own heart"; Singer, for his part, has called Bill and Melinda

Gates and Warren Buffett "the most effective altruists in history" (Singer, "The Why and How of Effective Altruism").

17. Banerjee and Duflo, *Poor Economics*, 5.

18. Ibid., 3.

19. Ibid., 3.

20. For examples of the former criticism (all in essays reviewing books by Singer, MacAskill, or both), see, e.g., Gray, "How & How Not to Be Good"; Srinivasan, "Stop the Robot Apocalypse"; and Lichtenberg, "Peter Singer's Extremely Altruistic Heirs." I discuss the latter criticism—that effective altruism neglects systemic or institutional change—below at note 58.

21. MacAskill, "The Definition of Effective Altruism," 15–17.

22. I develop the argument that effective altruism and other welfare-oriented approaches to giving can be objectionably paternalistic in Saunders-Hastings, "Benevolent Giving and the Problem of Paternalism." The analysis in this paragraph and the next draws on that chapter's arguments.

23. Note that there are two distinct issues here: whether undemocratic or paternalizing giving will produce greater welfare benefits and whether undemocratic or paternalizing giving will produce greater *measurable* welfare benefits. The latter condition might hold even where the former does not—for example, if EA-favored instruments for measuring giving, such as randomized controlled trials (RCTs), register some important contributors to welfare (e.g., short-term health outcomes) with more precision than others. That is, if effective altruism and other welfare-maximizing approaches have relational blind spots, this could be a product of their favored research methodologies and not only of their conception of the good(s) to be pursued through giving. For criticisms of the limitations and blind spots of RCTs, see, e.g., Reddy, "Economics' Biggest Success Story Is a Cautionary Tale"; Deaton, "Randomization in the Tropics"; and Clough, "Effective Altruism's Political Blind Spot."

24. Pummer, "Whether and Where to Give," 78. For a related argument, see Horton, "The All or Nothing Problem." For criticism of a "conditional obligation" to give effectively, see Sinclair, "Are We Conditionally Obligated to Be Effective Altruists?"

25. Pummer, "Whether and Where to Give," 84. This principle is later extended to cover cases in which it is only slightly costlier to perform the better act (e.g., because of a donor's personal preference for giving to a less effective charity).

26. MacAskill, "Definition of Effective Altruism," 14–15.

27. Including Kenya, Uganda, Rwanda, Liberia, Malawi, the Democratic Republic of the Congo, and Morocco. GiveDirectly has also operated disaster relief programs and (more recently) a coronavirus response fund in the United States.

28. See William MacAskill, "GiveWell's Recommendation of GiveDirectly," *Giving What We Can* (blog), November 30, 2012, https://www.givingwhatwecan.org/post/2012/11/givewells-recommendation-of-givedirectly/; Andreas Morgensen, "Why

We (Still) Don't Recommend GiveDirectly," *Giving What We Can* (blog), February 27, 2014, https://www.givingwhatwecan.org/post/2014/02/why-we-still-dont-recommend-givedirectly/.

29. MacAskill, *Doing Good Better*, 111.

30. Ibid.

31. Ibid., 115–16.

32. The "less" acknowledges that, on Shiffrin's definition of paternalism (as attempts to substitute one's judgment for that of the paternalized not only with regard to the latter's *own* good but also with regard to something that properly lies within her domain of authority), some such cases might still count as paternalistic. This would depend on claims about the appropriate loci and scope of authority within the family.

33. See, e.g., Clough, "Effective Altruism's Political Blind Spot"; Lisa Herzog, "(One of) Effective Altruism's Blind Spot(s), or: Why Moral Theory Needs Institutional Theory," *Justice Everywhere* (blog), October 21, 2015, http://justice-everywhere.org/international/one-of-effective-altruisms-blind-spots-or-why-moral-theory-needs-institutional-theory/.

34. MacAskill, *Doing Good Better*, 41–42.

35. Lichtenberg, "Peter Singer's Extremely Altruistic Heirs"; Srinivasan, "Stop the Robot Apocalypse."

36. To be clear, I take it that the morally relevant relationship is between MacAskill and the specific women whom he met, not between MacAskill and the Fistula Foundation; therefore, my suggestion that he might have reasons, grounded in respect or reciprocity, to donate to the Fistula Foundation would not extend very far into the future.

37. Whether effective altruists themselves can accept these arguments depends both on the degree to which hierarchical or paternalistic interventions lead to welfare improvements and on whether conceptions of the impersonal good to be promoted can incorporate considerations of relational equality. To the degree that egalitarian and antipaternalistic relationships are instrumentally important for promoting people's welfare (especially over the long term), effective altruists could agree about the general value of promoting such relationships. However, it is likely that in at least some cases there will be trade-offs between the demands of respect or relational equality and immediate welfare improvements.

38. Banerjee and Duflo, *Poor Economics*, 69–70.

39. Wenar, "Poverty Is No Pond." Consider New Incentives, an organization that received GiveWell's endorsement as a "top charity" for the first time in November 2020. New Incentives operates in North West Nigeria and offers conditional cash transfers (CCTs) to caregivers who bring infants to receive routine childhood vaccines (information available at newincentives.org). As GiveWell argues, this program has the potential to produce important welfare benefits by

increasing rates of immunization among children. On the other hand, GiveWell's report on New Incentives also notes some risks, including that of "caregivers bringing infants to receive the same vaccine multiple times within a short interval"; it estimates that "a relatively small percentage (roughly 10 percent) of children enrolled in the program receive repeated immunizations" and that the effects are unlikely to be life-threatening or cause serious harm ("New Incentives," November 2020, https://www.givewell.org/charities/new-incentives). As of December 15, 2020, New Incentives' website reports having enrolled over 240,000 infants in the program, so even GiveWell's "relatively small" 10 percent estimate would suggest that 24,000 infants have received repeated immunizations (and risked the associated side effects), presumably due to the economic incentives for their caregivers.

40. If international giving is an obligation of justice, this might compound the wrongs associated with philanthropic paternalism. To attach paternalistic conditions to the provision of something that I owe someone as a matter of justice is wrong, even on more restrictive definitions of paternalism than the one for which I argued in chapter 4. If, for example, one accepts the argument that citizens of rich countries are culpable of ongoing injustices or even rights violations against the global poor, many philanthropists might then be in the moral position of thieves attaching paternalistic conditions to the return of stolen goods (see, e.g., Pogge, *World Poverty and Human Rights* and "Severe Poverty as a Violation of Negative Duties"). However, internationally, as well as domestically, objectionable paternalism can occur without this aggravating condition.

41. As Barry puts it, "the crucial characteristic of justice is that the obligation to make the transfers required by it does not depend upon the use made of them by the recipient" ("Humanity and Justice in Global Perspective," 248).

42. Scanlon, "Preference and Urgency," 659.

43. Ibid., 659–60.

44. Rubenstein, "The Misuse of Power," 218. Clearly this definition would cover many actors beyond international NGOs, and Rubenstein leaves open the question of who else might be bound by the guidelines she sets out regarding how actors can avoid misusing their power. In particular, she does not say whether donors, as well as the operational NGOs that receive donations, must avoid misusing their power (and how).

45. Ibid., 223.

46. Ibid., 210. For examples of theorists who interpret INGOs as engaging in (unelected) representation, see Saward, "Authorisation and Authenticity"; and Montanaro, "The Democratic Legitimacy of Self-Appointed Representatives" and *Who Elected Oxfam?*

47. See Alcoff, "The Problem of Speaking for Others."

48. Freedom House consistently rates Botswana as "free." Although the country has held free elections since independence in 1966, its politics have been

dominated by the Botswana Democratic Party (BPD), raising some concerns about the competitiveness of elections.

49. The HIV prevalence rate among adults has improved since its peak around 2000 but is still estimated by UNAIDS to stand at 20.7 percent. (This number masks a significant gender disparity: among women aged 15–49, the estimated prevalence rate for 2019 was 25.1 percent, compared with 16.5 percent for men in the same age group.) UNAIDS, "Country Factsheet: Botswana 2019," accessed September 22, 2020, https://www.unaids.org/en/regionscountries/countries/botswana.

50. See Bill and Melinda Gates Foundation, "Working with Botswana to Confront Its Devastating AIDS Crisis," Bill and Melinda Gates Foundation, June 2006, https://docs.gatesfoundation.org/Documents/achap.pdf; Stover et al., "Estimated HIV Trends and Program Effects in Botswana"; and Ramiah and Reich, "Public-Private Partnerships and Antiretroviral Drugs for HIV/AIDS: Lessons from Botswana." Both the Stover and the Ramiah and Reich studies were funded by grants from ACHAP itself.

51. Charles Piller and Doug Smith, "Unintended Victims of Gates Foundation Generosity," *Los Angeles Times*, December 16, 2007, http://articles.latimes.com/2007/dec/16/nation/la-na-gates16dec16.

52. Interview (March 2004) quoted in Ramiah and Reich, "Building Effective Public-Private Partnerships," 400.

53. Ibid., 401.

54. Ibid., 400.

55. Sen, *Poverty and Famines*, 3. See also Drèze and Sen, *Hunger and Public Action*.

56. De Waal, *Famine Crimes*, 2. For concerns about welfare-oriented philanthropy displacing or subverting domestic accountability relations, see also Wenar, "Poverty Is No Pond"; Clough, "Effective Altruism's Political Blind Spot"; and Daron Acemoglu's and Angus Deaton's responses to Singer's essay, "The Logic of Effective Altruism," *Boston Review*, July 1, 2015. The latter two essays apply to effective altruism some arguments previously developed in relation to humanitarian and development aid generally (i.e., including aid from foreign governments and multilateral agencies); see Acemoglu and Robinson, *Why Nations Fail*; and Deaton, *The Great Escape*, chap. 7.

57. De Waal, *Famine Crimes*, 138.

58. Objections to the displacement of democratic actors and relationships can be distinguished from (at least some versions of) what Brian Berkey has called the "institutional critique" of effective altruism, and from the objection that effective altruism fails to promote "systemic change." For philosophical discussion of such criticisms, see Berkey, "The Institutional Critique of Effective Altruism"; Gabriel, "Effective Altruism and Its Critics"; Gabriel and McElwee, "Effective Altruism, Global Poverty, and Systemic Change"; and Lechterman, "The Effective Altruist's Political Problem." Frequently cited examples of "institutional"

or "systemic" criticisms of effective altruism include Srinivasan, "Stop the Robot Apocalypse"; and Lisa Herzog, "(One of) Effective Altruism's Blind Spot(s), or: Why Moral Theory Needs Institutional Theory," *Justice Everywhere* (blog), October 21, 2015, http://justice-everywhere.org/international/one-of-effective-al truisms-blind-spots-or-why-moral-theory-needs-institutional-theory/; and "Can 'Effective Altruism' Really Change the World?" openDemocracy, February 22, 2016, https://www.opendemocracy.net/en/transformation/can-effective-altruism-really -change-world/#. Sometimes, such criticisms charge effective altruism with overlooking opportunities to promote welfare by seeking political influence or structural transformations. Often, the implication is that effective altruists aren't doing *enough*, politically; a displacement critique, on the other hand, will often prescribe political forbearance rather than magnified attempts at political influence. The charge is that philanthropists undervalue other people's democratic institutions and relationships (or the conditions that will allow them to develop), not that they fail adequately to leverage them.

59. On vertical and horizontal approaches see, e.g., Oliveira-Cuz, Kurowski, and Mills, "Delivery of Priority Health Services," 68–69; and Atun, Bennett, and Duran, "When Do Vertical (Stand-Alone) Programmes Have a Place in Health Systems?"

60. See e.g., Atun, Bennett, and Duran, "When Do Vertical (Stand-Alone) Programmes Have a Place in Health Systems?"; and Msuya, "Horizontal and Vertical Delivery of Health Services."

61. See, e.g., Farmer, *Infections and Inequalities*.

62. Nellie Bristol, "NGO Code of Conduct Hopes to Stem Internal Brain Drain." Signatories include Oxfam UK and Physicians for Human Rights.

63. Quoted in Piller and Smith, "Unintended Victims of Gates Foundation Generosity."

64. Ibid.

65. Ibid.

66. Rubenstein, "Misuse of Power," 207.

67. Sabah Hamid, "Why I Resigned from the Gates Foundation," *New York Times*, September 26, 2019, https://www.nytimes.com/2019/09/26/opinion/modi-gates -award.html.

68. Aparna Alluri, "'Toilet trouble' for Narendra Modi and Bill Gates," BBC News, September 23, 2019, https://www.bbc.com/news/world-asia-india-49738605. In an earlier blog post, Bill Gates enthused about the Clean India program in similar terms: "What I love most about Clean India is that it identified a big problem, got everyone working on it, and is using measurement to show where things need to be done differently. As the old saying goes, What gets measured gets done." Bill Gates, "India Is Winning Its War on Human Waste," *GatesNotes* (blog), April 25, 2017, https://www.gatesnotes.com/Development/Indias-War-on-Human-Waste.

69. If it were, the solution might be simpler—to always turn over control of philanthropic funds to host-country governments. But, because such governments

often enjoy considerably less democratic legitimacy than in the Botswana case, this advice also would generate significant risks of empowering undemocratic actors.

70. This claim does not require implausibly strong premises about people *always* being reliable judges or promoters of their own good. It is consistent, for example, with behavioral science evidence of pervasive biases in human decision-making (e.g., procrastination, wishful thinking, and misleading heuristics). But since paternalizers have biases, too, the important questions are comparative and institutional: Whom is it safest to empower with decision-making authority, and how?

71. O. O'Neill, "Global Justice," 245.

72. Tanasoca and Dryzek, "Democratic Altruism." Tanasoca and Dryzek do not think that respect for the poor and their "formative agency" can be satisfied by giving to individuals, since "the global poor's rights to have a say in transnational altruism—to act as formative agents of justice—are best conceived as collective rights. They belong to the poor collectively rather than to any given individual" (224). This is the most important way their arguments differ from the relational egalitarian perspective developed in this chapter.

73. See Fung, "Deliberation Before the Revolution," on the important question of how deliberative democratic ideals can orient action in adverse circumstances and how a deliberative political ethic can be enacted and promoted in the absence of just deliberative institutions.

Conclusion

1. Eliot, *The Waste Land*, 78–79 and 85 (n401).

2. Mauss, *The Gift*, 65.

3. See, e.g., Thompson, "Representing Future Generations."

4. Tocqueville, *Democracy in America*, vol. 2, 585.

5. Ibid.

6. Ibid., 586.

7. Allen, *Talking to Strangers*, 29.

8. Ibid., 28–29.

9. I draw here on McKean, who argues that being effectively oriented to one's social and political circumstances requires accounting for "how social and political arrangements operate," "how those operations are generally made intelligible and legitimate," and "the normative values that one's actions should promote" in the relevant context (*Disorienting Neoliberalism*, 6). McKean defends orientation as a valuable way for political theory to guide action in real life—without providing "a 'to do' list for political action or a set of rules that, if followed, would put one beyond reproach" (10).

10. See, e.g., and in different ways, Anderson, *Private Government*; Zacka, *When the State Meets the Street*; Herzog, *Reclaiming the System*; and Banerjee and

Singer, "Race and the Meso-Level Sources of Domination." Of course, this is also a theme of much longer standing in feminist political thought; see, e.g., Okin, *Justice, Gender, and the Family*.

11. Soss and Weaver, "Police Are Our Government"; Anderson, *Private Government*.

Bibliography

Acemoglu, Daron. "The Logic of Effective Altruism: Response." *Boston Review*, July 1, 2015. http://bostonreview.net/forum/logic-effective-altruism/daron-ace moglu-response-effective-altruism.

Acemoglu, Daron, and James A. Robinson. *Why Nations Fail: The Origins of Power, Prosperity, and Poverty*. New York: Crown Business, 2013.

Acs, Zoltan J. *Why Philanthropy Matters: How the Wealthy Give, and What It Means for Our Economic Well-Being*. Princeton, NJ: Princeton University Press, 2013.

Addams, Jane. "A Modern Lear." *Survey* 29, no. 5 (November 2, 1912): 131–37.

———. "The Objective Value of a Social Settlement." In *Philanthropy and Social Progress: Seven Essays*. New York: T. Y. Crowell, 1893, 27–56.

———. "The Subjective Necessity for Social Settlements." In *Philanthropy and Social Progress: Seven Essays*. New York: T. Y. Crowell, 1893, 1–26.

Alcoff, Linda. "The Problem of Speaking for Others." *Cultural Critique* 20 (Winter 1991–1992): 5–32.

Allen, Danielle S. *Talking to Strangers: Anxieties of Citizenship since Brown v. Board of Education*. Chicago: University of Chicago Press, 2004.

Amarante, Eric Franklin. "Unregulated Charity." *Washington Law Review* 94, no. 4 (December 2019): 1503–76.

Anderson, Elizabeth. "Democracy: Instrumental vs. Non-Instrumental Value." In *Contemporary Debates in Political Philosophy*, edited by Thomas Christiano and John Christman, 213–28. Chichester, West Sussex: Wiley-Blackwell, 2009.

———. "The Epistemology of Democracy." *Episteme* 3, no. 1–2 (2006): 8–22.

———. "The Ethical Limitations of the Market." *Economics and Philosophy* 6, no. 2 (1990): 179–205.

———. *Private Government: How Employers Rule Our Lives (and Why We Don't Talk about It)*. Princeton, NJ: Princeton University Press, 2017.

———. *Value in Ethics and Economics*. Cambridge, MA: Harvard University Press, 1993.

———. "What Is the Point of Equality?" *Ethics* 109, no. 2 (January 1999): 287–337.

Andreoni, James. "The Benefits and Costs of Donor-Advised Funds." *Tax Policy and the Economy* 32 (2018): 1–44.

———. "Impure Altruism and Donations to Public Goods: A Theory of Warm-Glow Giving." *Economic Journal* 100 (1990): 464–77.

Andrews, William. "Personal Deductions in an Ideal Income Tax." *Harvard Law Review* 86 (1972): 309–85.

Arneson, Richard. "Equality and Equal Opportunity for Welfare." *Philosophical Studies* 56 (1989): 77–93.

———. "Mill versus Paternalism." *Ethics* 90, no. 4 (1980): 470–89.

Arrow, Kenneth J. "Gifts and Exchanges." *Philosophy & Public Affairs* 1, no. 4 (Summer 1972): 343–62.

Ascoli, Peter M. *Julius Rosenwald: The Man Who Built Sears, Roebuck and Advanced the Cause of Black Education in the American South*. Bloomington: Indiana University Press, 2006.

Atkinson, Rob. "The Low Road to Cy Pres Reform: Principled Practice to Remove Dead Hand Control of Charitable Assets." *Case Western Reserve Law Review* 58, no. 1 (Fall 2007): 97–166.

———. "Reforming Cy Pres Reform." *Hastings Law Journal* 44, no. 5 (1993): 1111–58.

Atun, Rifat A., Sara Bennett, and Antonio Duran. "When Do Vertical (Stand-Alone) Programmes Have a Place in Health Systems?" Copenhagen: World Health Organization, June 2008.

Aubrey, John. *Brief Lives*. Edited by John Buchanan-Brown. New York: Penguin, 2000.

Banerjee, Abhijit V., and Esther Duflo. *Poor Economics: A Radical Rethinking of the Way to Fight Global Poverty*. New York: PublicAffairs, 2011.

Banerjee, Kiran, and Abraham Singer. "Race and the Meso-Level Sources of Domination." *Political Research Quarterly* 71, no. 1 (2018): 215–27.

Barber, Benjamin R. "Searching for Civil Society." *National Civic Review* 84, no. 2 (Spring 1995): 114–18.

Barkan, Joanne. "Got Dough? How Billionaires Rule Our Schools." *Dissent* 51, no. 1 (Winter 2011): 49–57.

Barry, Brian. "Humanity and Justice in Global Perspective." *Nomos* 24 (1982): 219–52.

———. *Justice as Impartiality*. Oxford: Oxford University Press, 1995.

Bartels, Larry M. *Unequal Democracy: The Political Economy of the New Gilded Age*. Princeton, NJ: Princeton University Press, 2008.

Beerbohm, Eric. "The Free Provider Problem." In *Philanthropy in Democratic Societies: History, Institutions, Values*, edited by Rob Reich, Chiara Cordelli, and Lucy Bernholz, 207–25. Chicago: University of Chicago Press, 2016.

———. *In Our Name: The Ethics of Democracy*. Princeton, NJ: Princeton University Press, 2012.

Beitz, Charles R. *Political Theory and International Relations*. Princeton, NJ: Princeton University Press, 1979.

Ben-Porath, Sigal R. *Tough Choices: Structured Paternalism and the Landscape of Choice*. Princeton, NJ: Princeton University Press, 2010.

Berger, Ken, and Robert M. Penna. "The Elitist Philanthropy of So-Called Effective Altruism." *Stanford Social Innovation Review*, November 23, 2013. https://ssir.org/articles/entry/the_elitist_philanthropy_of_so_called_effective_altruism.

Berkey, Brian. "The Institutional Critique of Effective Altruism." *Utilitas* 30, no. 2 (June 2018): 143–71.

Bill and Melinda Gates Foundation. "Working with Botswana to Confront Its Devastating AIDS Crisis." Bill and Melinda Gates Foundation, June 2006. https://docs.gatesfoundation.org/Documents/achap.pdf.

Bishop, Matthew, and Michael Green. *Philanthrocapitalism: How the Rich Can Save the World*. New York: Bloomsbury, 2008.

Bittker, Boris. "Charitable Contributions: Tax Deductions or Matching Grants?" *Tax Law Review* 28 (1972): 37–63.

Brackman Reiser, Dana. "Dismembering Civil Society: The Social Cost of Internally Undemocratic Nonprofits." *Oregon Law Review* 82 (2003): 829–900.

Brennan, Jason, and Peter Martin Jaworski. "Markets without Symbolic Limits." *Ethics* 125, no. 2 (2015): 1053–77.

Brighouse, Harry. "Neutrality, Publicity, and State Funding of the Arts." *Philosophy & Public Affairs* 24, no. 1 (Winter 1995): 35–63.

Bristol, Nellie. "NGO Code of Conduct Hopes to Stem Internal Brain Drain." *Lancet* 371. June 28, 2008.

Brody, Evelyn. "Agents without Principals: The Economic Convergence of the Nonprofit and For-Profit Organizational Forms." *New York Law School Law Review* 40 (1996): 457–536.

Brody, Evelyn, and Marcus Owens. "Exile to Main Street: The I.R.S.'s Diminished Role in Overseeing Tax-Exempt Organizations." *Chicago-Kent Law Review* 91, no. 3 (2016): 859–94.

Burns, Nancy, Kay Lehman Schlozman, and Sidney Verba. *The Private Roots of Public Action: Gender, Equality, and Political Participation*. Cambridge, MA: Harvard University Press, 2001.

Buteau, Ellie, Satia Marotta, Hannah Martin, Naomi Orensten, and Kate Gehling. "New Attitudes, Old Practices: The Provision of Multiyear General Operating Support." Center for Effective Philanthropy, 2020. http://cep.org/wp-content/uploads/2020/10/CEP_MYGOS_Report_FNL.pdf.

Caney, Simon. *Justice beyond Borders: A Global Political Theory*. Oxford: Oxford University Press, 2005.

Carnegie, Andrew. *The Gospel of Wealth and Other Timely Essays*. New York: The Century Co., 1901.

Christiano, Thomas. *The Constitution of Equality: Democratic Authority and Its Limits*. Oxford: Oxford University Press, 2008.

Clark, Robert Charles. "Does the Nonprofit Form Fit the Hospital Industry?" *Harvard Law Review* 93 (May 1980): 1416–89.

Clough, Emily. "Effective Altruism's Political Blind Spot." *Boston Review*, July 14, 2015. http://bostonreview.net/world/lura-clough-effective-altruism-ngos.

Cohen, G. A. "Incentives, Inequality, and Community." *The Tanner Lectures on Human Values*. Salt Lake City: University of Utah Press, 1992.

———. "On the Currency of Egalitarian Justice." *Ethics* 99 (1989): 906–44.

———. *Rescuing Justice and Equality*. Cambridge, MA: Harvard University Press, 2008.

———. "Where the Action Is: On the Site of Distributive Justice." *Philosophy & Public Affairs* 26, no. 1 (January 1997): 3–30.

Cohen, Joshua, and Charles Sabel. "Extra Rempublicam Nulla Justitia?" *Philosophy & Public Affairs* 34, no. 2 (March 2006): 147–75.

Conly, Sarah. *Against Autonomy: Justifying Coercive Paternalism*. Cambridge: Cambridge University Press, 2013.

Cordelli, Chiara. "Democratizing Organized Religion." *Journal of Politics* 79, no. 2 (2017): 576–90.

———. "How Privatization Threatens the Private." *Critical Review of International Social and Political Philosophy* 16, no. 1 (2013): 65–87.

———. "The Institutional Division of Labor and the Egalitarian Obligations of Nonprofits." *Journal of Political Philosophy* 20, no. 2 (June 2012): 131–55.

———. *The Privatized State*. Princeton, NJ: Princeton University Press, 2020.

———. "Reparative Justice and the Moral Limits of Discretionary Philanthropy." In *Philanthropy in Democratic Societies*, edited by Rob Reich, Lucy Bernholz, and Chiara Cordelli, 244–65. Chicago: University of Chicago Press, 2016.

Cornell, Nicolas. "A Third Theory of Paternalism." *Michigan Law Review* 113 (June 2015): 1295–1336.

Cullman, Lewis B., and Ray Madoff. "The Undermining of American Charity." *New York Review of Books*, July 14, 2016.

Cureton, Adam. "Offensive Beneficence." *Journal of the American Philosophical Association* 2, no. 1 (Spring 2016): 74–90.

Deaton, Angus. *The Great Escape: Health, Wealth, and the Origins of Inequality*. Princeton, NJ: Princeton University Press, 2013.

———. "The Logic of Effective Altruism: Response" *Boston Review*, July 1, 2015. http://bostonreview.net/forum/logic-effective-altruism/angus-deaton-response-effective-altruism.

———. "Randomization in the Tropics Revisited: A Theme and Eleven Variations." NBER Working Paper 27600. National Bureau of Economic Research Working Paper July 2020. https://www.nber.org/papers/w27600.

de Marneffe, Peter. "Avoiding Paternalism." *Philosophy & Public Affairs* 34, no. 1 (2006): 68–94.

de Waal, Alex. *Famine Crimes: Politics and the Disaster Relief Industry in Africa.* Oxford: James Currey, 1997.

Dewey, John. *The Public and Its Problems.* 1927. Reprint, Athens, OH: Swallow Press/Ohio University Press, 1991.

Dickens, Charles. *Bleak House.* New York: Bantam Classics, 2006.

Diner, Hasia R. *Julius Rosenwald: Repairing the World.* New Haven, CT: Yale University Press, 2017.

Douglass, Frederick. *My Bondage and My Freedom.* In *Autobiographies,* edited by Henry Louis Gates Jr., 103–452. New York: Library of America, 1994.

Drèze, Jean, and Amartya Sen. *Hunger and Public Action.* Oxford: Clarendon, 1989.

Du Bois, W. E. B. *Black Reconstruction in America, 1860–1880.* 1935. Reprint, New York: The Free Press, 1998.

———. "Negro Education." *The Crisis,* February 1918. 173–78.

———. "Postscript." *The Crisis,* February 1932. 58.

Dworkin, Gerald. "Paternalism." *The Monist* 56, no. 1 (1972): 64–84.

Dworkin, Ronald. *A Matter of Principle.* Cambridge, MA: Harvard University Press, 1985.

———. *Sovereign Virtue.* Cambridge, MA: Harvard University Press, 2000.

Eikenberry, Angela M. *Giving Circles: Philanthropy, Voluntary Association, and Democracy.* Bloomington: Indiana University Press, 2009.

Elford, Gideon. "Relational Equality and Distribution." *Journal of Political Philosophy* 35, no. 4 (2017): 80–99.

Eliasoph, Nina. *Making Volunteers: Civic Life after Welfare's End.* Princeton, NJ: Princeton University Press, 2011.

Eliot, T. S. *The Waste Land* [1922], in *Collected Poems, 1909–1962.* London: Faber and Faber, 1963. 61–86.

Estlund, David. *Democratic Authority: A Philosophical Framework.* Princeton, NJ: Princeton University Press, 2008.

———. *Utopophobia: On the Limits (If Any) of Political Philosophy.* Princeton, NJ: Princeton University Press, 2020.

Farmer, Paul. *Infections and Inequalities: The Modern Plagues.* Berkeley: University of California Press, 1999.

Feinberg, Joel. "Legal Paternalism." *Canadian Journal of Philosophy* 1, no. 1 (September 1971): 105–24.

Ferguson, Karen. *Top Down: The Ford Foundation, Black Power, and the Reinvention of Racial Liberalism.* Philadelphia: University of Pennsylvania Press, 2013.

Fleishman, Joel L. *The Foundation: A Great American Secret: How Private Wealth Is Changing the World.* New York: PublicAffairs, 2009.

Forrester, Katrina. *In the Shadow of Justice: Postwar Liberalism and the Remaking of Political Philosophy*. Princeton, NJ: Princeton University Press, 2019.

Fourie, Carina, Fabian Schuppert, and Ivo Wallimann-Helmer, eds. *Social Equality: On What It Means to Be Equals*. Oxford: Oxford University Press, 2015.

Francis, Megan Ming. "The Price of Civil Rights: Black Lives, White Funding, and Movement Capture." *Law & Society Review* 53, no. 1 (2019): 275–309.

Fremont-Smith, Marion R. *Governing Nonprofit Organizations: Federal and State Law and Regulation*. Cambridge, MA: Harvard University Press, 2008.

Friedman, Lawrence M. *Dead Hands: A Social History of Wills, Trusts, and Inheritance Law*. Stanford: Stanford Law Books, 2009.

Friedman, Milton. *Capitalism and Freedom*. 40th anniversary ed. Chicago: University of Chicago Press, 2002.

Frumkin, Peter. *On Being Nonprofit*. Cambridge, MA: Harvard University Press, 2002.

Fung, Archon. "Associations and Democracy: Between Theories, Hopes, and Realities." *Annual Review of Sociology* 29 (2003): 515–39.

———. "Deliberation Before the Revolution: Toward an Ethics of Deliberative Democracy in an Unjust World." *Political Theory* 33, no. 3 (June 2005): 397–419.

Gabriel, Iason. "Effective Altruism and Its Critics." *Journal of Applied Philosophy* 34, no. 4 (August 2017): 468–70.

Gabriel, Iason, and Brian McElwee. "Effective Altruism, Global Poverty, and Systemic Change." In *Effective Altruism: Philosophical Issues*, edited by Hilary Greaves and Theron Pummer, 99–114. Oxford: Oxford University Press, 2019.

Galston, William. "Realism in Political Theory." *European Journal of Political Theory* 9, no. 4 (October 2010): 385–411.

Gates, Bill. "Why Inequality Matters." *Gates Notes* (blog), October 13, 2014. http://www.gatesnotes.com/Books/Why-Inequality-Matters-Capital-in-21st-Century-Review#.

Gert, Bernard, and Charles M. Culver. "Paternalistic Behavior." *Philosophy & Public Affairs* 6, no. 1 (1976): 45–57.

Geuss, Raymond. *Philosophy and Real Politics*. Princeton, NJ: Princeton University Press, 2008.

Gilens, Martin. *Affluence and Influence: Economic Inequality and Political Power in America*. Princeton, NJ: Princeton University Press and Russell Sage Foundation, 2012.

Gilens, Martin, and Benjamin I. Page. "Testing Theories of American Politics: Elites, Interest Groups, and Average Citizens." *Perspectives on Politics* 12, no. 3 (September 2014): 564–81.

Gilman, Michele Estrin. "Charitable Choice and the Accountability Challenge: Reconciling the Need for Regulation with the First Amendment Religion Clauses." *Vanderbilt Law Review* 55, no. 3 (April 2002): 799–888.

Giridharadas, Anand. *Winners Take All: The Elite Charade of Changing the World*. New York: Knopf, 2018.

Giving USA. *Giving USA 2020: The Annual Report on Philanthropy for the Year 2019*. Chicago: Giving USA Foundation, 2020.

Goodwin, Iris J. "Ask Not What Your Charity Can Do for You: *Robertson v. Princeton* Provides Liberal-Democratic Insights into the Dilemma of *Cy Pres* Reform." *Arizona Law Review* 51, no. 75 (2009): 75–125.

Grant, Ruth W. *Strings Attached: Untangling the Ethics of Incentives*. Princeton, NJ: Princeton University Press, 2012.

Gravelle, Jane G., Donald J. Marples, and Molly F. Sherlock. "Tax Issues Relating to Charitable Contributions and Organizations." Congressional Research Service Report R45922, June 15, 2020. https://crsreports.congress.gov/product /pdf/R/R45922.

Gray, John. "How & How Not to Be Good." *New York Review of Books*. May 21, 2015. https://www.nybooks.com/articles/2015/05/21/how-and-how-not-to-be-good/

Green, Jeffrey Edward. *The Shadow of Unfairness: A Plebeian Theory of Liberal Democracy*. New York: Oxford University Press, 2016.

Greene, Jay P. "Buckets into the Sea: Why Philanthropy Isn't Changing Schools, and How It Could." In *With the Best of Intentions: How Philanthropy Is Reshaping K–12 Education*, edited by Frederick M. Hess, 49–76. Cambridge, MA: Harvard Education Press, 2005.

Hacker, Jacob S., and Paul Pierson. *Winner-Take-All Politics: How Washington Made the Rich Richer—And Turned Its Back on the Middle Class*. New York: Simon & Schuster, 2010.

Hamid, Sabah. "Why I Resigned from the Gates Foundation." *New York Times*, September 26, 2019. https://www.nytimes.com/2019/09/26/opinion/modi-gates -award.html

Hamington, Maurice. "Community Organizing: Addams and Alinsky." In *Feminist Interpretations of Jane Addams*, edited by Maurice Hamington, 255–74. University Park: Pennsylvania State University Press, 2010.

Hansmann, Henry. "Economic Theories of Nonprofit Organizations." In *The Nonprofit Sector: A Research Handbook*, edited by Walter W. Powell. 1st ed. 27–42. New Haven, CT: Yale University Press, 1987.

Harbaugh, William T. "What Do Donations Buy? A Model of Philanthropy Based on Prestige and Warm Glow." *Journal of Public Economics* 67, no. 2 (February 1998): 269–84.

Harding, Matthew. *Charity Law and the Liberal State*. Cambridge: Cambridge University Press, 2014.

Harmon, Elizabeth A. "The Transformation of American Philanthropy: From Public Trust to Private Foundation, 1785–1917." PhD diss., University of Michigan, 2017.

Healy, Kieran. *Last Best Gifts: Altruism and the Market for Human Blood and Organs*. Chicago: University of Chicago Press, 2006.

Hertel-Fernandez, Alexander. *State Capture: How Conservative Activists, Big Businesses, and Wealthy Donors Reshaped the American States—and the Nation.* New York: Oxford University Press, 2019.

Herzog, Lisa. *Reclaiming the System: Moral Responsibility, Divided Labour, and the Role of Organizations in Society.* Oxford: Oxford University Press, 2018.

Hill, Octavia. "Homes of the London Poor." U.S. reprint. New York: State Charities Aid Association, 1875.

Himmelfarb, Gertrude. *Poverty and Compassion: The Moral Imagination of the Late Victorians.* New York: Vintage, 1991.

Hinton, Timothy. "Must Egalitarians Choose between Fairness and Respect?" *Philosophy & Public Affairs* 30, no. 1 (Winter 2001): 72–87.

Hirschman, Albert O. *Exit, Voice, and Loyalty: Responses to Decline in Firms, Organizations, and States.* Cambridge, MA: Harvard University Press, 1970.

Horton, Joe. "The All or Nothing Problem." *Journal of Philosophy* 114, no. 2 (2017): 94–104.

Hume, David. *The History of England from the Invasion of Julius Caesar to the Revolution in 1688.* [1778]. Edited by William B. Todd. 6 vols. Indianapolis: Liberty Fund, 1983.

Huyssen, David. *Progressive Inequality: Rich and Poor in New York, 1890–1920.* Cambridge, MA: Harvard University Press, 2014.

Incite!, eds. *The Revolution Will Not Be Funded: Beyond the Non-Profit Industrial Complex.* Durham, NC: Duke University Press, 2007.

Issacharoff, Samuel, and Pamela S. Karlan. "The Hydraulics of Campaign Finance Reform." *77 Texas Law Review* 1705 (1998–1999).

Jubb, Robert. "The Real Value of Equality," *Journal of Politics* 77, no. 3 (July 2015): 679–91.

Julius, A. J. "Basic Structure and the Value of Equality." *Philosophy & Public Affairs* 31, no. 4 (Fall 2003): 321–55.

———. "Nagel's Atlas." *Philosophy & Public Affairs* 34, no. 2 (2006): 176–92.

Kamm, Frances. *Intricate Ethics.* Oxford: Oxford University Press, 2007.

Kant, Immanuel. *Groundwork for the Metaphysics of Morals.* Edited and translated by Allen Wood. New Haven, CT: Yale University Press, 2002.

Katz, Michael B. *In the Shadow of the Poorhouse: A Social History of Welfare in America.* Revised ed. New York: Basic Books, 1996.

———. *The Undeserving Poor: America's Enduring Confrontation with Poverty.* 2nd ed. New York: Oxford University Press, 2013.

Kennedy, Sheila Suess, and Wolfgang Bielefeld. "Government Shekels Without Government Shackles? The Administrative Challenges of Charitable Choice." *Public Administration Review* 62, no. 1 (January/February 2002): 4–11.

"Key Facts on U.S. Nonprofits and Foundations." Candid.org, April 22, 2020. https://www.issuelab.org/resources/36381/36381.pdf.

Knight, Louise W. *Citizen: Jane Addams and the Struggle for Democracy*. Chicago: University of Chicago Press, 2005.

Kogan, Vladimir, Stéphane Lavertu, and Zachary Peskowitz. "The Democratic Deficit in U.S. Education Governance" (EdWorkingPaper: 20-196). Retrieved from Annenberg Institute at Brown University. https://doi.org/10.26300/2dqg -w009.

Kohl-Arenas, Erica. *The Self-Help Myth: How Philanthropy Fails to Alleviate Poverty*. Oakland: University of California Press, 2016.

Kolodny, Niko. "Being under the Power of Others." In *Republicanism and the Future of Democracy*, edited by Yiftah Elazar and Geneviève Rousselière, 94–114. Cambridge: Cambridge University Press, 2019.

———. "Rule Over None II: Social Equality and the Justification of Democracy." *Philosophy & Public Affairs* 42, no. 4 (2014): 287–336.

Landemore, Hélène. *Democratic Reason: Politics, Collective Intelligence, and the Rule of the Many*. Princeton, NJ: Princeton University Press, 2013.

Larmore, Charles. *Patterns of Moral Complexity*. Cambridge: Cambridge University Press, 1987.

Lechterman, Theodore M. "The Effective Altruist's Political Problem." *Polity* 52, no. 1 (January 2020): 88–115.

Lessig, Lawrence. "Institutional Corruption Defined." *Journal of Law, Medicine and Ethics* 41, no. 3 (Fall 2013): 553–55.

———. *Republic, Lost: How Money Corrupts Congress—and a Plan to Stop It*. New York: Twelve, 2011.

Letts, Christine W., William Ryan, and Allen Grossman. "Virtuous Capital: What Foundations Can Learn from Venture Capitalists." *Harvard Business Review* (March–April 1997): 37–44.

Levy, Jacob T. *Rationalism, Pluralism, and Freedom*. Oxford: Oxford University Press, 2015.

———. "There's No Such Thing as Ideal Theory." *Social Philosophy and Policy* 33, no. 1 –2 (October 2016): 312–33.

Lewis, Michael. "The Speculator." *New Republic*, January 10, 1994. http://www.new republic.com/article/politics/the-speculator.

Lichtenberg, Judith. "Peter Singer's Extremely Altruistic Heirs." *New Republic*, November 30, 2015. https://newrepublic.com/article/124690/peter-singers-extremely -altruistic-heirs.

Lindsey, Almont. "Paternalism and the Pullman Strike." *American Historical Review* 44, no. 2 (January 1939): 272–89.

Livy, Titus. *The Early History of Rome*. Translated by Aubrey de Sélincourt. New York: Penguin, 1960.

MacAskill, William. "The Definition of Effective Altruism." In *Effective Altruism: Philosophical Issues*, edited by Hilary Greaves and Theron Pummer, 10–28. Oxford: Oxford University Press, 2019.

———. *Doing Good Better: How Effective Altruism Can Help You Make a Difference*. New York: Penguin Random House, 2015.

Macdonald, Dwight. *The Ford Foundation: The Men and the Millions*. New Brunswick, NJ: Transaction Publishers, 1989.

Machiavelli, Niccolò. *Discourses on Livy*. Translated by Harvey C. Mansfield and Nathan Tarcov. Chicago: University of Chicago Press, 1996.

Madoff, Ray D. *Immortality and the Law: The Rising Power of the American Dead*. New Haven, CT: Yale University Press, 2010.

———. "When Is Philanthropy? How the Tax Code's Answer to This Question Has Given Rise to the Growth of Donor-Advised Funds and Why It's a Problem." In *Philanthropy in Democratic Societies: History, Institutions, Values*, edited by Rob Reich, Lucy Bernholz, and Chiara Cordelli, 158–77. Chicago: University of Chicago Press, 2016.

Mandeville, Bernard. *The Fable of the Bees or Private Vices, Publick Benefits*. 2 vols. Indianapolis: Liberty Fund, 1988.

Markell, Patchen. "The Insufficiency of Non-Domination." *Political Theory* 36, no. 1 (February 2008): 9–36.

Marx, Karl, and Friedrich Engels. *Manifesto of the Communist Party*. In *The Marx-Engels Reader*, edited by Robert C. Tucker, 469–500. New York: Norton, 1978.

Mauss, Marcel. *The Gift: The Form and Reason for Exchange in Archaic Societies*. Translated by W. D. Halls. New York: Norton, 1990.

Mayer, Jane. *Dark Money: The Hidden History of the Billionaires behind the Rise of the Radical Right*. New York: Doubleday, 2016.

McCormick, John P. *Machiavellian Democracy*. Cambridge: Cambridge University Press, 2011.

McKay, Douglas. "Basic Income, Cash Transfers, and Welfare State Paternalism." *Journal of Political Philosophy* 27, no. 4 (2019): 422–47.

McKean, Benjamin Laing. *Disorienting Neoliberalism: Global Justice and the Outer Limit of Freedom*. Oxford: Oxford University Press, 2020.

Mill, John Stuart. *On Liberty*. In *The Collected Works of John Stuart Mill*. Vol. 18. Edited by J. M. Robson. Toronto: University of Toronto Press, 1977.

———. *Principles of Political Economy*. In *The Collected Works of John Stuart Mill*. Vol. 3. Edited by J. M. Robson. Toronto: University of Toronto Press, 1965.

———. *The Subjection of Women*. In *The Collected Works of John Stuart Mill*. Vol. 21. Edited by J. M. Robson. Toronto: University of Toronto Press, 1977.

Miller, David. "Equality and Justice." *Ratio* 10, no. 3 (1997): 222–37.

———. *Justice for Earthlings: Essays in Political Philosophy*. Cambridge: Cambridge University Press, 2013.

Miller, John J., and Karl Zinsmeister, with Ashley May. *Agenda Setting: A Wise Giver's Guide to Influencing Public Policy*. Washington, DC: Philanthropy Roundtable, 2015.

Mills, Charles W. "Ideal Theory as Ideology." *Hypatia* 20, no. 3 (August 2005): 165–83.

Minow, Martha. *Partners, Not Rivals: Privatization and the Public Good*. Boston, MA: Beacon, 2002.

Montanaro, Laura. "The Democratic Legitimacy of Self-Appointed Representatives." *Journal of Politics* 74, no. 4 (October 2012): 1094–1107.

———. *Who Elected Oxfam? A Democratic Defense of Self-Appointed Representation*. Cambridge: Cambridge University Press, 2018.

Msuya, Joyce. "Horizontal and Vertical Delivery of Health Services: What Are the Trade Offs?" Washington, DC: World Bank, January 2003. http://www-wds .worldbank.org/external/default/WDSContentServer/IW3P/IB/2003/10/15/0 00160016_20031015125129/additional/310436360_200502761000211.pdf.

Murphy, Liam B. "Institutions and the Demands of Justice." *Philosophy & Public Affairs* 27, no. 4 (1999): 251–91.

Murphy, Liam, and Thomas Nagel. *The Myth of Ownership: Taxes and Justice*. Oxford: Oxford University Press, 2002.

Nagel, Thomas. *Equality and Partiality*. New York: Oxford University Press, 1993.

———. "The Problem of Global Justice." *Philosophy & Public Affairs* 33, no. 2 (2005): 113–47.

Norman, Richard. "The Social Basis of Equality." *Ratio* 10, no. 3 (1997): 238–52.

Nozick, Robert. *Anarchy, State, and Utopia*. New York: Basic Books, 1974.

———. "Coercion." In *Philosophy, Science, and Method: Essays in Honor of Ernest Nagel*, edited by Sidney Morgenbesser, Patrick Suppes, and Morton White, 440–72. New York: St. Martin's, 1969.

Odendahl, Teresa. *Charity Begins at Home: Generosity and Self-Interest Among the Philanthropic Elite*. New York: Basic Books, 1990.

Okin, Susan Moller. *Justice, Gender, and the Family*. New York: Basic Books, 1989.

———. "Justice and Gender: An Unfinished Debate." *Fordham Law Review* 72 (2004). 1537–67.

Oliveira-Cruz, Valeria, Christoph Kurowski, and Anne Mills. "Delivery of Priority Health Services: Searching for Synergies Within the Vertical Versus Horizontal Debate." *Journal of International Development* 15 (2003): 67–86.

Olsen, Frances. "The Myth of State Intervention in the Family." *University of Michigan Journal of Law Reform* 18 (1985): 835–64.

O'Neill, Martin. "What Should Egalitarians Believe?" *Philosophy & Public Affairs* 36, no. 2 (Spring 2008): 119–56.

O'Neill, Onora. "Global Justice: Whose Obligations?" In *The Ethics of Assistance: Morality and the Distant Needy*, edited by Deen K. Chatterjee, 242–59. Cambridge: Cambridge University Press, 2004.

Ostrower, Francie. *Why the Wealthy Give: The Culture of Elite Philanthropy*. Princeton, NJ: Princeton University Press, 1995.

Page, Benjamin I., Larry M. Bartels, and Jason Seawright. "Democracy and the Policy Preferences of Wealthy Americans." *Perspectives on Politics* 11, no. 1 (March 2013): 51–73.

Page, Benjamin I., and Martin Gilens. *Democracy in America: What Has Gone Wrong and What We Can Do About It*. Chicago: University of Chicago Press, 2017.

Page, Benjamin I., Jason Seawright, and Matthew J. Lacombe. *Billionaires and Stealth Politics*. Chicago: University of Chicago Press, 2019.

Paine, Thomas. *Agrarian Justice*. In *Political Writings*, edited by Bruce Kuklick. Cambridge: Cambridge University Press, 2000.

Pettit, Philip. *On the People's Terms: A Republican Theory and Model of Democracy*. Cambridge: Cambridge University Press, 2012.

———. *Republicanism: A Theory of Freedom and Government*. Oxford: Oxford University Press, 1997.

Pevnick, Ryan. "Democratizing the Nonprofit Sector." *Journal of Political Philosophy* 21, no. 3 (September 2013): 260–82.

———. "Does the Egalitarian Rationale for Campaign Finance Reform Succeed?" *Philosophy & Public Affairs* 44, no. 1 (2016): 46–76.

———. "Philanthropy and Democratic Ideals." In *Philanthropy in Democratic Societies: History, Institutions, Values*, edited by Rob Reich, Chiara Cordelli, and Lucy Bernholz, 226–43. Chicago: University of Chicago Press, 2016.

Phulwani, Vijay. "The Poor Man's Machiavelli: Saul Alinsky and the Morality of Power." *American Political Science Review* 110, no. 4 (November 2016): 863–64.

Piketty, Thomas. *Capital in the Twenty-First Century*. Translated by Arthur Goldhammer. Cambridge, MA: Harvard University Press, 2014.

Piketty, Thomas, and Emmanuel Saez. "Income Inequality in the United States, 1913–1998." *Quarterly Journal of Economics* 118, no. 1 (2003): 1–39.

Pogge, Thomas W. "How International Nongovernmental Organizations Should Act." In *Giving Well: The Ethics of Philanthropy*, edited by Patricia Illingworth, Thomas Pogge, and Leif Wenar, 46–66. New York: Oxford University Press, 2011.

———. "On the Site of Distributive Justice: Reflections on Cohen and Murphy." *Philosophy & Public Affairs* 29, no. 2 (April 2000): 137–69.

———. "Severe Poverty as a Violation of Negative Duties." *Ethics & International Affairs* 19, no. 1 (March 2005): 55–83.

———. *World Poverty and Human Rights*. 2nd ed. Malden, MA: Polity, 2002.

Pummer, Theron. "Whether and Where to Give." *Philosophy & Public Affairs* 44, no. 1 (2016): 77–95.

Putnam, Robert D. "Bowling Alone: America's Declining Social Capital." *Journal of Democracy* 6, no. 1 (1995): 65–78.

———. *Bowling Alone: The Collapse and Revival of American Community*. New York: Simon & Schuster, 2000.

———. *Making Democracy Work: Civic Traditions in Modern Italy*. Princeton, NJ: Princeton University Press, 1993.

Quong, Jonathan. *Liberalism Without Perfection*. Oxford: Oxford University Press, 2011.

Radin, Margaret Jane. *Contested Commodities: The Trouble with Trade in Sex, Children, Body Parts, and Other Things.* Cambridge, MA: Harvard University Press, 1996.

Ramiah, Ilavenil, and Michael R. Reich. "Building Effective Public-Private Partnerships: Experiences and Lessons from the African Comprehensive HIV/AIDS Partnerships (ACHAP)." *Social Science and Medicine* 63 (2006): 397–408.

———. "Public-Private Partnerships and Antiretroviral Drugs for HIV/AIDS: Lessons from Botswana." *Health Affairs* 24, no. 1 (March/April 2005): 545–51.

Ransby, Barbara. *Ella Baker and the Black Freedom Movement: A Radical Democratic Vision.* Chapel Hill, NC: University of North Carolina Press, 2003.

Rauch, Jonathan. "This Is Not Charity." *Atlantic.* October 1, 2007. http://www.theatlantic.com/magazine/archive/2007/10/-this-is-not-charity/306197/.

Ravitch, Diane. *The Death and Life of the Great American School System: How Testing and Choice are Undermining Education.* New York: Basic Books, 2010.

Rawls, John. *A Theory of Justice.* Cambridge, MA: Belknap, 1971.

———. *Justice as Fairness: A Restatement.* Edited by Erin Kelly. Cambridge, MA: Belknap, 2001.

———. *The Law of Peoples: With "The Idea of Public Reason Revisited."* Cambridge, MA: Harvard University Press, 2001.

———. *Political Liberalism.* 2nd ed. New York: Columbia University Press, 2005.

Reckhow, Sarah. *Follow the Money: How Foundation Dollars Change Public School Politics.* Oxford: Oxford University Press, 2015.

Reddy, Sanjay G. "Economics' Biggest Success Story Is a Cautionary Tale." *Foreign Policy*, October 19, 2019. https://foreignpolicy.com/2019/10/22/economics-development-rcts-esther-duflo-abhijit-banerjee-michael-kremer-nobel/.

Reese, Ellen. *Backlash Against Welfare Mothers: Past and Present.* Berkeley: University of California Press, 2005.

Reich, Rob. "A Failure of Philanthropy: American Charity Shortchanges the Poor, and Public Policy Is Partly to Blame." *Stanford Social Innovation Review* (Winter 2005): 24–33.

———. *Just Giving: Why Philanthropy Is Failing Democracy and How It Can Do Better.* Princeton, NJ: Princeton University Press, 2018.

———. "Toward a Political Theory of Philanthropy." In *Giving Well: The Ethics of Philanthropy*, edited by Patricia Illingworth, Thomas Pogge, and Leif Wenar, 177–95. New York: Oxford University Press, 2011.

———. "What Are Foundations For?" *Boston Review* (March/April 2013): 10–15.

Reich, Rob, Chiara Cordelli, and Lucy Bernholz, eds. *Philanthropy in Democratic Societies: History, Institutions, Values.* Chicago: University of Chicago Press, 2016.

Reich, Rob, Lacey Dorn, and Stefanie Sutton. "Anything Goes: Approval of Nonprofit Status by the IRS." Stanford University Center on Philanthropy and Civil Society, October 2009. http://www.stanford.edu/~sdsachs/AnythingGoesPACS1109.pdf.

Richardson, Henry S. "Only in the Ballpark of Paternalism: Arrogance and Liberty-Limitation in International Humanitarian Aid." In *Paternalism beyond Borders*, edited by Michael N. Barnett, 47–74. Cambridge: Cambridge University Press, 2017.

Richmond, Mary E. *Friendly Visiting Among the Poor: A Handbook for Charity Workers*. New York: MacMillan, 1903.

Ridzi, Frank. *Selling Welfare Reform: Work-first and the New Common Sense of Employment*. New York: New York University Press, 2009.

Rockefeller, John D., Senior. *Random Reminiscences of Men and Events*. New York: Doubleday, Page, 1909.

Roelofs, Joan. *Foundations and Public Policy: The Mask of Pluralism*. Albany: State University of New York Press, 2003.

Rooks, Noliwe. *Cutting School: Privatization, Segregation, and the End of Public Education*. New York: The New Press, 2017.

Rosenblum, Nancy L. *Good Neighbors: The Democracy of Everyday Life in America*. Princeton, NJ: Princeton University Press, 2016.

———. *Membership and Morals: The Personal Uses of Pluralism in America*. Princeton, NJ: Princeton University Press, 2000.

Rossi, Enzo, and Matt Sleat. "Realism in Normative Political Theory." *Philosophy Compass* 9, no. 10 (2014): 689–701.

Rubenstein, Jennifer C. *Between Samaritans and States: The Political Ethics of Humanitarian INGOs*. Oxford: Oxford University Press, 2015.

———. "The Misuse of Power, Not Bad Representation: Why It Is Beside the Point that No One Elected Oxfam." *Journal of Political Philosophy* 22, no. 2 (June 2014): 204–30.

Russakoff, Dale. *The Prize: Who's in Charge of America's School's?* New York: Houghton Mifflin Harcourt, 2015.

Sabl, Andrew. "Community Organizing as Tocquevillean Politics: The Art, Practices, and Ethos of Association." *American Journal of Political Science* 46, no. 1 (January 2002): 1–19.

———. "History and Reality: Idealist Pathologies and 'Harvard School' Remedies." In *Political Philosophy versus History? Contextualism and Real Politics in Contemporary Political Thought*, edited by Jonathan Floyd and Marc Stears, 151–76. Cambridge: Cambridge University Press, 2011.

———. *Hume's Politics: Coordination and Crisis in the History of England*. Princeton, NJ: Princeton University Press, 2012.

Sandel, Michael J. *What Money Can't Buy: The Moral Limits of Markets*. New York: Farrar, Straus and Giroux, 2012.

Satz, Debra. *Why Some Things Should Not Be for Sale: The Moral Limits of Markets*. Oxford: Oxford University Press, 2010.

Saunders-Hastings, Emma. "Benevolent Giving and the Problem of Paternalism."

In *Effective Altruism: Philosophical Issues*, edited by Hilary Greaves and Theron Pummer, 115–36. Oxford: Oxford University Press, 2019.

———. "No Better to Give than to Receive: Charity and Women's Subjection in J.S. Mill." *Polity* 46, no. 2 (April 2014): 233–54.

———. "Plutocratic Philanthropy." *Journal of Politics* 80, no. 1 (January 2018): 149–61.

Saward, Michael. "Authorisation and Authenticity: Representation and the Unelected." *Journal of Political Philosophy* 17, no. 1 (March 2009): 1–22.

Scanlon, T. M. "Preference and Urgency." *Journal of Philosophy* 72, no. 19 (1975): 655–69.

———. *Why Does Inequality Matter?* Oxford: Oxford University Press, 2018.

Schambra, William. "By the People: The Old Values of the New Citizenship." *National Civic Review* 84, no. 2 (Spring 1995): 101–13.

Scheffler, Samuel. "Choice, Circumstance, and the Value of Equality." *Politics, Philosophy & Economics* 4, no. 1 (2005): 5–28.

———. "What Is Egalitarianism?" *Philosophy & Public Affairs* 31, no. 1 (2003): 5–39.

Schemmel, Christian. "Distributive and Relational Equality." *Politics, Philosophy & Economics* 11, no. 2 (2011): 123–48.

———. "Why Relational Egalitarians Should Care about Distributions." *Social Theory and Practice* 37, no.3 (2011): 365–90.

Schlozman, Kay Lehman, Sidney Verba, and Henry E. Brady. *The Unheavenly Chorus: Unequal Political Voice and the Broken Promise of American Democracy*. Princeton, NJ: Princeton University Press, 2012.

Scott, Janelle. "The Politics of Venture Philanthropy in Charter School Policy and Advocacy." *Educational Policy* 23, no. 1 (January 2009): 106–36.

Sen, Amartya. *The Idea of Justice*. Cambridge, MA: Belknap, 2009.

———. *Poverty and Famines: An Essay on Entitlement and Deprivation*. New York: Oxford University Press, 1982.

Seneca, Lucius Annaeus. *On Benefits*. Translated by Aubrey Stewart. London: George Bell & Sons, 1887.

Shiffrin, Seana Valentine. "Paternalism, Unconscionability Doctrine, and Accommodation." *Philosophy & Public Affairs* 29, no. 3 (Summer 2000): 205–50.

———. "The Power and Influence of Grantors." (Comment on Rob Reich's "What Are Foundations For?") *Boston Review*, March 1, 2013. http://bostonreview.net/forum/what-are-foundations/power-and-influence-grantors

Shklar, Judith. *The Faces of Injustice*. New Haven, CT: Yale University Press, 1992.

———. "The Liberalism of Fear." In *Liberalism and the Moral Life*, edited by Nancy L. Rosenblum, 21–28. Cambridge, MA: Harvard University Press, 1989.

Simmons, A. John. "Ideal and Non-ideal Theory." *Philosophy & Public Affairs* 38, no. 1 (Winter 2010): 5–36.

Sinclair, Thomas. "Are We Conditionally Obligated to Be Effective Altruists?" *Philosophy & Public Affairs* 46, no. 1 (2018): 36–59.

Singer, Peter. "Altruism and Commerce: A Defense of Titmuss against Arrow." *Philosophy & Public Affairs* 2, no. 3 (1973): 312–20.

———. "Famine, Affluence, and Morality." *Philosophy & Public Affairs* 1, no. 3 (Spring 1972): 229–43.

———. *The Life You Can Save: Acting Now to End World Poverty*. New York: Random House, 2010.

———. "The Logic of Effective Altruism." *Boston Review*, July 1, 2015. http:// bostonreview.net/forum/peter-singer-logic-effective-altruism.

———. *The Most Good You Can Do*. New Haven, CT: Yale University Press, 2015.

———. "What Should a Billionaire Give—and What Should You?" *New York Times Magazine*, December 17, 2006. https://www.nytimes.com/2006/12/17 /magazine/17charity.t.html.

———. "The Why and How of Effective Altruism." March 2013. TED video, 17:06. http://www.ted.com/talks/peter_singer_the_why_and_how_of_effective _altruism/transcript.

Skocpol, Theda. "Advocates without Members: The Recent Transformation of American Civic Life." In *Civic Engagement in American Democracy*, edited by Theda Skocpol and Morris P. Fiorina, 461–510. New York: Brookings Institution and Russell Sage Foundation, 1999.

———. *Diminished Democracy: From Membership to Management in American Civic Life*. Norman: University of Oklahoma Press, 2003.

———. "The Tocqueville Problem: Civic Engagement in American Democracy." *Social Science History* 21, no. 4 (Winter 1997): 455–79.

Skocpol, Theda, and Alexander Hertel-Fernandez. "The Koch Network and Republican Party Extremism." *Perspectives on Politics* 14, no. 3 (September 2016): 681–99.

Smith, Adam. *An Inquiry into the Nature and Causes of the Wealth of Nations*. Edited by R. H. Campbell and A. S. Skinner. 2 vols. Indianapolis: Liberty Fund, 1981.

Smith, Steven Rathgeb, and Michael Lipsky. *Nonprofits for Hire: The Welfare State in the Age of Contracting*. Cambridge, MA: Harvard University Press, 1993.

Soss, Joe, and Vesla Weaver. "Police Are Our Government: Politics, Political Science, and the Policing of Race-Class Subjugated Communities." *Annual Review of Political Science* 20 (2017): 565 –91.

Spencer, Herbert. "The Proper Sphere of Government." In *The Man versus the State, with Six Essays on Government, Society and Freedom* [1842–43], edited by Eric Mack. Indianapolis: LibertyClassics, 1981.

Srinivasan, Amia. "Stop the Robot Apocalypse." *London Review of Books* 37, no. 18 (September 24, 2015): 3–6.

Steinberg, Richard, and Walter W. Powell. Introduction to *The Nonprofit Sector: A Research Handbook*. 2nd ed. Edited by Walter W. Powell and Richard Steinberg, 1–10. New Haven, CT: Yale University Press, 2006.

Stemplowska, Zofia. "What's Ideal about Ideal Theory?" *Social Theory and Practice* 34, no. 3 (July 2008): 319–40.

Stout, Jeffrey. *Blessed Are the Organized: Grassroots Democracy in America.* Princeton, NJ: Princeton University Press, 2010.

Stover, John, Boga Fidzani, Batho Chris Molomo, Themba Moeti, and Godfrey Musuka. "Estimated HIV Trends and Program Effects in Botswana." *PLOS One* 3, no. 11 (November 2008). http://www.plosone.org/article/info%3Adoi%2F10.1371%2Fjournal.pone.0003729.

Tan, Kok-Chor. *Justice without Borders: Cosmopolitanism, Nationalism, and Patriotism.* Cambridge: Cambridge University Press, 2004.

Tanasoca, Ana, and John Dryzek. "Democratic Altruism." *International Theory* 13, no. 2 (July 2021): 205–30.

Tawney, R. H. *Equality.* 1931. Revised ed., London: Allen and Unwin, 1964.

Taylor, Robert S. "Donation without Domination: Private Charity and Republican Liberty." *Journal of Political Philosophy* 26, no. 4 (2018): 441–62.

Thaler, Richard H., and Cass R. Sunstein. *Nudge: Improving Decisions about Health, Wealth, and Happiness.* New York: Penguin, 2009.

Thompson, Dennis F. *Ethics in Congress: From Individual to Institutional Corruption.* Washington, DC: Brookings Institution, 1995.

———. *Political Ethics and Public Office.* Cambridge, MA: Harvard University Press, 1987.

———. "Representing Future Generations: Political Presentism and Democratic Trusteeship." *Critical Review of International Social and Political Philosophy* 13, no. 1 (2010): 17–37.

Titmuss, Richard. *The Gift Relationship: From Human Blood to Social Policy.* London: Allen & Unwin, 1970.

Tocqueville, Alexis de. *Democracy in America.* 2 vols. Translated by Arthur Goldhammer. New York: Library of America, 2004.

———. *Memoir on Pauperism.* Translated by Seymour Drescher. London: Civitas, 1997.

Tolentino, Jia. "What Mutual Aid Can Do during a Pandemic." *New Yorker,* May 18, 2020.

Tompkins-Stange, Megan E. *Policy Patrons: Philanthropy, Education Reform, and the Politics of Influence.* Cambridge, MA: Harvard Education Press, 2016.

Toobin, Jeffrey. "Rich Bitch: The Legal Battel over Trust Funds for Pets." *New Yorker,* September 29, 2008. 38–47.

Tsai, George. "Rational Persuasion as Paternalism." *Philosophy & Public Affairs* 42, no. 1 (2014): 78–112.

Unger, Peter. *Living High and Letting Die: Our Illusion of Innocence.* New York: Oxford University Press, 1996.

Valentini, Laura. "Ideal vs. Non-ideal Theory: A Conceptual Map." *Philosophy Compass* 7/9 (2012): 654–64.

———. "On the Apparent Paradox of Ideal Theory." *Journal of Political Philosophy* 17, no. 3 (2009): 332–55.

Veyne, Paul. *Le pain et le cirque: Sociologie historique d'un pluralisme politique.* Paris: Le Seuil, 1976.

Viehoff, Daniel. "Democratic Equality and Political Authority." *Philosophy & Public Affairs* 42, no. 4 (2014): 337–75.

Waldron, Jeremy. "Legislation and Moral Neutrality." In *Liberal Neutrality,* edited by Robert E. Goodin and Andrew Reeve, 61–83. New York: Routledge, 1989.

———. "Mill on Liberty and on the Contagious Diseases Acts." In *J. S. Mill's Political Thought: A Bicentennial Reassessment,* edited by Nadia Urbinati and Alex Zakaras, 11–42. Cambridge: Cambridge University Press, 2007.

Walzer, Michael. "Socialism and the Gift Relationship." *Dissent* 29, no. 4 (September 1, 1982).

———. *Spheres of Justice: A Defense of Pluralism and Equality.* New York: Basic Books, 1983.

Weisbrod, Burton A. *The Nonprofit Economy.* Cambridge, MA: Harvard University Press, 1988.

Weiss, Jeffrey. "Donations: Can They Reduce a Donor's Welfare?" In *The Economics of Nonprofit Institutions: Studies in Structure and Policy,* edited by Susan Rose-Ackerman, 45–56. Oxford: Oxford University Press, 1986.

Wenar, Leif. "Poverty Is No Pond." In *Giving Well: The Ethics of Philanthropy,* edited by Patricia Illingworth, Thomas Pogge, and Leif Wenar, 104–32. New York: Oxford University Press, 2011.

Wertheimer, Alan. *Exploitation.* Princeton, NJ: Princeton University Press, 1996.

White, Curtis. "The Idols of Environmentalism." *Orion.* March/April 2007. https://orionmagazine.org/article/the-idols-of-environmentalis/.

Wiens, David. "Against Ideal Guidance." *Journal of Politics* 77, no. 2 (April 2015): 433–46.

Wiesel, Elie. *A Passover Haggadah, As Commented Upon by Elie Wiesel and Illustrated by Mark Podwal.* New York: Simon & Schuster, 1993.

Williams, Bernard. *In the Beginning Was the Deed: Realism and Moralism in Political Argument.* Princeton, NJ: Princeton University Press, 2005.

Wilson, James Lindley. *Democratic Equality.* Princeton, NJ: Princeton University Press, 2019.

Winters, Jeffrey A. *Oligarchy.* New York: Cambridge University Press, 2011.

Wolff, Jonathan. "Fairness, Respect, and the Egalitarian Ethos." *Philosophy & Public Affairs* 27, no. 2 (April 1998): 97–122.

———. "Fairness, Respect and the Egalitarian Ethos Revisited," *Journal of Ethics* 14 (2010): 335–50.

Young, Iris Marion. *Justice and the Politics of Difference.* Princeton, NJ: Princeton University Press, 1990.

Yunus, Muhammad, with Alan Jolis. *Banker to the Poor: Micro-Lending and the Battle against World Poverty.* New York: PublicAffairs, 1997.

Zacka, Bernardo. *When the State Meets the Street: Public Service and Moral Agency.* Cambridge, MA: Harvard University Press, 2017.

Zakaras, Alex. *Individuality and Mass Democracy: Mill, Emerson, and the Burdens of Citizenship.* New York: Oxford University Press, 2009.

Zelizer, Viviana A. *The Social Meaning of Money: Pin Money, Paychecks, Poor Relief & Other Currencies.* New York: Basic Books, 1994.

Zuiderhoek, Arjan. *The Politics of Munificence in the Roman Empire: Citizens, Elites and Benefactors in Asia Minor.* Cambridge: Cambridge University Press, 2009.

Zunz, Oliver. *Philanthropy in America: A History.* Princeton, NJ: Princeton University Press, 2011.

Zwolinski, Matt. "The Pragmatic Libertarian Case for a Basic Income Guarantee." Cato Unbound, August 4, 2014. https://www.cato-unbound.org/2014/08/04/matt-zwolinski/pragmatic-libertarian-case-basic-income-guarantee.

Index

Lightning Source UK Ltd.
Milton Keynes UK
UKHW022050040722
405363UK00007B/1116